Advisory Boards in Medium-Sized Companies

Advisory Boards in Medium-Sized Companies

—

An International Comparison

Edited by
Daniel Graewe

DE GRUYTER

ISBN 978-3-11-066551-2
e-ISBN (PDF) 978-3-11-066618-2
e-ISBN (EPUB) 978-3-11-066571-0

Library of Congress Control Number: 2021930700

Bibliographic information published by the Deutsche Nationalbibliothek
The Deutsche Nationalbibliothek lists this publication in the Deutsche Nationalbibliografie;
detailed bibliographic data are available on the Internet at http://dnb.dnb.de.

© 2021 Walter de Gruyter GmbH, Berlin/Boston
Cover image: Sidekick/Getty Images/E+
Typesetting: Integra Software Services Pvt. Ltd.
Printing and binding: CPI books GmbH, Leck

www.degruyter.com

To Carlotta and Antonia

Preface

The initiative for this book came from an enquiry by the German Lawyers' Institute (Deutsches Anwalts Institut, DAI) to the publisher. The DAI was looking for a summary of the economic and legal framework for advisory boards in medium-sized companies. This presentation was to be used in the further education of lawyers specialising in commercial and corporate law and therefore required a more detailed study of the legal matter. In the course of the preparation of the document at the Institute of Applied Business Law in Hamburg, it quickly became clear that a "brief" presentation of legal matters in other countries was not possible due to the fundamentally different regulations and legal traditions for the document to be prepared. Nevertheless, a comparison of the regulations on advisory boards on an international level was identified as equally interesting and quite uncharted territory. At the end of this rather coincidental process of development you will find, dear reader, the present work. It is dedicated to the basics of the legal framework of advisory boards in medium-sized companies and provides an overview of their situation in the economically most important national economies with regard to the GDP. We hope that in this way we will be able to make an additional contribution to the further mutual understanding of corporate law at the international level.

The editor thanks the international authors of this work for their efforts and their contribution to the international understanding of this – not always easy to grasp – corporate law subject matter.

Last but not least, the untiring work of Johanna Tensi, research associate at the Institute for Applied Business Law, should be mentioned as an important factor in the success of this book. Without her organisational talent, her empathetic approach to the international colleagues and her great patience with the editor, this work would not have been possible. Thank you very much, Johanna.

Daniel Graewe
Hamburg, Germany, Autumn 2020

https://doi.org/10.1515/9783110666182-202

Foreword

This is a useful and timely book.

Cross-border mergers, acquisitions and joint ventures – and generally businesses expanding into new jurisdictions – are an ever-prevalent phenomenon. There is plenty of literature on the mechanics of setting up, or taking over, a foreign company. There is rather less on how to run companies across different countries to ensure that integration is successful once the merger has happened. There is even less literature specifically geared towards small and medium-sized enterprises (SMEs) operating internationally.

This is a significant issue in light of the widely diverging, and constantly changing, array of governance and participation rules internationally for companies to be aware of. Such factors are far too rarely given full consideration at the outset of a deal. It is well-documented that many a venture fails because of this.[1] This risk is particularly critical for SMEs, where the success of international expansion often determines the long-term viability of the business.

This book on the role of corporate advisory boards in key jurisdictions around the world, with a particular focus on SMEs, therefore helps to fill a gap. These consultative bodies are perhaps the most frequently overlooked aspect of international corporate governance. They can be a vital instrument both for driving innovation and for maintaining stability within a corporation. They can also, especially for SMEs, be a handy channel for the influx of external talent. In some jurisdictions they are enshrined in law (mainly in the civil law world). In other countries – especially those following the common law tradition as France or Germany but also, for instance, China – they are much less regulated.

Familiarising oneself at the outset with the requirements for advisory boards as important tools of corporate governance is bound to help prevent the clash of cultures that all too often follows in the wake of cross-border mergers, acquisitions and joint ventures.

This being the first work of its kind, Professor Daniel Graewe and his globe-spanning team of authors have also made a seminal contribution to the academic

---

1 By way of example, a 2019 Deloitte survey of the worldwide merger activities of US companies suggests that roughly one-third of failed mergers are due to the regulatory and legal environment not having been properly considered. Another third fail because of gaps in integration execution (see https://www2.deloitte.com/content/dam/Deloitte/us/Documents/mergers-acqisitions/us-mergers-acquisitions-trends-2019-report.pdf). See also the recent reports by *Financier Worldwide* magazine (https://www.financierworldwide.com/cross-border-ma-integration#.X32D6mhKiUl), *Financial Management* magazine (https://www.fm-magazine.com/issues/2019/feb/cross-border-mergers-acquisitions-planning.html) and the Boston Consulting Group (BCG) (https://media-publications.bcg.com/pdf/Understanding-Overcoming-Challenges-Cross-Border-PMI.pdf). All web resources accessed on November 25, 2020.

https://doi.org/10.1515/9783110666182-203

study of comparative corporate governance law. They have produced a clear and easy-to-handle reference guide for practitioners and scholars alike. I for one am sure that I, my clients and my colleagues will make regular use of it.

Hendrik Puschmann[†]
London, UK, Autumn 2020

[†] Partner and head of international arbitration, Farrer & Co. Associate fellow of Green Templeton College in the University of Oxford and Clare Hall in the University of Cambridge. Member of the academic advisory board of the Institute for Applied Business Law, Nordakademie, Hamburg. Visiting senior lecturer in international law and commerce, Johannes Kepler University Linz.

Contents

Daniel Graewe
Chapter 1
Introduction

Small and medium-sized companies (SMEs) differ from large corporations in their independent business models, leaner structures and special culture. Many strategic questions must be answered differently than with blue chip companies. Although medium-sized companies often occupy niches, at the same time they can be world market leaders or operate in the top group worldwide. Given such a background, internationality is not a vision of the future; it is part of everyday life. Especially medium-sized companies know their customers personally and are extraordinarily flexible. Flat hierarchies are their shortest path to success. Private ownership and visionary leaders establish a direct link between future orientation and risk balancing.

However, a (medium-sized) company cannot be successful in the long term if it is not also constantly able to adapt to new internal and external circumstances. An important factor for this is the quality of the governance structures and processes within the company. A well thought out and well-functioning management and control structure is not only an important instrument for realising the interests and will of the shareholders and stakeholders, but also an essential prerequisite for recruiting and retaining capable managers and employees.

However, the aftermath of the financial and economic crisis, globalisation, COVID-19 and increased complexity due to growth and increasing density of regulation also pose major challenges for owner-managed companies, especially in the coming post-corona period. In addition, numerous medium-sized companies are confronted with a growing circle of shareholders, the increasing unequal distribution of the shares of different shareholders and the resulting diverging interests, also between the various stakeholders. These are central hurdles for the future viability of medium-sized businesses. In this situation, a properly staffed, competent and responsible advisory board in the sense of good governance contributes significantly to the success of the company and its sustainable development.

In the economic literature, there are essentially three approaches for explaining the existence and benefits of such bodies.

The principal–agent theory attributes the existence of advisory boards to the conflicting goals and information asymmetries between the owner of the company (the principal) and its management (the agent). Accordingly, the principal and the agent pursue different goals and interests, which can lead to a threat to the success of the company. In this context, the agent has an information advantage due to his

https://doi.org/10.1515/9783110666182-001

operative activity, which he can use for opportunistic behaviour.[1] For this reason, the principal can and must take measures to limit such benefit-maximising management behaviour, in particular an internal control and incentive system. For this task, principals set up a (voluntary) advisory board to reduce conflicts between such parties.

In family owned companies, these conflicts of objectives are not the primary concern since ownership and control do not necessarily have to fall apart. Here, the stewardship theory is primarily applied, according to which managers do not primarily pursue their own but rather collectivist goals and work towards the common corporate good for intrinsic motives. In these constellations, advisory boards are not primarily used for control, but rather to advise and support the management. In addition, through staffing, networking and know-how, the advisory board can provide important access to rare corporate resources that are difficult to imitate and substitute (the so-called resource-based approach), which promises competitive advantages.

However, to achieve the desired effect, the advisory board first needs a clear understanding of its own function. Primarily, it must be ensured that the rights and duties assigned to it are exercised in such a way that the interests of the shareholders, but also those of the other stakeholders, are adequately safeguarded; this includes in any case forward-looking advice, but may also include a control component based on past experience.

Having a clear focus is also another important characteristic of a well-functioning advisory board. Experienced advisory boards direct their attention to the long-term success and consistency of the business model and are able to focus on the relevant topics. The best supervisory boards spend at least two-thirds of their time on questions about the future instead of coming to terms with the past and questioning completed processes. An effective advisory board must therefore also ensure that operational management is in the hands of the best possible management talents. This means finding, attracting, hiring, integrating and monitoring excellent board members, but also supporting, challenging and promoting them. And that also includes paying them appropriately, retaining them in the company and, if necessary, replacing them (in good time).

After all, the value that an advisory board can generate for the company depends heavily on its composition. Advisory board work can be stimulating and fulfilling, but above all it is a demanding and complex task. The members must be individually suited for it, but also be able to use their potential as a group for the benefit of the company, its owners and the other stakeholders. Advisory boards are sometimes made up of quite different members, and discrepancies in experience, expertise, attitudes, perspectives and interests can create considerable tension.

---

1 For reasons of readability only the male form is used in this book although it addresses all genders; male and female.

Productive interaction therefore does not happen by itself, but requires a lot of openness, goodwill and discipline and a certain amount of experience and willingness to cooperate. Here, much depends on the experience and ability of the members of the advisory board, and in particular the chairman of the advisory board, to adequately penetrate and deal with issues in a short period of time. In the best case, the chairman of the advisory board is a valuable sparring partner for the operative management. Another important function, especially for the chairman of the advisory board, is the mediation between shareholders and management and between the shareholders. This can be done informally and inconspicuously, but sometimes it develops into a conciliation procedure with high publicity.

Besides this globally applicable economic basis, advisory boards worldwide very much differ from one another. Whether advisory boards in SMEs are required by law or can be set up voluntarily, what their rights and obligations are, how much they can adapt to the respective companies and change their internal structure and if/how they can be dismissed varies from country to country and legal system to legal system.

This book aims to help to classify, compare and understand the role of advisory boards in SMEs in the main legal and economic systems. Experienced practitioners from each country have brought together their experiences to improve understanding of these particular bodies through up-to-date and practice-oriented country reports and to raise awareness of the benefits of such a corporate body.

Daniel Graewe
Chapter 2
Germany

2.1 Introduction

In Germany, the law only provides for a mandatory advisory and controlling body – the so-called supervisory board (*Aufsichtsrat*) – for stock corporations (*Aktiengesellschaften (AG)*), the Societas Europaea (SE) and for larger cooperatives (*Genossenschaften*). In other enterprises, mandatory supervisory bodies are either not regulated by law at all or are only mandatory from a certain number of employees.

In most cases, medium-sized enterprises and in particular family owned companies do not exceed the legal size requirements for the mandatory establishment of supervisory boards, namely 500 employees. For them, the only question that usually arises is the formation of voluntary advisory boards. The term "advisory board" is generally used as a generic term for the various forms of advisory bodies, supervisory boards, administrative boards with management powers or shareholders' committees, etc.

Voluntary advisory boards are not limited to special legal forms of companies typical for medium-sized businesses. However, the possibility of an advisory board is expressly provided for in Section 52 of the German Law concerning limited liability companies (GmbHG). With more than one million registered entities, the company with limited liability is also the most economically important form of company in the field of medium-sized and family enterprises in Germany. The following considerations therefore focus on this legal form.

2.2 Concept and definition, delimitation from other corporate bodies

On closer examination of the advisory board in medium-sized enterprises, it must first be clarified what is meant by such a body and how an advisory board distinguishes itself from other bodies, in particular the supervisory board.

2.2.1 Concept

There is no legal definition of the term "advisory board". However, an advisory board is generally defined as a body that can be formed in partnerships and corporations

https://doi.org/10.1515/9783110666182-002

(and also in foundations or cooperatives) and to which various tasks can be assigned. It is a body set up by the shareholders/partners on a voluntary basis, but not a legally prescribed body.

Other terms are used synonymously for the advisory board: board of directors, supervisory board, family board, shareholders' committee, board of trustees, working committee or board of elders. However, it is recommended to use the term "advisory board", which has become widely used and established.

2.2.2 Distinction from supervisory boards

The German Stock Corporation Act (Aktiengesetz (AktG)) contains mandatory provisions for the establishment of a supervisory board for stock corporations in Sections 95 et seq. AktG. The formation of an advisory board is nevertheless permissible but may not change the mandatory competence regulations in favour of the supervisory board under stock corporation law; the advisory board of a stock corporation may therefore only have consulting/advisory functions.

The legal form of a limited liability company frequently used in medium-sized or family owned enterprises does not initially provide by law for the formation of a third body in addition to a shareholders' meeting (*Gesellschafterversammlung*) and the managing directors (*Geschäftsführer*). However, according to Section 52 GmbHG, an optional supervisory board can be set up if it does not have to be set up by law anyway on the basis of other statutory provisions (Section 52 Para. 2 GmbHG). In the case of a GmbH, this includes forming a supervisory board with a so-called employee parity, if the requirements under the German One-Third Participation Act (Drittelbeteiligungsgesetz (DrittelbG)), starting from 500 employees, the German Co-Determination Act (Mitbestimmungsgesetz (MitbestG)), starting from 2,000 employees or other co-determination acts are met; the powers of the co-determined supervisory board are prescribed by law and cannot be changed (Section 25 Para. 1 sentence 1 no. 1 MitBestG, Section 1 Para. 1 no. 3 DrittelbG).

Voluntary supervisory boards are those supervisory boards that are set up by the shareholders without legal obligation, irrespective of the legal form or size of a company. A supervisory board within the meaning of Section 52 GmbHG exists if the authority of the body corresponds to the model set by stock corporation law. This depends on an overall assessment, in particular the question of whether, for example, supervisory and personnel competencies have also been transferred to the board, or only advisory/consultancy tasks.

If there is no supervisory board as defined by stock corporation law, it is a – voluntary – body to which Section 52 GmbHG and the provisions of the stock corporation law do not apply. It can then be an advisory board. In this case, the legal limits for the formation of an advisory board are merely drawn from the principle of the sovereignty of the association and the principle of self-governance. The principle of the association sovereignty demands that the shareholders/partners must always have the possibility (if the necessary majorities are met) to abolish the advisory board again, to curtail its competences or also to revoke decisions of the advisory board.

Higher Regional Court of Berlin, Judgment of 23 July 2015 – file no. 23 U 18/15
The Higher Regional Court of Berlin (*Kammergericht, KG*) has ruled in favour of the establish-ment of an optional supervisory board (not: advisory board) in a GmbH in accordance with Sec-tion 52 GmbHG as follows:

The subsequently resolved establishment of a supervisory board in a GmbH must be nota-rized and registered with the competent commercial register, even if there is an opening clause to establish such a body in its articles of association.

The court rejects the unanimous view in legal literature that the establishment of a supervi-sory board can be decided with a simple majority without any certification/notarization and be-comes effective without registration with the commercial register if the articles of association provide for the establishment of a supervisory board as a possibility.

Most authors are rather vague on these questions. In some cases, for example, there is only the remark that the establishment of an advisory board must be stipulated in the articles of association or introduced retrospectively by amending the articles of association. Only in a further half sentence is it noted succinctly that at least the articles of association must contain a corre-sponding authorization to the shareholders' meeting. What majorities the resolutions adopted on the basis of the authorisation must have, whether they require notarisation and whether their reg-istration is necessary is not stated.

Insofar as in the literature justifications are given for the more or less vaguely indicated admissi-bility of the establishment of a supervisory board by simple majority resolution, these are ex-hausted in a reference to a judgment of the Reich Court from the mid-19th century. This decision, however, does not indicate whether a supervisory board was established in this case with a simple majority or with a qualified majority amending the articles of association. The judgment only refers to a "resolution of the shareholders' meeting"; the circumstances of the case (adoption of a resolu-tion immediately following the formation process), however, point to an unanimous adoption of the resolution. In any case, it is not clear from the decision that a supervisory board can be set up with a simple majority if the articles of association provide for an optional supervisory board.

2.2.3 Name of advisory boards in the articles of association

Even if there is agreement in legal literature and jurisdiction (*Rechtsprechung*) that the denomination of a corporate body is ultimately not decisive for its real nature, the use of the term "advisory board" instead of "supervisory board" or a term other than that of the supervisory board prima facie suggests that the body should not have the control rights of a (voluntary or mandatory) supervisory board within the meaning of Section 52 GmbHG that goes far beyond simple advisory/consultancy. However, even if the term "advisory board" or a denomination other than that of the board was chosen, the body may still be a supervisory board within the meaning of Section 52 GmbHG. The decisive factor is rather the design of its tasks, rights and duties. In view of the expectations associated with the term "supervisory board" by the public, an optional supervisory board within the meaning of Section 52 GmbHG can only be assumed if a minimum degree of inalienable control rights is assigned to the body. The advisory board, on the other hand, should typically not control/supervise the management, but merely advise and support it. Such an allocation of competence does not point to more far-reaching rights than purely future-oriented advice. If there are no objective indications of any control rights, the tasks of the supervisory board cannot be used analogously. The term "advisory board" rather indicates an implied exclusion of the control-rights from Section 52 GmbHG. This suggests that a purely consulting advisory board has been formed which does not have the far-reaching rights of an optional supervisory board.

Whereas in individual cases the body may also be an optional supervisory board even if the body is not referred to as a supervisory board in the articles of association of the respective enterprise, the use of the term "supervisory board" as the *terminus technicus* defined by Section 52 GmbHG, however, can be more likely to be based on a supervisory board with the powers specified in Section 52 GmbHG. The designation of the body as a "supervisory board" initially arouses the expectation of the public that the body has at least similar rights (and duties) as the supervisory board under stock corporation law. This, however, is not likely to be the case with a body designated as an "advisory board".

However, the terminology is not decisive in the end. Rather, it depends on the actual competence of the body to supervise the management. The public has different expectations of a supervisory board than of an advisory board or a body with another denomination. If, however, the articles of association contain provisions that clearly speak against the competence of the board to supervise the management – for example, if the "supervisory board" only has the task of "advising" the management – these express provisions take precedence over the fundamental expectations of the public to a body referred to as the "supervisory board". However, in the case of a denomination of the body as a supervisory board with unclear or incomplete provisions in the articles of association, recourse to provisions under stock corporation law according to general principles can be made for interpretation purposes, which is not the case with a denomination as "advisory board". This means that an advisory board has been formed that is referred to as a "supervisory board" and is not entitled to the rights under Section 52 GmbHG in accordance with the articles of association.

2.3 Establishment, organisation and operations

An advisory board in a medium-sized company must first be set up before it can commence its operations. In addition to questions relating to the establishment of the body itself, questions relating to its internal organisation and its subsequent activities must also be regulated.

2.3.1 Establishment

In principle, an advisory board can be set up in two different ways. It can first be implemented in the articles of association either when the company is founded or at a later date. However, it is also conceivable to establish the advisory board solely on the basis of the law of obligations (*schuldrechtlicher Beirat*). In the case of family companies, the establishment of an advisory board should be tackled at an early stage before the participation of the next generation with a view to generational succession. Since the number of family members being/becoming shareholders tends to increase from generation to generation, it is becoming increasingly difficult to organise the necessary majorities and convince the family to establish a strong advisory board. In terms of organisation, the articles of association can stipulate that an (independent) advisory board must automatically be constituted as a corporate body when a certain number of shareholders is reached. The assignment of rights and duties can also be made dependent on certain conditions.

2.3.1.1 Statutory advisory boards in the articles of association

There are no explicit legal regulations for the establishment of an advisory board. However, it can be seen from the provisions of the GmbHG that for limited liability companies the existence of an advisory board is permitted in general. An advisory board can therefore be set up at the same time as the company is founded or only later by amending its articles of association. The establishment of an advisory board at the same time as the formation of the company is possible if a company is either newly established or arises by way of a change of legal form (e.g., by merger, carve-out or separation). In most cases, however, an advisory board is only established retrospectively if a specific need for its establishment arises due to a particular development or problem, such as a pending business succession. The articles of association of a company may initially be limited to authorising or, if necessary, obliging the shareholders to set up an advisory board at a later date. In this way, in the event that the wish or need for an advisory board arises later, the shareholders can set up such a body without having to amend the articles of association. An advisory board may also exist alongside a supervisory board that must be set up on a mandatory basis; it may be set up as a group or individual body.

The articles of association of a company can and must in any case regulate all details with regard to the tasks and competences of the (statutory) advisory board as well as its composition. Gaps in regulation should be avoided by including detailed provisions. Depending on the structure of these provisions, the advisory board may then be entrusted with advisory/consultancy or monitoring tasks. There are no legal requirements or restrictions regarding the allocation of tasks. The shareholders' meeting can therefore to a large extent transfer the rights to which it is entitled to the advisory board. However, the competence of the shareholders' meeting to make fundamental decisions (amendments to the articles of association, etc.) must necessarily remain with the shareholders' meeting itself. It is also indispensable for the managing directors to have exclusive authority to represent the company as an organ.

With the transfer of tasks and rights/duties to an advisory board, the organisational structure of the company is changed as a result and a (partial) reorganisation with a change in competences within the company takes place. When setting up the advisory board, all regulations that change the previous organisational structure of the company or the regulations required for the reorganisation must then be taken into account and the legal documentation of the company must be adapted accordingly.

> **Higher Regional Court of Munich, Judgment of 9 August 2012 – file no. 23 U 4173/11**
> The Higher Regional Court of Munich has decided that the possibility provided for in the articles of association of a GmbH to set up an advisory board with a simple majority of votes cannot be forfeited. The voting of the majority shareholder for the establishment of the advisory board is also not unfair because in the past a deletion of the clause in the articles of association was discussed but ultimately not implemented.

2.3.1.2 Advisory boards on the law of obligations

The shareholders of a company can also set up an advisory board beyond the articles of association of the company on the basis of the law of obligations (*Schuldrecht*), e.g., in the form of a shareholders' agreement. However, an advisory board established under the law of obligations cannot interfere with the company's structure of competences due to a lack of authorisation in the articles of association, because an advisory board exclusively established under the law of obligations is not considered to be a corporate body of the company. The rights and duties of the (already existing) corporate bodies are therefore not changed by an advisory board under the law of obligations. The advisory board established under the law of obligations can therefore neither make its own corporative decisions nor can information claims under company law be transferred to it. Rather, only a transfer of advisory/consultancy tasks can be considered, which, however, the advisory board can fulfil with expertise and quality.

Members of an advisory board under the law of obligations logically only have a legal relationship with the company under the law of obligations. Their responsibility therefore depends exclusively on the content of the agreement on the basis of which they act. In practice, advisory boards based on the law of obligations are therefore less common. They are particularly important in the context of credit financing, when banks demand the establishment of such a body in order to achieve greater transparency about the company's business activities and to have a say and control rights, or to monitor compliance with covenants.

It has already been mentioned that an advisory board can be formed not only by a statutory provision in the articles of association, but also by a simple shareholder resolution that does not change the articles of association and by agreements under the law of obligations with the individual members of the advisory board. If the advisory board is established in accordance with the law of obligations, the rights and duties of the advisory board on the one hand and the advisory board members on the other – in particular information rights and advisory duties – result solely from the contractual relationships due to the lack of a position in the corporate bodies. Since these are legal transactions under individual law, the interpretation of the provisions remains governed by the general civil law basic rules resulting from Sections 133, 157 German civil code (*Buergerliches Gesetzbuch (BGB)*); in particular the recognisable individual will of the contracting parties must be taken into account rather than the very word laid down in a contract. However, due to the lack of a corporate and contractual unity, no corporative rights can be granted to an advisory board under the law of obligations, such as control and supervising rights. Such rights can at best have effect under the law of obligations vis-à-vis the managing directors of the company, whereby this presupposes a corresponding obligation on the part of the managing directors. A mention of the advisory board in the articles of association naturally speaks in favour of an advisory board established on a corporate basis rather than on a contractual one. If, however, the articles of association only refer to an advisory board based on a contract, a false provision in the articles of association and as a result an advisory board based on the law of obligations only are to be assumed. In this respect, the tasks assigned to the advisory board for advising the management of the company are unproblematic. If the advisory board is also to supervise/control the managing directors of the company, such provisions are not legally binding for the managing directors.

2.3.1.3 First members of the advisory board

With regard to the size and composition of an advisory board, the shareholders are free to choose their own structure. The size of the advisory board should be based on the interests of the company, its expediency and efficiency. Decisive for a good and successful work of an advisory board is the appointment of the right people. It depends on the quality of the members, a high degree of integrity as well as the personal competences.

Professional competence
The professional competencies can depend on a broad, general professional or industry knowledge, or on specific specialist competencies. Management experience is usually desirable, as the advisory board is normally involved as an advisory and

monitoring/consultancy body. The members should also have experience in dealing with medium-sized or family owned companies as well as entrepreneurial experience.

Social competences
Social competences of an advisory board member are also indispensable, because the activities of the advisory board must serve the well-being of the company. However, employees and other stakeholder interests should be taken into account as well as other social aspects. Advisory board members must therefore work productively with one another, but also with the management, shareholders and other stakeholders of the company.

Further requirements
Advisory board members should also be skilled in analytical thinking, creativity and assertiveness, and have a good reputation and strong motivation. The ability to work in a team and the courage to make changes are also prerequisites that an advisory board member should have. A good mixture of different characters, a team of thought leaders, fellow thinkers, and lateral thinkers is recommended.

2.3.1.4 Appointment of advisory board members

The appointment of an advisory board member represents an act of decision making based on the organisational constitution of the respective company. The service contract (possibly under additional provisions applicable under labour law), which regulates the relationship under the law of obligations between the member of the advisory board and the company, must be separated from the appointment as an organ.

Specifications in the articles of association
The articles of association can be the legal basis for the appointment of one or more advisory board members. In practice, the advisory board established by the articles of association represents the normal case without mentioning the appointment of individual members of the advisory board.

Election at the shareholders' meeting
However, the election of advisory board members can also often be within the responsibility of the shareholders' meeting. The provisions in the articles of association can then provide for qualified majority requirements for the specification of concrete details or determine the rights of individual shareholders to make proposals.

Appointment by other corporate bodies

The appointment of advisory board members can also be left to other corporate bodies. However, there must be a strict separation between the management and control bodies. Therefore, the management may not appoint its own supervisory body.

Delegation rights

It is also possible to agree on delegation rights for individual shareholders or shareholder groups. However, preference should be given to the election of an advisory board member in order to achieve greater acceptance among the shareholders.

2.3.1.5 Compensation

Whether advisory board members receive remuneration is in principle at the discretion of the shareholders. In practice, it is customary to pay members of an advisory board at least an expense allowance (whereby the applicable German tax exemption limits should be taken into account when deciding on the amount of compensation). It is then advisable to already provide for the payment of a remuneration and regulations for determining its amount in the articles of association of the company.

Details of the remuneration can be provided in the articles of association, by shareholder resolution or by a provision in the service contract or the advisory board regulations. Since the articles of association (depending on the legal form) are subject to the publicity of the commercial register, the law of obligations should be preferred for confidentiality reasons.

German Federal Court, Judgement of 24 June 24 1991 – file no. II ZR 268/90
The German Federal Court (*Bundesgerichtshof, BGH*) has commented on the question of the appropriateness of advisory board remuneration. The guiding principles of its above-mentioned decision are as follows:
1. Whether the shareholders' meeting or the advisory board itself has to determine the amount of the remuneration of the advisory board members is to be determined by interpreting the articles of association.
2. In the event of a dispute, the court may not impose its own standard for the appropriateness of the remuneration on the parties.
3. A judicial examination of the remuneration is limited to whether the person/corporate body entitled to determine has exceeded the scope of discretion granted to him.

With regard to the scope of discretion, the German Federal Court states in this respect:
The contracting party that has to make the determination has to do so at its reasonable discretion. Not only a single "correct" result is conceivable. The person/corporate body entitled to determine is entitled to a margin of discretion; the determination is only to be replaced by the court if the limits drawn by fairness are exceeded, but not if the court itself considers another determination to be correct.

In the present case, the overall content would appear to suggest that the advisory board it-self, which had largely also received tasks from the shareholders' meeting, should determine the remuneration of its members. Even if the provisions included in the articles of association at the time may to a large extent have infringed mandatory statutory law, this would not apply to the advisory board's right of determination. This would correspond to the statutory provision according to which, in case of doubt, the provision is due to the party to the contract who has to demand the consideration. It will also have to be taken into account that, according to com-mon practice, the chairman of a supervisory or advisory board is granted a higher remuneration than the other members since his workload is considerably greater than that of the other mem-bers of the advisory board.

2.3.1.6 Transfer of competences to the advisory board

Before an advisory board is set up, the legally permissible transfer of authority must be clarified. A distinction must be made between the absolutely indispensable and the relatively irrevocable membership rights and duties.

In principle, the following applies: unless otherwise expressly stipulated, the re-sponsibilities of the advisory board also lie with the shareholders' meeting in case of doubt (so-called competing responsibilities).

Decisive for the rights and duties of the advisory board is the question to what extent competences from the shareholders and/or managing directors may be trans-ferred to the advisory board. In this context, attention must be paid to the composi-tion in which the advisory board is formed, whether with or without the participation of third parties, as certain rights may not be transferred to third parties outside the company. This means that tasks that are exclusively the responsibility of the manag-ing directors or the shareholders' meeting based on a mandatory statutory regulation may not be transferred to an advisory board. This primarily concerns the represen-tation of a GmbH as an organ pursuant to Section 35 GmbHG, the preparation of the annual financial statements, the appropriation of the annual results, the filing of commercial register applications or the filing of an insolvency petition.

This must not affect the core area of the company law position according to the so-called core area theory. The shareholders must retain a residual competence as their sovereignty over the company may not be completely withdrawn. Among other things, this residual competence also includes the right to decide on the dissolution of the company, to withdraw certain competences from the advisory board or to abol-ish it completely and to dismiss members of the advisory board for good cause. The competence for amendments to the articles of association (Section 52 GmbHG) or resolutions on conversion may also not be transferred to the advisory board. It is furthermore inadmissible to grant the advisory board a reservation of consent for amendments to the articles of association. The competence for structuring resolutions that are equivalent to an amendment of the articles of association cannot be delegated either. The shareholder's right to information as a preventive right of control (Sections 716 Para. 2 BGB, 118 Para. 2 HGB, Sections 51a, b GmbHG) is also mandatory and therefore not transferrable. The right of action against shareholder resolutions is also deemed to be a (subsequent) right of control. It is excluded that a shareholder waives his control rights in favour of an advisory board. Even the core area of voting rights cannot be fully transferred, although voting rights can be largely restricted.

For partnerships (in particular, partnerships under civil law, limited partnerships and general partnerships), the principle of self-organisation also applies (Sections 709 ff. BGB, 114, 125 German Trade Law [Handelsgesetzbuch, HGB]). This states that management and representation powers must be located with the partners/shareholders and may only be transferred to the extent that the organ status of the (managing) partners/shareholders is not impaired in its essence.

However, there are also rights that can be transferred with the consent of the shareholder concerned. These include, for example, preferential or special rights of a shareholder.

2.3.2 Organisation and operations

Regarding the organisation of an advisory board one can differentiate between the internal organisation and its operations.

2.3.2.1 Internal order

The newly established advisory board shall take up its duties after the appointment of its members. A first constituent meeting is convened regularly for this purpose. This serves to appoint a chairman and, if necessary or desired, a deputy chairman. However, there is no legal obligation to appoint a chairman of the advisory board.

There are also no legal regulations on the convening of an advisory board, on the rights of its members and on the adoption of its resolutions. It is therefore advisable to lay down rules for the internal order in the statutes or in rules of procedure of the advisory board (even if only by a corresponding reference) in order to facilitate the implementation of the tasks.

In this respect, it is advisable to foresee in the articles of association whether the rules of procedure are specified by the shareholders or whether the advisory board issues its rules of procedure itself. Even if the rules of procedure are prescribed by the shareholders, they should be laid down outside the articles of association by shareholders' resolution in order to facilitate subsequent changes.

The chairman of the advisory board, who should have special leadership competence, convenes the meetings of the advisory board and chairs them. If the chairperson of the management board is a family member, the chairperson of the advisory board should be an external member (and vice versa) in order to form a counterpart. Meetings must be convened in sufficient time to allow all members to prepare sufficiently. The number of meetings in the financial year should normally be four, and the frequency of meetings should be increased in the case of special challenges (restructurings, mergers and acquisitions (m&a) measures, compliance investigations, etc.). Depending on the size of the advisory board and the tasks, it also makes sense to form committees in order to be able to process the tasks efficiently and effectively. The larger the advisory board, the more use should be made of this possibility.

2.3.2.2 Advisory board committees

An advisory board committee represents a committee composed of some members of the advisory board, which supports as a subdivision of the advisory board its activities as a whole.

The support may take the form of deliberations, negotiations or decisions; the monitoring of the implementation of decisions may also be entrusted to an advisory board committee. In practice, however, the establishment of advisory board committees – in contrast to supervisory board committees – is only of minor importance, since most advisory boards consist of only a few people and a further subdivision does not appear to make sense.

Nevertheless, the establishment of an advisory board committee can be carried out by the advisory board members within the scope of their freedom of organisation. However, an advisory board committee may not be formed if the shareholders stipulate that no advisory board committee is to be formed, which is unusual as a general rule. When deciding for or against an advisory board committee, the shareholders should be guided in particular by the intended size as well as the intended competencies.

In any case, it is not permissible for the advisory board to transfer competences granted to it as a whole by the shareholders to an advisory board committee for decision by the committee. This would constitute an inadmissible encroachment on the sole competence of the shareholders to organise the corporate constitutions of the company. Only the shareholders themselves can transfer competences to a committee of the advisory board.

There is no minimum number of members for the composition of an advisory board committee, but in any case more than one person will have to be assigned. This follows, on the one hand, from the fact that the composition of an advisory board is not subject to any fixed rules on its establishment and, on the other, from the fact that one person alone cannot form a "committee" in the conceptual sense. However, only one person from the advisory board itself can be a member of an advisory board committee.

The activities of an advisory board committee are governed by the same principles as those of the advisory board itself. It is possible that the advisory board committee organises itself without any further instructions from the advisory board.

If an advisory board committee is to be able to make decisions in exceptional
cases, the shareholders must make corresponding arrangements. These include, for
example, provisions on quorum. If the activity requires the involvement of third
parties, the admissibility depends on whether the advisory board should have or
may have consulted the third party.

The advisory board committee must fulfil its duties – as the advisory board itself does – properly and with the necessary duty of care. If the advisory board de-
tects misconduct on the part of the advisory board committee, it is obliged to take
measures following appropriate examination. It is important for the monitoring
task of the advisory board through the advisory board committee that the advisory
board obtains regular reports on the committee's activities.

2.3.3 Operations of the advisory board

The advisory board's activities may relate only to an internal impact, but they may
also have an external impact. In addition, an advisory board, which not only provides non-binding advisory services, will make decisions, which are usually made
at meetings.

2.3.3.1 Adoption of resolutions

Insofar as the advisory board does not only exercise advisory/consultancy functions,
the members of the advisory board must pass resolutions on its respective agenda
items.

The advisory board exercises its activities predominantly in meetings at which
it passes resolutions. The chairman of the advisory board therefore regularly convenes the meetings for which minutes (for purposes of proof) should be drawn up.

A prerequisite for the quorum of the advisory board is that all members of the
advisory board have been duly invited. The decision-making process of the advisory
board takes place through the casting of votes.

2.3.3.2 External activities of the advisory board

The advisory board is mainly assigned tasks and advisory/consultancy functions
with an internal impact, but there are activities of the advisory board that can have
an external impact.

For example, a personnel decision taken by the advisory board on behalf of the managing directors can be communicated to the outside world. The chairman of the advisory board makes an external declaration of intent (if the rules on the respective advisory board allow such kind of declaration).

Activities of an advisory board also have an external effect if employees of the company communicate with the advisory board or third parties contact it, e.g., in compliance matters.

The advisory board may also be entrusted with management responsibilities, which may also be used as a basis for external activities of the advisory board. It may then be entitled to conclude legal transactions with third parties, such as a service contract with a managing director of the company.

2.4 Members, breach of duty and liability

The advisory board is being composed of its members. In addition to the fundamental question of who can become a member of an advisory board and how the appointment and election process is structured, questions arise in particular about the possibility of breaches of duty and their consequences.

2.4.1 Members

In principle, (objectively justified) conditions for the appointment of advisory board members may be laid down, such as a minimum/maximum age, academic background, industry experience, member of the owner family, etc. Once suitable candidates have been identified, they must be appointed and, if necessary, an employment contract must be concluded. Both the position as an organ and the employment contract can determine the specific rights and duties of the members. If the members of the advisory board violate this, they may be held liable.

2.4.1.1 Eligibility requirements

There are various legal conditions for eligibility, in addition to which there can be optional requirements in the articles of association, as already pointed out above.

Furthermore, a member of the advisory board must be a natural person (not another partnership or corporation) who is not the legal representative of the company itself (managing directors, supervisory board members, etc.). However, certain groups of persons are denied the right of being professionally active in an area, even if they fulfil these requirements. For example, an appointment as a managing director of the same company usually excludes a parallel advisory board membership due to possible conflicts of interest. The member of the advisory board may also not make an arbitral decision about himself. The handling of so-called cross-involvements, i.e., advisory boards active in one company and at the same time managing directors in another and vice versa, is controversial.

2.4.1.2 Appointment and service agreement

The appointment of an advisory board member, i.e., the admission of a person to the advisory board, requires an organisational act based on company law. This act is referred to as an appointment. In this case, either an appointment from another corporate body or other third party (in particular by the shareholders' meeting or a single shareholder) or a co-optation can be considered. Co-optation means that the advisory board itself determines the successors for its departing members.

In addition to the appointment, it may also be necessary to conclude a service contract between the advisory board member and the company. The predominant opinion in the literature and jurisdiction recommends the conclusion of such a contract of service under the law of obligations.

2.4.1.3 Rights and duties of advisory board members

Advisory board responsibilities entail rights and duties for the advisory board members in general; an overview is shown in Figure 2.1. The personal rights and duties

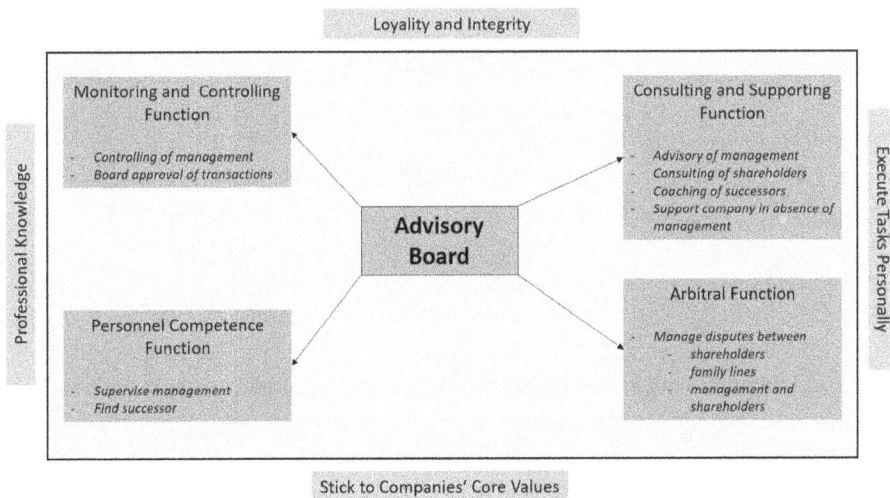

Figure 2.1: Typical responsibilities of advisory boards.

of the advisory board members generally correspond to those of the members of a (voluntary) supervisory board. Details, however, are derived from the individual tasks and structure of the respective advisory board.

In addition to the right to participate in advisory board meetings, the essential rights of an advisory board member are the right to vote (in the case of a decision-making advisory board), the right to receive minutes/protocols of meetings and a remuneration usually paid as well as reimbursement of expenses. Further rights may arise from a claim to be discharged, from any contractually agreed limitation of liability and from a right to the premature termination of one's own appointment.

The duties of the advisory board member result from the competences and tasks assigned by the shareholders. The tasks of the advisory board can be hugely different according to the purposes pursued by its appointment. The competences may be limited to a purely non-binding consultancy/advisory function, but may also include monitoring and control duties that are significant in terms of liability law.

In detail, the tasks differ according to the competences assigned to the advisory board as follows:

Consulting function

In the basic form of an advisory board, the latter is merely intended to "advise" the management.

In this constellation, the scope of the advice to be provided by the members of the advisory board depends upon the situation of the company and the mandate given; the more difficult or crisis-driven, the more intensive the advisory services must be rendered.

However, on the basis of an objective standard of interpretation, the assignment of "advice" alone cannot entitle the advisory board to any other right than to support the management in the sense of future-oriented advice with regard to all fields relevant to the company. A limitation of the consulting fields is not necessary, although it may actually be necessary.

In principle, the expert opinion of the advisory board is required, both for specific questions of the management, but also unsolicited, if the advisory board recognises a corresponding need. It is a permanent, continuous task that is future oriented. This requires a constant flow of information on the part of the managing directors, which may have to be reinforced if there is a specific need for advice.

The most important task of the advisory board is to accompany the management in leading the company into a promising future. It can support the management in the development and implementation of the corporate strategy and provide new ideas and thought-provoking impulses for the management. In a family business – in relation to the (owner) family – the advisory board can contribute to the family safeguarding its financial interests and exercising information and disclosure rights.

For the transfer of further tasks beyond the consultation it requires a basis in the articles of association of the company. If the articles of association do not describe any of the tasks of the advisory board, at least in general terms, its range of tasks is also reduced to mere advice to the managing directors. On the other hand, the tasks of the facultative supervisory board cannot be resorted to.

Supporting function

If the articles of association of the company stipulate that the advisory board should "support" the management, this also entails a purely advisory task for the advisory board. In any case, it cannot be assumed without further indications that the tasks and powers referred to in Section 52 GmbHG have been transferred to the advisory board. At most, it is questionable whether this will change if the task of supporting the management is supplemented by the transfer of specific powers of instruction (in practice, the committee is then frequently referred to as a "shareholders' committee" or "administrative (advisory) board"). Since, however, instruction powers also have a forward-looking effect, it can also be assumed in this case that no supervisory board within the meaning of Section 52 GmbHG has been formed and that the advisory board, apart from the specifically designated instruction powers, merely exercises an advisory function.

Monitoring function

In an advisory board with a supervisory function, control and monitoring tasks are regularly at the forefront of its duties; in contrast to advisory/consultancy tasks, it is thus oriented towards the past. The advisory board is then obliged to monitor the management regarding the legality, regularity and cost-effectiveness of its actions. The monitoring of legality means that the advisory board must ensure that the management acts within the legal and contractual limits. In a comparable way, it assumes (at least a part of) the function of a supervisory board in a stock corporation.

The control of the regularity is directed to the question whether the organisation of the enterprise is economically meaningful in the sense of the expediency.

Things are more complicated if the committee has been assigned the task of supervising the management. "Monitoring" is the *terminus technicus* of Section 111 Para. 1 AktG. Objectively, therefore, the assignment of a supervisory task indicates that the rights of the body should at least correspond to those rights that are assigned to an optional supervisory board pursuant to Section 52 Para. 1 GmbHG in conjunction with Section 111 Para. 1 AktG. If the articles of association do not relate to the validity of Section 52 Para. 1 GmbHG, it can be further assumed that an optional supervisory board has been formed due to the use of the *terminus technicus* of Section 111 Para. 1 AktG. If there is no clear provision in the articles of association regarding the rights of the "supervising" body, this is to be regarded as an optional supervisory board within the meaning of Section 52 Para. 1 GmbHG, irrespective of whether it is also referred to in the articles of association as a supervisory board or as an advisory board, committee or family board, etc.

Controlling function

There is no difference in a legal sense if the term "monitor" is replaced by the term "control" alone or in addition. Although this term does not appear in Section 111 Para.1 AktG, this cannot result in a minus in powers if an objective standard of interpretation is applied. The terms "monitor" and "control" are therefore also equated in company law jurisdiction and in company law literature. If the advisory board is to control the managing directors, it has – if no further indications are given – also the minimum tasks of an optional supervisory board according to Section 52 Para. 1 GmbHG in conjunction with Section 111 Para. 1 AktG. Unless individual provisions are waived, it can also be assumed in principle that the "controlling" advisory board is entitled to all the powers (and duties) of the facultative supervisory board within the meaning of Section 52 GmbHG.

Arbitral tasks

Sometimes an advisory board is also assigned the task of "arbitrating" disputes between the company and shareholders, the shareholders and the managing directors or among the shareholders. The member of the advisory board to whom arbitral functions have been delegated assumes the duty, with his office, to take note of, discuss, formulate his opinion neutrally and impartially without regard to any person or matter, and to cast his vote accordingly, i.e., to arbitrate the matter. This duty also includes the task of bringing up possible conflicts of interest of the arbitrating advisory board member in good time and, if necessary, even to refrain from discussion or voting and to temporarily refrain from exercising his office in this respect.

Such an assignment of tasks is then typically specified in more detail, for example, by the provision that a court can only be called upon after an attempt at conciliation before the advisory board has failed, whereby the duration and procedure of the conciliation attempt are regularly regulated in more detail. If the articles of association merely stipulate that the advisory board "arbitrates" disputes, only this one field of competence can be opened up to the advisory board from the outset. A further task to advise the management or even to supervise the management is then excluded.

A conciliatory or arbitrational function of the advisory board will be considered in particular in companies in whose shareholders' meetings equally strong "blocks", such as different family groups or 50/50 participants, face one another.

Obligation to find a successor

It can also be the task of an advisory board to facilitate the succession in the management of the respective company. The assignment of an advisory board in the area of company succession has proven itself in practice in order to maintain the continuity and ability to act, of a family business in particular. Then the advisory board has the duty to ensure the best possible succession with regard to the new management director's position to be filled.

In this context, it can also be the task of an advisory board to merely accompany a harmonious generation change with experience and know-how. An advisory board can also perform a coaching function in this respect.

On the other hand, the mediating advisory board can also compensate for existing conflicts between or within the shareholders or family groups. In this respect, it can have a moderating and mediating function.

Ultimately, an advisory board can also be available as a management corporate body – for example, in the event of the unexpected departure of a strong shareholder – and ensure the appointment of a successor.

Obligation of personal participation

The tasks and powers delegated to the advisory board shall be exercised by its members themselves in person (*höchstpersönlich*). Tasks may not be transferred to third parties, but it may be permissible to entrust third parties with the procurement of information and input. The third party must then comply with the confidentiality obligations of the advisory board. Depending on the provision in the articles of association or rules of procedure, a member of the advisory board may be represented at meetings or accompanied by experts, which does not prevent any confidentiality needs.

Duty of loyalty

The advisory board and its members are committed to the interests of the company. The interests of individual (minority) shareholders or specific family groups shall only be considered to the extent that they form part of the overall interests of the company to be considered by the advisory board.

The individual duties of the advisory board members, which are indexed under company law, are based on this. The interests of the company must be safeguarded and there is an obligation not to take into account any own or other interests in the exercise of the advisory board rights and duties, although a general reconciliation of different interests should generally be harmless.

The obligation of fiduciary duty thus applies to each individual board member and obliges any individual member of the advisory board to safeguard the interests of the company.

Duty of confidentiality

Members of an advisory board shall maintain secrecy regarding confidential tasks and business secrets of the company that have become known to them through their activities on the advisory board. The obligation to maintain secrecy applies to all confidential tasks and information that are not intended to become obvious according to an objectively assessed need for secrecy on the part of the company. The same applies to all facts, such as the design of production processes, corporate planning, including investment and sales projects, as well as financial planning and other company-specific information. Decisive for classification as a "business secret" is the company's interest in not disclosing the information and the company's objective need for confidentiality.

The obligation to maintain secrecy applies during the period of an advisory board member's term of office, but also beyond the term of office of an advisory board member. It is possible to further regulate, restrict or extend the obligation of confidentiality (also only for individual advisory board members) in the articles of association, in the service agreements of the advisory board members or in the rules of procedure of the advisory board.

Instruction commitment

Shareholders of the company may be entitled to issue instructions to the advisory board. The articles of association, the rules of procedure or the service agreements may further stipulate that the members of an advisory board are bound by (other) instructions. In this case, the members of the advisory board are obliged to observe the relevant instructions; they may not carry out their own discretionary or expediency control, even if they consider the instructions to be materially incorrect. The individual member of the advisory board merely has the opportunity to raise his objections in the advisory board or to refuse to participate in a resolution; a resignation from the office of member of the advisory board, possibly with immediate effect, may be considered as a last resort. As far as a member of the advisory board observes instructions to them, they are not liable for any damages that occur while they have obeyed such binding instructions.

However, it is generally not advisable to include general rights of instruction vis-à-vis an advisory board, since the value of advisory boards lies precisely in the fact that they bring their own experience, specialist knowledge and judgement to their work. It will also be difficult to win qualified and independent personalities for an activity in the advisory board of a company, if this activity is subject to extensive instruction rights of the partners.

Specific rights and obligations in the case of open statutes

In the case of open statutes in which the rights and duties of the advisory board are not regulated in more detail than just "advisory", "supervising" or "controlling", the field of competence of the advisory board can be defined on the basis of an analysis of its name and the abstract-general task assignments contained in the articles of association. Since the specific rights and duties of the advisory board members depend quite decisively on the tasks assigned to the advisory board and thus on the provisions of the articles of association to be interpreted in the individual case, they can be very different. On the other hand, open statutes are characterised by the fact that they only contain a highly incomplete regulation.

However, it is possible to make some fundamental observations:

Consulting advisory board

In the basic form of the advisory board, the latter has the task of advising the management. Accordingly, the individual member of the advisory board is entitled and obliged to advise the managing directors and thereby support them in the management of the company. The members of the advisory board shall therefore comment individually or together with the other members of the advisory board on questions arising from the development of the company as well as current business activities and/or plans of the management. The scope of the consultation naturally depends on the specific situation of the company. The right to advice is condensed into a corresponding duty of the members of the advisory board in particular when unusual or complex decisions are involved. For the basic obligation of the members of the advisory board to provide advice in accordance with the diligence of a prudent and conscientious member of the advisory board it is ultimately irrelevant whether they act on the basis as a corporative member of an advisory board or (also) on the basis of a service contract under the law of obligations. The duty of the members of the advisory board to advise the company also entails a fundamental duty to participate in the meetings of the advisory board, as this is the only way to provide orderly information on relevant business transactions and appropriate advice. Furthermore, it should be noted that the members of an advisory board are also subject to a duty of loyalty under company law. After all, the members of the advisory board are bound to confidentiality. Considering that, in the interest of high-quality advice, the advisory boards are generally given a comprehensive insight into the company, the relevance of this obligation is assessed.

The basis for any consultation is sufficient information about the specific subject matter. Nevertheless, the advisory board member's advisory task does not necessarily correspond to a comprehensive claim for information on the part of the advisory board member vis-à-vis the management; for shareholders, however, reference is made to Sections 51a and b GmbHG. In this respect, it cannot go unnoticed that the information claim for the facultative supervisory board is only established by the reference to Section 90 AktG contained in Section 52 Para. 1 GmbHG. On the other hand, expert advice to the management requires comprehensive information of the advisory board members on relevant business transactions and the company's situation. If the consulting fields are therefore not limited – which will not normally be the case with open statutes – and if accordingly nothing can be derived from the articles of association for a limitation of the claim to information, the advisory board has the right to be informed about the essential actions and decisions of the management and their effects on the situation of the company. If special business decisions or measures are pending, this claim to information is condensed and updated accordingly.

Advisory board as voluntary supervisory board

If, after interpretation of the articles of association, the advisory board is to be qualified as a voluntary supervisory board, its rights shall be determined in accordance with the provisions of the German Stock Corporation Act referred to in Section 52 Para. 1 GmbHG, subject to deviating provisions in the articles of association. Even if this country report cannot constitute a compendium of the tasks and powers of an optional GmbH supervisory board for reasons of space, the following tasks are nevertheless outlined at least briefly:

Supervision of the management. In accordance with Section 52 Para. 1 GmbHG in conjunction with Section 111 AktG, the voluntary supervisory board has in particular the task of supervising the managing directors of the company. Controlling is the core task of the facultative supervisory board as a decisive differentiation criterion from the advisory board in the narrower sense. It extends to supervise compliance with the law, the articles of association, the rules of procedure, the proper business management of the company and the economic efficiency of the management's actions. It may relate to past as well as current and future management measures.

In order for the voluntary supervisory board to be able to fulfil its supervisory task, sufficient and timely information from the managing directors is required. For the voluntary supervisory board, corresponding reporting rights result directly from the reference to Section 90 Para. 3, 4 and 5 sentence 1 and 2 AktG contained in Section 52 Para. 1 GmbHG. However, the absence of a reference to the reporting obligations of the managing directors leads to the conclusion that the voluntary supervisory board itself must act. Since the voluntary supervisory board remains at liberty to make regular enquiries, regular reporting can nevertheless be achieved as a result.

German Federal Court, Judgment of 2 February 2016 – file no. II ZB 2/15
In this respect, the German Federal Court has clarified the competences of advisory boards with regard to litigation against (former) managing directors:

If the advisory board, which acts instead of the shareholders' meeting in accordance with the articles of association, has made use of its authority to conduct a lawsuit against a (retired) managing director, a managing director of the company may not grant a power of attorney for the company and, for example, lodge an appeal.

According to the established case law of the German Federal Court, Section 46 no. 8 alt. 2 GmbHG provides for the shareholders' meeting (or the advisory board, if this competence has been transferred to it), to appoint a representative of the company in lawsuits, insofar as these are conducted against current or former managing directors. This is intended to ensure unbiased litigation in legal disputes. The company is only represented by the managing directors if the shareholders' meeting or the advisory board does not make use of this authority.

Managing directors of a company are therefore well advised to first take care of a shareholders' or advisory board resolution on the legal representation of the company in a law suit
against a managing director in order to avoid liability risks.

Accounting system. From an analogous application of the Sections 170 et. seq.
AktG a right of the voluntary supervisory board exists to take note of and to audit
the company's annual financial statements and consolidated financial statements.
Accordingly, the voluntary supervisory board may analyse the annual financial
statements and submit corresponding statements to the shareholders' meeting.

Personnel expertise. Subject to a corresponding explicit allocation in the articles
of association, however, the voluntary supervisory board lacks any personnel competence. It is therefore neither responsible for the appointment and dismissal of a
managing director nor for the conclusion or amendment of his service contract. The
competence of the shareholders' meeting (Section 46 no. 5 GmbHG) remains unaffected in this respect.

Enforcement opportunities. To carry out its supervisory tasks, the voluntary supervisory board is entitled to formally criticise the management, report to the shareholders'
meeting and, if necessary, convene a shareholders' meeting. The reorganisation or dismissal of individual managing directors, on the other hand, can only be carried out –
as already pointed out above – if expressly assigned by the articles of association.

2.4.2 Breach of duty and liability

Members of an advisory board who fail to comply with the standard of care incumbent upon them may be held liable for breaches of duty. It is questionable who is
the claimant of claims for damages and what possibilities exist for the advisory
board as a whole or the individual member of the advisory board to reduce his
liability.

2.4.2.1 Breach of duty

Members of an advisory board shall perform their duties carefully and conscientiously. Otherwise there may be a breach of duty. An advisory board that acts
against the interests of the company commits a breach of duty as well as one that
does not fulfil its supervisory duties or one that violates its duty of confidentiality.
The duties of each member of the advisory board shall be determined based on his
general and specific duties.

A breach of duties can lead to (immediate) dismissal as an advisory board member and thus to termination of the corporative relationship to the company and, as a rule, also to termination of the service contract for good cause without notice period.

In addition to the termination of the position as an advisory board member, claims for damages against the member may also arise. However, there are no separate statutory provisions on the liability of advisory boards with respect to its members, as the duties of the advisory board can largely be structured individually. However, similar liability regulations exist for corporations in Section 52 GmbHG, as well as Sections 116 and 93 AktG. If the advisory board is set up with a corporation, such as a GmbH, the quite prevailing opinion assumes a corresponding application of the legal organ liability as a basis for a compensation liability of the advisory board member (Sections 93, 116 AktG, Sections 43, 52 GmbHG).

Furthermore, the member of the advisory board may be liable for a breach of his service contract.

For partnerships, however, there are no direct statutory provisions for the assertion of claims for damages. However, according to the case-law of the German Federal Court, the liability principles for limited partnerships serving as a public closed fund vehicle (*Publikumsgesellschaft*) according to Sections 93, 116 AktG are basically applicable accordingly. On the other hand, this jurisdiction is not to be applicable to companies with only a small circle of shareholders. For members of an advisory board under the law of obligations, there is only liability for breach of contract.

2.4.2.2 Standard of care

Advisory board members have the obligation to perform their duties conscientiously and carefully. If, however, a member of the advisory board commits a breach of duty, this must be by fault. Fault means that the advisory board member must have acted intentionally or negligently, Section 276 BGB. Here, the standard of an ordinary and conscientious member of the advisory board applies, i.e., an objectified standard of care. Each member of the advisory board must therefore have at least the knowledge and abilities of an average member of the advisory board necessary for the specific company and task.

For advisory board members in corporations the same standard of care applies as for supervisory board members of a stock corporation. For advisory board members of a partnership, on the other hand, it is disputed whether the due diligence standard of the advisory board members is to be applied objectively or subjectively.

2.4.2.3 Assertion

The company shall be entitled to claim damages from a member of the advisory board. If the company does not assert a claim for damages, it must be considered in the individual case whether a shareholder can proceed directly against an advisory board member by way of a so-called *actio pro socio*, which is possible in principle. This is understood to mean the conduct of a shareholder who asserts claims of the company directly against another shareholder in his own name for payment to the company in court. The claim is then directed against the member of the advisory board who committed the breach of duty.

2.4.2.4 Discharge and waiver of claims for damages

Measures of the advisory board may be approved by the shareholders' meeting. The consequence of this is that for claims for damages against advisory board members that have already arisen, breaches of duty that are recognisable to the shareholders and are included in the discharge resolution can no longer be claimed against the advisory board members. However, a discharge does not refer to unknown facts. It is further disputed whether a restrictive function of the discharge in the sense of a waiver is also to apply to advisory boards, as is the case in stock corporation law when it comes to mandatory supervisory boards. The company may also expressly waive known claims for damages against members of the advisory board to which it is entitled. This requires a waiver contract to be concluded between the advisory board member and the company in accordance with Section 387 BGB.

2.4.2.5 Limitation of liability

Due to the contractual freedom in the establishment of advisory boards, there are no fundamental objections to including liability limitations in favour of the advisory board members in the articles of association or the individual service agreements. However, a limitation of liability that a company wishes to impose on its advisory board members, and that has no basis in the articles of association or the service agreements must be approved by the shareholders' meeting.

A limitation of liability can also be achieved by determining the duties to be fulfilled by the advisory board members, e.g., if restrictions are provided for, e.g., by introducing a broad discretion or changing the burden of proof. The shareholders can apply (i.e., reduce) the liability standard up to the limits of Section 276 Para. 3 BGB. However, when limiting liability, the shareholders should bear in mind that the members of the advisory board, depending on the tasks resulting from the transfer of competence, sometimes assume very extensive responsibility and that liability can and should therefore be a correlate to this responsibility. A limitation of liability should therefore, if it is to be introduced at all, take into account the interests of both sides.

2.4.2.6 Liability towards third parties and shareholders

Advisory board members may be liable not only to the company, but also to third parties and shareholders. In particular, a member of the advisory board may be liable pursuant to Sections 823 et seq. BGB if it commits an unlawful act or violates protective laws (in particular if it makes itself liable to prosecution to the detriment of the company because of the broadly defined offence of breach of trust in accordance with Section 266 German criminal law [*Strafgesetzbuch, StGB*]).

2.5 Termination

Upon termination, the termination of the appointment of a member of the advisory board and the termination of the advisory board itself must be separated from each other.

2.5.1 Termination with regard to a certain member

The membership of a member of the advisory board may be duly terminated at the end of the specified period, upon completion of tasks or prematurely by dismissal of the member of the advisory board or resignation from office (or by death) by the member of the advisory board.

The appointment and term of office of an advisory board member shall be governed by the rules laid down in the statutes/bylaws or may be terminated extraordinarily – and thus also without express regulation. Insofar as the articles of association do not contain any provisions, the shareholders' meeting shall be responsible for specifying the necessary details.

A distinction must also be made between the position of an executive body and the service relationship when the advisory board membership of an advisory board member is terminated.

2.5.1.1 Automatic termination

If the term of office of an advisory board member is stipulated in the articles of association for a fixed period (typically three to five years), the term of office of the member shall end automatically at the end of that period, unless the articles of association contain an automatic renewal clause until the election of a new member. If the memorandum and articles of association contain no provisions on the term of office and if no time limit is specified in the appointment, the member is appointed for an indefinite term, which is also possible. If the advisory board is abolished due to a change in the articles of association, the term of office of the advisory board members ends automatically, as does the expiry of the company.

The abolition of personal requirements can also lead to a termination of the advisory board office, for example if an age limit set in the articles of association is reached or if an advisory board member becomes incapable of acting. However, the advisory board office ends in any case with the death of the advisory board member. As the office is highly personal, inheritance is out of the question.

The service contract agreed with the member of the advisory board can also end due to the expiry of time, the death of a member of the advisory board, the loss of personal prerequisites, the abolition of the advisory board or the extinction of the company.

2.5.1.2 Dismissal

There are no legal regulations on the dismissal of advisory board members; hence, the general principles of company law apply.

The advisory board membership can then be terminated by dismissal, whereby it must be differentiated whether the advisory board member is appointed for a certain period of time or for an indefinite period of time (in particular lifetime). If an advisory board member has been appointed for life, dismissal will only be considered for good cause.

The appointing body is responsible for the dismissal, i.e., either the shareholders' meeting or the shareholder entitled to delegate (so-called *actus contrarius* theory). A dismissal has to take place expressly the opposite way than the appointment. It can take place without form, unless something else is provided for in the articles of association. The termination of the service relationship must be separated from the dismissal and is independent from it.

2.5.1.3 Resignation

The resignation from office of an advisory board member is also not regulated by law, but its admissibility is generally recognised. In the articles of association, resignation from office may be regulated by an advisory board member. A specific fact or an important reason may entitle the member to resign from office, even without any prior notice period.

If there is no provision in the articles of association, an advisory board member can resign from office in any case if there is a good cause. Apart from this, it has not yet been clarified by the German Federal Court whether a good cause is always required for resignation in the absence of provisions in the articles of association, or whether it can take place at any time – except at an inopportune time (during an ongoing restructuring or take-over). It may also be necessary to differentiate whether the activity of the member of the advisory board is carried out against payment or free of charge.

Unless otherwise stipulated in the articles of association, the statement of resignation may be made informally, i.e., also orally.

The termination of the employment contract under the law of obligations must be distinguished from the corporative resignation, which terminates the position under company law as an advisory board member. Here, the content of the service contract is decisive. This can be terminated by mutual consent, which is also possible informally. Furthermore, the service contract may end due to the expiry of time, death of the member of the advisory board, the loss of personal prerequisites (age limit, etc.), the abolition of the advisory board itself or the termination of the company.

If the service contract is limited in time, it ends on the agreed expiry date, unless there is an extraordinary reason for termination. If the service contract is concluded for an indefinite period, it can be terminated in accordance with Sections 620 Para. 2, 621 BGB. An unscheduled termination of a paid service contract can be effected by an extraordinary termination, Sections 627, 626 BGB.

2.5.1.4 Termination of service contract by a member of the advisory board

The termination of a service contract by a member of the advisory board also leads to the premature termination of the corporate status of an advisory board member, although the initiative for this is taken by the member of the advisory board himself.

A distinction must be made between the termination of a paid service contract and the termination of a free-of-charge service contract. If no remuneration is paid to the member of the advisory board, the contractual relationship between the company and the member of the advisory board may be regarded as a contractual relationship (*Auftrag*), Sections 662 et seq. BGB. The contractual relationship may be terminated by the member of the advisory board at any time in accordance with Section 671 Para. 1 BGB. However, the termination may not take place at an inopportune time, unless there is an important reason for the inopportune termination, Section 671 Para. 2 sentence 1 BGB. If the non-remunerated member of the advisory board is authorised to resign, he may also terminate his service contract.

If a member of an advisory board has declared a termination of his service contract without having simultaneously or previously declared a resignation, his declaration will have to be understood as a simultaneous resignation of the position under company law.

In the case of a paid membership, which as a rule should be classified as an agency agreement with service contract character, Sections 675, 611 et seq. BGB shall apply. This depends upon the question whether the service contract was concluded for a limited or unlimited period or whether there is an important reason or not.

In addition to the scheduled termination facts, the unscheduled termination by extraordinary termination is also possible for an advisory board member if the statutory or, if applicable, contractually agreed prerequisites are fulfilled.

2.5.1.5 Termination of office by mutual agreement

A consensual termination of an advisory board mandate is possible at any time and does not require a good cause.

2.5.2 Termination of advisory board itself

The existence of an advisory board itself may end temporarily or permanently.

2.5.2.1 Advisory board incapable of acting

An advisory board is incapable of acting if it no longer fulfils or is unable to fulfil the tasks assigned to it. The inability to act can be due to various reasons. "No being able" means that the conditions necessary for the action of the advisory board and particularly for a resolution, such as the quorum, are not given. An inability to act can exist among other things for the following reasons:

- prevention of one or more advisory board members, e.g., due to illness or overlapping appointments at an advisory board meeting
- withdrawal of a member from the advisory board, e.g., by resignation from office, dismissal, loss of personal prerequisites or death
- conflict of interests of an advisory board member
- stalemate in the advisory board or
- boycott of advisory board measures or even simple failure to act (omission)

The inability to act can vary in length depending on the individual constellations.

However, not every inability of an advisory board to act also has legal relevance. Insofar as the prerequisites for the advisory board to act have ceased to exist, the remaining members of the advisory board are obliged to ensure that the ability to act is restored as soon as possible.

Many problems of incapacity to act can be avoided by certain regulations provided for in the articles of association, etc. For example, resolutions should not depend on the presence of all members, there should be regulations to avoid stalemate situations or the possibility of passing resolutions outside meetings.

If the advisory board is unable to act but a resolution is urgently required the question arises whether the shareholders' meeting is appointed to decide instead of the advisory board (so-called recidivism competence (*Rückfallkompetenz*) of the shareholders' meeting), which will be the case in case of doubt.

2.5.2.2 Non-acting advisory board

A "non-acting" advisory board is an advisory board that is in principle capable of acting but – intentionally or slightly negligently – does not act. Normally, all advisory board members are obliged to participate in the omission. In practice, however, there are always cases in which an advisory board proactively does not wish to act. The advisory board members who do not act then violate their duties, can be dismissed immediately and may be liable to pay damages.

2.5.2.3 Temporary advisory board

The temporary advisory board is not usual in practice. A temporary advisory board should only be considered if advisory and controlling measures are only to be provided for a limited period of time by expert persons to support the management or if genuine management activities are also to be ensured, for example in the aftermath of a company takeover, in order to support downstream integration or in restructuring scenarios.

2.5.2.4 Faulty advisory board

A defective advisory board was one not set up effectively, but nevertheless became legally binding. If the advisory board was set up correctly but only the appointment of an advisory board member was ineffective, this is not a question of the end of an advisory board as a corporate body; it must then be examined whether the advisory board could act effectively without the ineffectively appointed member of the advisory board or not.

2.5.2.5 Restricted advisory board

Shareholders may limit the powers of an advisory board from the outset or at a later date. To the extent that the shareholders' meeting limits the competences of the advisory board, its competence ends. The decision of the shareholders leads to a limited field of responsibility of the advisory board, but has no effect on its existence.

2.5.2.6 Abolition of the advisory board

The shareholders of a company can abolish the advisory board. This is an amendment to the organisational structure of the company so that the regulations applicable to amendments to the articles of association must be observed. With the abolition of the advisory board, the powers exercised by it revert to the originally competent corporate body. The rights and duties of the members of the advisory board will cease to apply in the future. Until the date of abolition, the advisory board must continue to exercise its activities; resolutions adopted by it remain effective even after the end of the advisory board.

However, the advisory board cannot be tacitly abolished. The abolition of the advisory board – just as the establishment – must be carried by a clearly recognisable outward will formation of the shareholders. The advisory board also cannot abolish itself; only the advisory board members can resign their mandate in each case and thus effectively terminate the advisory board activity indirectly.

2.5.2.7 Advisory boards in crisis and insolvency

The crisis of a company does not immediately affect the existence of the advisory board. However, the scope of the advisory board's activities can be influenced, and the members of the advisory board must also pay attention to any delay in insolvency to avoid personal liability later. In principle, the members of the advisory board are not obliged to file for the opening of insolvency proceedings. In provisional insolvency proceedings, the members of the advisory board usually act at their own risk. An agreed remuneration may only be asserted as an insolvency claim. At this stage, advisory board members can consider whether they have a reason for resigning their memberships and terminating their service contracts due to the insolvency.

If the company's assets are not sufficient to cover the costs of the insolvency proceedings, the insolvency court will reject the application to open insolvency proceedings for lack of assets, Section 26 Para. 1 InsO. The advisory board shall be dissolved by operation of law, Sections 131 Para. 2, 161 Para. 2 HGB, 60 Para. 1 no. 5 GmbHG, 262 Para. 1 no. 4, 289 AktG. With the deletion of the advisory board also any rights and obligations of the advisory board members are abolished for the future.

2.5.2.8 Advisory boards in dissolved companies

The existence of an advisory board may also depend on the decision of the shareholders on the continued existence of the advisory board company. As soon as the shareholders decide to dissolve their company (Sections 131 Para. 2 no. 2, 161 HGB, 60 Para. 1 no. 2 GmbHG, 262 Para. 1 no. 2, 289 AktG), the "living" company is transformed into a liquidation company with the aim of liquidating the assets and (fully) terminating the dissolved company.

If the shareholders do not pass any resolutions concerning the advisory board on the occasion of the dissolution, the dissolution resolution has no direct effect on the existence of the advisory board. In future, however, the advisory board must realign its activities towards the liquidation purpose.

Dietmar Lux and Julius Ecker

Chapter 3
Austria

3.1 Introduction

Medium-sized and family owned companies and private foundations in many cases set up an authority/body organised according to individually set rules alongside the mandatory bodies. They call it an advisory board, administrative board, a shareholders' committee, board of partners, family board, standing committee, an advisory committee, a board of trustees, committee, an arbitration committee, etc.[1] These bodies are charged with a wide range of tasks: "No two advisory boards are alike."[2] Any general statement on the conception of such bodies fails because of their diversity. In practice, the advisory board's main purpose is to provide advice to the management, control and supervise the management, perform certain shareholder or management duties and act as arbitrator in disputes or decide controversies.[3]

3.2 Concept and definition, demarcation from the company's other bodies

3.2.1 Concept and definition

Austrian corporate law contains no legal definition nor any explicit rules for advisory boards. Setting up an advisory board on the basis of corporate law is one option. Although Austrian law contains no specific provisions on advisory boards, it expressly allows the establishment of "additional bodies" in the articles of association (e.g., § 14 para 2 PSG [Private Foundation Act]). If such an additional body is laid down in the articles of association, memorandum of association or deed of foundation or set up on the basis of an authorisation enshrined there by means of a shareholders' resolution, it will have the quality of a body under corporate law (see Section 3.3.1.1). The second possibility is to set up an advisory board purely on a contractual basis under the law of obligations (see Section 3.3.1.3).

---

1 *Kalss* in Kalss/Kunz, Handbuch Aufsichtsrat[2] Rz 39/1; *Kalss/Probst*, Familienunternehmen Rz 13/149.
2 *Kalss* in Kalss/Kunz, Handbuch Aufsichtsrat[2] Rz 39/1.
3 Cf. *M. Heidinger*, Aufgaben und Verantwortlichkeit von Aufsichtsrat und Beirat der GmbH (1988) 363.

https://doi.org/10.1515/9783110666182-003

3.2.2 Demarcation from supervisory board and other bodies

The conceptual distinction between the company's bodies is of decisive importance. Extensive discussion and case-law on the demarcation and admissibility of advisory boards versus supervisory boards – which are regulated by law – have evolved in Austria.

3.2.2.1 The Stock Corporation (AG)

The mandatory provisions of §§ 86 et seq. AktG (Stock Corporation Act) regulate the formation of a supervisory board and its powers. Forming an advisory board is acceptable, provided that the supervisory board's powers are not restricted by it.[4] There are no objections to the rights to be heard or provide advice.[5] This does not apply to the transfer of decision-making powers[6] if such transfer interfered with the rigid body structure of a stock corporation; thus, the advisory board does not play a major role alongside the supervisory board – which is mandatory in stock corporations in any case[7] – in practice. The advisory board is, therefore, typically created as a panel of advisors (e.g., advisory board for environmental matters, scientific committee[8]) or set up for specific projects (e.g., architecture committee).

3.2.2.2 The Limited Liability Company (GmbH)

This legal form is of particular relevance to medium-sized (often family run) businesses. That an advisory board is generally admissible is derived from § 20 para 2 GmbHG (Limited Liability Companies Act), which refers to the consent of the shareholders, the supervisory board or "another body of the company". Moreover – irrespective of the legal form – the materials on § 239 UGB (Austrian Commercial Code) explicitly mention the advisory board, referring to it as being a body "similar to" the supervisory board and the management board.[9] The great flexibility provided by the legislation on limited liability companies gives ample scope for the implementation of

---

4 *Kastner* in FS Strasser (1983) 843 (862) et seq.; *Kalss* in Doralt/Nowotny/Kalss, AktG² up to § 86 Rz 33; *Nowotny*, Beirat – Aufsichtsrat – Ausschuss, RdW 2008, 699 (699).
5 *Kalss/Probst*, Familienunternehmen Rz 13/149.
6 *Nowotny*, RdW 2008, 699 (699).
7 See *Kastner*, Beiräte im österreichischen Gesellschaftsrecht, RdW 1983, 98 (98 et seq.); *Kalss* in Doralt/Nowotny/Kalss, AktG² Vor § 86 Rz 32 and *Nowotny*, RdW 2008, 699 (699).
8 *Kalss* in Kalss/Kunz, Handbuch Aufsichtsrat² Rz 39/15 et seq.
9 ErlRV 1270 BlgNR XVII. GP 60.

an advisory board as compared to stock corporations.[10] In principle, powers of other bodies – provided that they are of a discretionary nature – may be transferred to the advisory board of a limited liability company.[11]

Only in specifically defined cases is the creation of a supervisory board for a limited liability company mandatory, for example, if the share capital exceeds 70,000 Euros and the number of shareholders exceeds 50 (§ 29 para 1 subpara 1 GmbHG) or if the number of employees averages more than 300 (§ 29 para 1 subpara 2 GmbHG). If none of these cases applies, setting up a supervisory board is no requirement – unlike in a stock corporation. Nevertheless, the articles of association may provide for the creation of a voluntary supervisory board (§ 29 para 7 GmbHG). If a supervisory board is set up voluntarily, according to prevailing opinion[12] the same legal requirements on organisation and powers and in particular employee participation as defined by § 110 ArbVG (Labor Constitution Act) as those applicable to mandatory supervisory boards shall apply (if the supervisory board consists of an even number of shareholder representatives, one member per two shareholder representatives on the supervisory board is appointed by the works council; in the case of an odd number, an additional works council representative is appointed). The reasoning behind this analogous application of said rules is to prevent creditors and the public from being deceived by the establishment of a voluntary but ineffective supervisory board.[13]

An advisory board may be set up alongside an optional or a mandatory supervisory board; in either case the supervisory board's statutory minimum set of powers must not be curtailed by the advisory board.[14]

An advisory board may also be set up where no (mandatory or optional) supervisory board exists. In such a case, if vested with a supervisory board's "key powers", the advisory board qualifies as a voluntary supervisory board in case-law[15] and parts

---

10 See *A. Heidinger* in Gruber/Harrer, GmbHG² § 29 Rz 56; *Kalss* in Kalss/Kunz, Handbuch Aufsichtsrat² Rz 39/1; for Germany *Reichert* in FS Maier-Reimer (2010) 543 (544).

11 OLG Vienna 27.9.1982, 5 R 106/82; *Kalss/Probst,* Familienunternehmen Rz 13/152.

12 *Reich-Rohrwig,* Der Beirat der GmbH, ÖJZ 1981, 509 (509 et seq.); *Reich-Rohrwig,* GmbH-Recht I² Rz 4/132; *M. Heidinger* Aufgaben 42; *A. Heidinger* in Gruber/Harrer, GmbHG² § 29 Rz 51; *Koppensteiner/Rüffler, GmbHG³* § 29 Rz 18; *Straube/Rauter* in Straube, WK GmbHG § 29 Rz 85; OGH 1 Ob 144/01k, GesRZ 2002, 86 on rights and obligations, and OGH 9 ObA 130/05s, DRdA 2008/15 (*Putzer*) on employee participation; in this regard doubts are only expressed by *P. Huber,* Fakultativer Aufsichtsrat, Beirat und Arbeitnehmermitwirkung in der GmbH, ecolex 1995, 807 (810).

13 This can be clearly seen from materials on GmbHG 1906 (ErlRV 236 BlgHH 17. Sess 67 et seq.); see also HHB 272 BlgHH 17. Sess 9: A voluntary supervisory board must not be a lure ("Lockspeise") for the public.

14 *Reich-Rohrwig,* Der Beirat der GmbH, ÖJZ 1981, 509 (510); *M. Heidinger,* Aufgaben 386; *A. Heidinger* in Gruber/Harrer, GmbHG² § 29 Rz 63.

15 OGH 9 ObA 130/05s, DRdA 2008/15 (*Putzer*).

of legal theory[16] regardless of it being called an advisory board. Consequently, all requirements applying to a supervisory board (including, but not limited to, employee participation as defined by § 110 ArbVG) will also apply to such an advisory board. If the power of appointment or removal of members of such advisory board is then restricted or (as in private foundations) mandatorily assigned directly to the court that keeps the commercial register, the shareholders will have a very limited influence on the composition of an advisory board vested with such excessive powers.

> **Supreme Court of Justice (OGH), Ruling of 27 September 2006, 9 ObA 130/05s**
> In sum the OGH ruled that a body formed on the basis of articles of association (as "advisory board" or "administrative board") that was vested with the "key powers" of a supervisory board must be considered "supervisory board-like" and the relevant legal provisions – including, but not limited to, those relating to employee participation (§ 110 ArbVG) – shall be applicable. According to § 110 ArbVG, in stock corporations but also in a limited liability company a minimum of one third of the members of the supervisory board must be employee representatives (one-third parity representation). The OGH ruled that the name of the board (in casu: "administrative board") is not the point in the assessment of whether a board is supervisory board-like or not.
> The OGH relies on the following argument: It cannot be concluded from the right to choose whether to set up a supervisory board or not that the key powers of the supervisory board may also be assigned to an "advisory board" without the other legal requirements being imposed as well. Thus, if a body is to be vested with key powers, form constraints apply – mainly according to the older literature:[17] If the participation of employee representatives is mandatory for a supervisory board set up under corporate law, the same must apply if such a supervisory board does not exist but a body called "advisory board" is formed on the basis of the articles of association. In such cases one may speak of "evasion", which must be judged on the basis of the shareholders' true will upon the formation of the body.
> The OGH followed the critical legal theory[18] at least insofar as it dismissed the arguments of protection of transactions and risk of deception: In practice, advisory boards are charged with a great variety of tasks; thus the audience cannot associate any specific functions with a body of that name. Incidentally, persons outside the company are typically unaware of whether an advisory board exists or not. Thus the point is solely whether the advisory board is actually given "key powers".
> Such "key powers" of a supervisory board as mentioned by the OGH, in addition to control and monitoring and exceptional representation of the company, include in particular the reservations of consent regarding the catalog of measures in § 30j GmbHG. The actions that are subject to the consent of the advisory board include:
> – Acquisition and sale of interests and acquisition, sale and closure of businesses and operating units (§ 30j para 5 subpara 1);
> – Acquisition and sale of and encumbrances on real estate properties, unless such transactions are part of the ordinary course of business (§ 30j para 5 subpara 2);
> – Establishment and closure of branches (§ 30j para 5 subpara 3).

---

16 *Reich-Rohrwig*, ÖJZ 1981, 509 (511).

17 *Reich-Rohrwig*, ÖJZ 1981, 509 (511), who has abandoned this view since, see *Reich-Rohrwig*, GmbH-Recht I² Rz 4/498; *Löschnigg*, Die Entsendung der Betriebsräte in den Aufsichtsrat – organisationsrechtliche Probleme des § 110 ArbVG (1985) 53 et seq.; *M. Heidinger*, Aufgaben 383 et seq.

18 E.g. *Koppensteiner/Rüffler*, GmbHG³ § 35 Rz 54, 55; *P. Huber*, ecolex 1995, 807 (807 et seq.); *Reich-Rohrwig*, GmbH-Recht I² Rz 4/498.

The transfer of minor powers to an advisory board is not sufficient for the advisory board to qualify as "supervisory board-like".

This court ruling has been discussed quite contentiously in recent jurisprudence[19] but must be considered consolidated by now, given the fact that in a similar form it is also upheld in private foundation law.[20]

The limits drawn by the OGH should absolutely be respected in the arrangements made concerning an advisory board to avoid a reinterpretation and/or application of the rules applying to a supervisory board. Resorting to a purely contract-based advisory board as an alternative is a possibility,[21] but then the board cannot have any corporate powers (see Section 3.3.1.3).

3.2.2.3 The private foundation

No opportunities to exert influence like shareholders

The advisory board in Austria is of special relevance to private foundations, a frequently used organisation. About three-quarters of all Austrian private foundations provide for the possibility of setting up an advisory board.[22] This is mainly because an Austrian private foundation has no owner and hence no equivalent to a shareholders' meeting or a general meeting of shareholders; therefore an inherent control deficit exists.[23] "The controlling eye and the controlling hand of the owner" are missing.[24] This deficit can be compensated within defined limits by appropriate provisions laid down in the deed of foundation, mainly by setting up, alongside the foundation's management board, an advisory board appointed or controlled by the founder, the founder's family or the beneficiaries of the private foundation.[25]

Mandatory structure places restrictions on advisory board design

Thus, § 14 para 2 PSG allows setting up additional bodies for "safeguarding the foundation's purpose" alongside the foundation's mandatory bodies: management

---

19 Critical jurisprudence e.g. *Feltl*, remarks on 9 ObA 130/05s, GesRZ 2007, 197 (201 et seq.); *Auer*, Zum GmbH-Beirat, der ein fakultativer Aufsichtsrat sein soll, GeS 2007, 183 et seq.; *Wenger*, Beirat als Aufsichtsrat, RWZ 2006, 356 (357); *Koppensteiner/Rüffler*, GmbHG³ § 35 Rz 54; in agreement with the case-law *Kalss/Probst*, Familienunternehmen Rz 13/157; *Kastner*, RdW 1983, 98 (101); *A. Heidinger* in Gruber/Harrer, GmbHG² § 29 Rz 61.
20 See Section 3.2.2.3.
21 *Nowotny*, RdW 2008, 699 (700); *Aburumieh/Hoppel* in Foglar-Deinhardstein/Aburumieh/Hoffenscher-Summer, GmbHG § 29 Rz 73.
22 See *Arnold*, Der Beirat einer Privatstiftung, AR aktuell 5/2005, 4 (4).
23 Example: OGH 6 Ob 195/10k, JBl 2011, 321 (*Karollus*); 6 Ob 82/11v, PSR 2011, 117 (*Hofmann*); 6 Ob 244/11t, GesRZ 2012, 311 (*Hochedlinger*).
24 Concise *Kalss* in Kalss/Kunz, Handbuch Aufsichtsrat² Rz 39/110.
25 Cf. *Kalss* in Kalss/Kunz, Handbuch Aufsichtsrat² Rz 39/111.

board, auditor and (under certain circumstances)[26] supervisory board. Such additional bodies must not be charged with the direct implementation of the foundation's purpose, however – and hence they cannot have power of representation but only fulfil control or advisory functions.[27] The powers and the distribution of responsibilities between the statutory bodies are laid down in mandatory provisions of the PSG and cannot be reassigned by the deed of foundation.[28]

Incompatibility rules

The legal concept of "third-party management" of the private foundation has been identified as problematic in practice: The beneficiaries and persons close to them are not allowed to be members of the foundation's management board[29] to ensure that impartiality in the implementation of the provisions regarding beneficiaries is maintained by the foundation's management board and to avoid any conflict of interests.[30] This principle is reinforced by an incompatibility provision for the foundation's supervisory board: According to § 23 para 2 PSG beneficiaries[31] or their families are not allowed to have a majority in the supervisory board; the power to appoint and remove persons lies solely with the court that keeps the commercial register and is thus beyond the founder's or the beneficiaries' control.

"Additional bodies" as defined by § 14 para 2 PSG – and hence also advisory boards – are basically not subject to any incompatibility rules. Any number of beneficiaries and their families may be appointed to the advisory board to meet their need for control and information.[32]

"Supervisory board-like" advisory boards

The founder and the beneficiaries – usually relatives of the founder – as the persons having a shareholder-like interest in the private foundation obviously take a great interest in giving such an advisory board comprehensive rights of control and

---

26 That is the case when the number of employees of the private foundation itself or the corporations or cooperatives controlled by it exceeds 300 (§ 22 para 1 PSG).

27 Expressly in ErlRV 1132 BlgNR XVIII. GP 26. The most powerful possibility of influencing the foundation's decision-making process, which can be granted to an "additional body" according to § 14 para 2 PSG, is the right to remove the management board or one of its members (OGH 6 Ob 141/20h, ZFS 2020, 126; ErlRV 981 BlgNR XXIV. GP 67).

28 ErlRV 1132 BlgNR XVIII. GP 26.

29 According to § 15 paras 2 and 3 and/or 3a PSG this applies to each beneficiary of the foundation, his or her spouse or partner and lineal relatives or up to third degree collateral relatives of the beneficiary.

30 *Arnold*, PSG³ § 15 Rz 21 with reference to ErlRV 1132 BlgNR XVIII. GP 26.

31 The same applies according to § 23 para 2 sentence 3 PSG also to persons tasked by beneficiaries or the latters' family (§ 15 para 2) to look after their interests in the supervisory board.

32 ErlRV 981 BlgNR XXIV. GP 67.

influence. But here, too, a careful demarcation of responsibilities between the advisory board and the supervisory board is required when the advisory board is set up: Austrian court rulings and jurisprudence have examined in great depth the "similarity to a supervisory board" and the "similarity to a management board" of such a body and the legal consequences:

> **Supreme Court of Justice (OGH), Ruling of 9 September 2013, 6 Ob 139/13d**
> Through an amendment to the deed of foundation in the year 2012 the advisory board was to be granted the right to remove members of the management board in certain cases. Moreover, the advisory board was to be granted extensive rights to reserve consent (inter alia with respect to certain transactions – e.g. taking out/granting loans, purchase/sale of real estate, assumption of liability and appointment of beneficiaries and disbursing of funds to them).
>
> The OGH concludes as follows: Whether an advisory board is a body comparable to the supervisory board or not must be determined in accordance with previous court rulings, taking primarily the set of responsibilities assigned to the supervisory board in § 25 para 1 PSG into account, which outlines the core of the supervisory board's (extendable but inalienable) powers.[33]
>
> In casu the OGH held that the assigned responsibilities and rights were typical responsibilities of a supervisory board as defined in § 25 para 1 PSG in conjunction with § 95 para 5 subparas 1, 2, 4, 5 and 6 AktG. The question of authority to set the amount of compensation the members of the management board shall receive was also addressed. In conclusion the advisory board in its current form was classified as "supervisory board-like" because a supervisory board's statutory responsibilities had been transferred to it, and therefore the incompatibility rule of § 23 para 2 PSG applied.[34]

This ruling has upheld previous court rulings on "supervisory board-like" advisory boards, although legal theory[35] had expected that the 2011 amendment to the PSG[36] would put an end to the instrument of the "supervisory board-like" advisory board (and/or the accompanying incompatibility provisions). This line of court rulings has mostly been met with disapproval in Austrian jurisprudence.[37]

---

33 Cf. the previous rulings OGH 6 Ob 49/07k; 6 Ob 50/07g; 6 Ob 42/09h.

34 With reference to OGH 6 Ob 42/09h.

35 In detail *Arnold*, PSG³ § 14 Rz 76e et seq. with further references in the discussion.

36 By the Budget Accompanying Act 2011 (BGBl I 2010/111).

37 See *Arnold*, PSG³ § 14 Rz 69 et seq. with further references; *Zollner*, Grenzen der Gestaltungsmöglichkeiten für Beiräte einer Privatstiftung, JBl 2009, 22 (23 et seq.); *Briem*, remarks on 6 Ob 139/13d, GesRZ 2014, 63 (66 et seq.); *Csoklich*, remarks on 6 Ob 139/13d, PSR 2013, 175 et seq.; *Nowotny*, Privatstiftungen "in troubles", RdW 2009, 834 (834 et seq.); *H. Torggler*, remarks on OGH 6 Ob 42/09h, JBl 2010, 336; of differing opinion e.g. *Micheler* in Doralt/Nowotny/Kalss, PSG § 14 Rz 22; *Pittl*, Der Stifter einer Privatstiftung und die ihm zustehenden Rechte, NZ 1999, 197 (203) and also *Karollus*, remarks on OGH 6 Ob 230/13m, ZFS 2014, 111 (116).

Notwithstanding the case-law there are probably no objections to the following tasks:

- appointment and removal of members of the management board (but only for cause as defined by § 27 PSG)[38]
- rights to be heard or to give advice
- rights to information and inspection[39]
- rights of consent to changes to the deed of foundation made by the founder[40]

Even in view of the court rulings so far, the questions which (individual) rights of consent may be granted to an advisory board of which one member or a majority of the members is/are beneficiary/beneficiaries and to what extent beneficiaries are allowed to be involved in the appointment of beneficiaries and/or the determination of payments to beneficiaries are still debatable.[41]

"Management board-like" advisory boards

Attention should be paid to the powers and responsibilities of the management board.[42] The (minimum) range of responsibilities assigned to the management board is mandatory and must not be compromised by the foundation's design.[43] If this demarcation of responsibilities is not respected and the advisory board is classified as "management board-like", the consequence will not only be the application of circumvented norms such as, e.g., the incompatibility rules – as in the case of a similarity to a supervisory board – but inadmissibility of the formation of the advisory board in this form. It will then be irrelevant whether beneficiaries are appointed to the advisory board. The powers and responsibilities of each body have been assigned in a specific way by the lawmaker on purpose to create a system of mutual control and to ensure that the foundation's purpose is achieved.[44] In this respect the case-law[45] examines

---

38 OGH 6 Ob 37/17k, GesRZ 2017, 269 (*Csoklich*); *Arnold*, PSG[3] § 14 Rz 67.

39 See OGH 6 Ob 37/17k, GesRZ 2017, 269 (*Csoklich*). Information rights are rightly considered unobjectionable, as the beneficiaries are entitled to information even according to § 30 PSG; cf. *Arnold*, Einschränkungen für begünstigtendominierte Beiräte und Stifter, GesRZ 2009, 348 (352); *Hartlieb/Zollner*, Der fehlerhafte Beirat, PSR 2019, 4 (9).

40 This seems to *Hartlieb/Zollner*, PSR 2019, 4 (9) unobjectionable, as it is no management board competence.

41 See *Hartlieb/Zollner*, PSR 2019, 4 (9); *Briem*, remarks on 6 Ob 139/13d, GesRZ 2014, 63 (67 et seq.); *Csoklich*, remarks on 6 Ob 139/13d, PSR 2013, 175 (180 et seq.) *Hasch* in Hasch, PSG[2] § 14 Rz 62.

42 Inter alia OGH 6 Ob 60/01v, GesRZ 2002, 27; 6 Ob 230/13m, ZfS 2014, 111 (*Karollus*); 6 Ob 139/13d, PSR 2013, 175 (*Csoklich*); 6 Ob 95/15m, GesRZ 2015, 333 (*Briem*); recently in particular 6 Ob 37/17k, GesRZ 2017, 269 (*Csoklich*).

43 ErläutRV 981 BlgNR 24. GP 67; *Karollus*, remarks on 6 Ob 230/13m, ZfS 2014, 111 (113); *Hartlieb/Zollner*, PSR 2019, 4 (10).

44 Cf. *Arnold*, PSG[3] § 14 Rz 14.

45 See particularly OGH 6 Ob 37/17k, GesRZ 2017, 269 (*Csoklich*).

whether the management board is not reduced to the level of a mere implementing body. Unlike the sharply criticised[46] court rulings on the similarity to a supervisory board, the OGH's premises regarding the demarcation of responsibilities between the advisory board and the management board are widely supported.[47] As to the powers mentioned below, relatively reliable statements on their admissibility and/or inadmissibility can be made, taking into account that an overall assessment of all criteria rather than an isolated examination is decisive for similarity to a management board:[48]

– Issuance of procedural rules for the management board: In recent court judgments[49] the advisory board's authority to issue procedural rules for the foundation's management board and to generally make the implementation of any legal transactions "of importance" to the foundation subject to its consent was judged to be illegal. Such a general reservation of consent could enable the founder and/or the advisory board to prevent, by designing the rules of procedure for the foundation's management board accordingly, any legal transaction intended by the management board by invoking their right of consent or veto. By contrast, obligations to consent as laid down in the statutory catalogue of § 95 AktG (extraordinary management) were recently judged to be admissible,[50] with the OGH emphasising the difference compared to a reservation of consent provision, which relates to all transactions "of importance" and thus could also include matters of little significance.

– Rights to issue directives: Since these rights allow a more serious interference with the management board's powers (management) compared to rights of consent, it is reasonable to be particularly prudent here to avoid being classified as "degrading" the management board.[51]

– Rights to be heard: The experts agree that a mere right to be heard does not affect the independence of the management board.[52]

– Right to appoint and remove members of the management board: As to the power to appoint and remove members of the management board for cause, the OGH identified concerns with respect to the similarity to a management board only in conjunction with further powers.[53] If there is no overstretch, granting the

---

46 See Footnote 37. Tending to advocate the established court practice, *Karollus*, remarks on 6 Ob 230/13m, ZFS 2014, 111 (116), who considers the case-law to be "understandable in terms of the method" and sees no reason for abandoning this established court practice in the Budget Accompanying Act 2011 either (*Karollus*, remarks on 6 Ob 195/10k, JBl 2011, 329 [332]).
47 See e.g. *Hartlieb/Zollner*, PSR 2019, 4 (13).
48 Cf. OGH 6 Ob 230/13m, ZfS 2014, 111 (*Karollus*).
49 OGH 6 Ob 95/15m, GesRZ 2015, 333 (*Briem*).
50 See E OGH 6 Ob 37/17k, GesRZ 2017, 269 (*Csoklich*).
51 Cf. ErläutRV 981 BlgNR 24. GP 67; and also *Hartlieb/Zollner*, PSR 2019, 4 (11).
52 OGH 6 Ob 37/17k, GesRZ 2017, 269 (*Csoklich*).
53 OGH 6 Ob 230/13m, ZfS 2014, 111 (*Karollus*).

authority to appoint and remove members is unlikely to be inadmissible:[54] § 14 para 3 PSG states exactly that the management board (or one of its members) can be removed by another body as defined by para 2 (undoubtedly also advisory boards) subject to a qualified majority.[55] In this context § 14 para 4 PSG must be borne in mind in any event, according to which the beneficiary and persons close to him must not be entitled to the decisive majority in this decision, if it is about a removal for reasons other than those mentioned in § 27 para 2 subparas 1 to 3 PSG (= removal for cause, e.g., gross breach of duty).[56]

– Authority to set up a compensation plan: From previous court rulings it is not clear whether the authority to set up a compensation plan was examined in the light of similarity to a supervisory board or management board (which leads to inadmissibility per se). Although according to the literature such an authority is inadmissible in exceptional cases, i.e., when the advisory board has a completely free hand in deciding the amount of compensation,[57] a cautious approach should be taken with such arrangements in practice – until the issue is finally clarified by the OGH.[58]

Summary

With due regard to the limits for similarities to supervisory boards and management boards the following powers of an advisory board do not appear to be problematic[59]

– the right to appoint members to the management board and remove them for cause
– rights of consent as defined by the catalogue of measures of § 95 para 5 AktG (also without the restriction that a measure is only subject to consent if it is taken outside the normal business operations)
– a right of consent to the foundation, acquisition and sale of companies and
– rights to be heard (generally without limits)

with the rights of consent and of being heard in practice being prescribed not only for measures taken by the private foundation itself but extended to measures taken

---

54 Accurately *Hartlieb/Zollner*, PSR 2019, 4 (12); cf. ErlRV 981 BlgNR XXIV. GP 67 and OGH 6 Ob 141/20h, ZFS 2020, 126, which describe the removal of the foundation's management board or one of its members as the the most powerful right that can be exercised by an "additional body" according of § 14 para 2 PSG.
55 A majority of at least three fourths of the votes cast is required; if the body has fewer than four members, unanimity is required.
56 Cf. also OGH 6 Ob 37/17k, GesRZ 2017, 269 (*Csoklich*), which expressly exclude the right of dismissal but point at § 14 PSG.
57 *Arnold*, PSG³ § 14 Rz 59 and/or § 19 Rz 1; *Hochedlinger*, Zulässige und unzulässige Regelungen zur Vorstandsvergütung, PSR 2014, 4 (10 et seq.); *Hartlieb/Zollner*, PSR 2019, 4 (12).
58 See *Hochedlinger*, PSR 2014, 4 (10 et seq.).
59 This conclusion was already drawn by *Hartlieb/Zollner*, PSR 2019, 4 (12 et seq.).

at the level of the companies controlled by the private foundation (which requires appropriate integration also in the relevant companies).

3.2.2.4 Advisory boards in partnerships

Partnerships (OG [general partnership], KG [limited partnership]) typically have also an advisory board. For these types of company the law does not mention the establishment of a supervisory board and the employee participation rules are not applicable, therefore the limits to the design of stock corporations, limited liability companies and private foundations do not apply here. An exception is a GmbH & Co KG, i.e., a limited partnership in which no natural person acts as fully liable partner. With regard to employee participation this so-called "camouflaged corporation" is ultimately treated as equal to the limited liability company (§ 110 para 7 ArbVG), so that the statements made on limited liability companies in this paper apply.

3.3 Establishment, organisation and operations

3.3.1 Establishment and operations

Basically an advisory board can be set up in two ways: The advisory board can either be laid down in the articles of association (or in the deed of foundation in the case of a private foundation) or set up purely on the basis of the law of obligations. The choice of how to set up the advisory board is decisive for the intended field of activity.[60] If an advisory board is laid down in the articles of association, tasks of an executive body may and typically are assigned to it, whereas an advisory board established under the law of obligations typically has the function of a body providing advice and information.[61] If the advisory board is formed under corporate law, usually also a contractual relationship under the law of obligations between the company and the advisory board members exists, which is the basis on which the advisory board members exercise their role; a contract for personal services (*Auftragsvertrag*) in return for payment or without payment or on the basis of a labour contract is possible.

Given the special importance of limited liability companies as a type of corporate structure for medium-sized enterprises and the fact that here – unlike in stock corporations – setting up a supervisory board to supervise and monitor the enterprise is only mandatory if the enterprise exceeds a certain size, the focus hereinafter

---

60 Cf. *Reich-Rohrwig*, ÖJZ 1981, 509 (509 et seq.).

61 See e.g. *A. Heidinger* in Gruber/Harrer, GmbHG^2 § 29 Rz 56 et seq.; *Reich-Rohrwig*, ÖJZ 1981, 509 (510).

will be on advisory boards in limited liability companies as they are by far the most significant ones in practice. For the advisory board in a private foundation and its possible powers and responsibilities, see Section 3.2.2.3 et seq.

The so-called "representatives' committee" (*Vertreterausschuss*), which is sometimes called a special form of an advisory board,[62] is neither a body of the company nor an advisory board established under the law of obligations: If individual shareholders give other shareholders enduring proxy to vote to exercise their shareholder rights, these proxies form the so-called representatives' committee in the period between the general meetings of shareholders where all members are present.[63] In such a case a contractual relationship defining the rights and obligations exists between the shareholders authorising a proxy and their representatives in the committee.[64]

3.3.1.1 Establishment of an advisory board in the articles of association

Owing to the absence of statutory requirements the organisation, tasks and composition of an advisory board and its interaction with other bodies require careful regulation in the articles of association. Only the organisational design and the allocation of rights and obligations provide the advisory board with the characteristics of a body of the company.[65] Depending on the tasks assigned to it the advisory board can be within the domain of the management, within the domain of supervision and control or within the domain of the shareholders' tasks.[66] Although the GmbHG provides considerable design flexibility, the mandatory allocation of key powers between the bodies of the limited liability company must be borne in mind; in case of doubt the least possible encroachment on the legal model of the organisational constitution of a limited liability company must be the basis.[67] Therefore, the advisory board can only have decision-making powers that were clearly assigned to it according to the articles of association;[68] otherwise its duties (in particular advising the managing director) are of an informal nature.[69] The minimum set of powers of a mandatory or an optional supervisory board must not be curtailed.

---

62 *Reich-Rohrwig*, ÖJZ 1981, 509 (510); *A. Heidinger* in Gruber/Harrer, GmbHG² § 29 Rz 58 speaks of a "perpetuated general meeting of shareholders".
63 *M. Heidinger*, Aufgaben 373 et seq.; *Koppensteiner/Rüffler*, GmbHG³ § 35 Rz 52; *Reich-Rohrwig*, ÖJZ 1981, 509 (510); *A. Heidinger* in Gruber/Harrer, GmbHG² § 29 Rz 58; *Enzinger* in Straube, WK-GmbHG § 35 Rz 120.
64 *A. Heidinger* in Gruber/Harrer, GmbHG² § 29 Rz 58 with further references.
65 *A. Heidinger* in Gruber/Harrer, GmbHG² § 29 Rz 56; cf. *M. Heidinger*, Aufgaben 376 et seq.
66 Cf. *Schneiderbauer/Krebs*, Die Reichweite der Delegierbarkeit von Gesellschafterkompetenzen an einen Beirat, GesRZ 2018, 285 (285).
67 E.g. *M. Heidinger*, Aufgaben 376 et seq. with further references.
68 *A. Heidinger* in Gruber/Harrer, GmbHG² § 29 Rz 56; *Reich-Rohrwig*, GmbH-Recht I² Rz 4/495.
69 *Reich-Rohrwig*, GmbH-Recht I² Rz 4/498.

As to the risk of qualifying as "supervisory board-like" in case of strong orientation towards the statutory powers of the supervisory board, see Section 3.2.2.2.

3.3.1.2 Possible tasks of an advisory board established in the articles of association

When the powers of the advisory board are laid down, it must be taken into account
whether the advisory board will exist alongside a supervisory board[70] because the latter's statutory minimum set of powers must not be undermined. The advisory board
can be charged with the following tasks even where a supervisory board exists:[71]

- implementation of specific management tasks (e.g., including the awarding of
  contracts through an advisory committee on procurement and contracts or architecture); the advisory board itself is subject to supervision by a supervisory
  board, since § 30j aims at supervising the management in functional terms and
  not only the managing directors;[72] the assignment of such tasks is admissible to
  the extent that the supervisory board keeps a right to exercise an overarching
  control and thus its status is not undermined[73]
- right to issue instructions to the managing directors in specific (or all) matters[74]
- deciding on personnel matters
- resolution of differences of opinion between managing directors with regard to the
  implementation of a specific management measure; assistance in the preparation
  of the annual accounts, including, but not limited to, the profit-sharing proposal
- laying down a reservation of consent for specific management activities (=
  negative instructions)
- providing advice to the management
- providing support and advice to the shareholders (e.g., preparations for the general meeting of shareholders)
- dispute settlement function

Mandatory statutory obligations that continue to apply to the managing directors
(e.g., adjudication in bankruptcy, accounting, registration in the commercial register)[75]

---

70 Cf. e.g. the description in *M. Heidinger*, Aufgaben 383 et seq.
71 See *Reich-Rohrwig*, ÖJZ 1981, 509 (511 et seq.); see also *Reich-Rohrwig*, GmbH-Recht I² Rz 4/491;
Kalss/Probst, Familienunternehmen Rz 13/161 et seq.
72 Cf. *Reich-Rohrwig*, ÖJZ 1981, 509 (512).
73 *Reich-Rohrwig*, ÖJZ 1981, 509 (512); but differently in GmbH-Recht I² Rz 4/502.
74 *M. Heidinger*, Aufgaben, 395; *Reich-Rohrwig*, ÖJZ 1981, 512 et seq.; *Reich-Rohrwig*, GmbH-Recht
I² Rz 4/506; of differing opinion *Kastner*, RdW 1983, 98 (102).
75 E.g. *M. Heidinger*, Aufgaben, 396 f and *Schneiderbauer/Krebs*, GesRZ 2018, 285 (287).

are not assignable; the same applies to external representation (according to § 18 para 1 GmbHG – exclusive nature of the power of representation).

To what extent the advisory board may be granted rights in competition with or complementary to the supervision and control rights of the existing supervisory board (e.g., additional rights of consent within the meaning of § 35j para 5 GmbHG) has been the object of controversies.[76] If no supervisory board exists, attention should be paid to the limits beyond which the advisory board would qualify as "supervisory board-like"; see Section 3.2.2.2.

Moreover, certain shareholder responsibilities may be delegated to the advisory board:[77]

- representation of the limited liability company in its relationship with the managing directors; the same applies to the conduct of litigation, provided that the advisory board was elected "special representative" according to § 30l para 2 GmbHG by the shareholders
- determination of the management's compensation, but not the appointment and removal of managing directors[78]
- claiming outstanding sums payable to the original capital contributions
- decision on whether or whom 'Prokura' (registered commercial power of attorney) or power of attorney is granted
- the right to convene the general meeting of shareholders
- rights of consent that are in the area of authority of the shareholders and not the supervisory board (e.g., assignment and division of shares)
- the right to be informed by the managing directors (§ 30j para 2 GmbHG; § 30l para 3 GmbHG)

Tasks that mandatorily fall within the exclusive area of authority of the general meeting of shareholders as such, e.g., amendments to the articles of association, resolutions on mergers and conversions as well as the utilisation of the company assets, dissolution of the company and appointment of managing directors, are non-assignable, however.[79] This does not apply if the advisory board is designed as a so-called representatives' committee (see Section 3.3.1) and thus acts on behalf of the shareholders within the scope of its power of attorney.[80]

---

76 In contrast *Kastner* in FS Strasser (1983) 843 (865 et seq.); in favor, inter alia, *M. Heidinger*, Aufgaben 390 et seq.; *Reich-Rohrwig*, GmbH-Recht I² Rz 4/501 and *Schneiderbauer/Krebs*, GesRZ 2018, 285 (288).

77 Examples taken from *Reich-Rohrwig*, ÖJZ 1981, 509 (511 et seq.) and *Schneiderbauer/Krebs*, GesRZ 2018, 285 (285 et seq.).

78 Now OGH 6 Ob 183/18g, GesRZ 2019, 272 (*Kalss*); previously controversial, cf. *Kalss/Probst*, Familienunternehmen Rz 13/162; *Kalss* in Kalss/Kunz, Handbuch Aufsichtsrat² Rz 39/38; *Koppensteiner/Rüffler*, GmbHG³ § 35 Rz 53; *Enzinger* in Straube, GmbHG § 35 Rz 123; *Reich-Rohrwig*, GmbH-Recht I² Rz 4/516; *M. Heidinger*, Aufgaben 399; *A. Heidinger* in Gruber/Harrer, GmbHG² § 29 Rz 63.

79 E.g. *Reich-Rohrwig*, ÖJZ 1981, 509 (513); in detail *Schneiderbauer/Krebs*, GesRZ 2018, 285 (285 et seq.).

80 Cf. *Reich-Rohrwig*, GmbH-Recht I² Rz 4/496.

The advisory board may also play the role of an arbitral institution or an arbitrator for the company.[81] In such a case it is expected to make decisions on disputes arising out of the shareholder relationship (cf. § 577 ZPO [Code of Civil Procedure]). The shareholders may decide what kinds of (corporate) legal transactions shall be made subject to arbitration proceedings. If the advisory board is to become active as arbitral tribunal, no personal ties to any individual shareholder or body of the company should exist, however; in such a case the general meeting of shareholders shall not have the right to issue instructions to the advisory board, of course.[82] Moreover, the establishment as an arbitral tribunal is entirely subject to the consent of all shareholders; a resolution changing the articles of association by any (otherwise sufficient) majority is not sufficient for this purpose.[83] In addition to an arbitration function, the advisory board may also be appointed an arbitrator, for example, establishing certain facts or taking a decision when the shareholders have a conflict in the general meeting (e.g., to resolve a deadlock situation).[84]

In the area of partnerships, particularly the limits arising from the principle that the management consists of members of the partnership must be respected.[85] Therefore, the advisory board frequently takes action as a partners' committee to which, e.g., rights of consent are assigned in the context of unusual transactions.[86]

In the case of a private foundation it is essential to respect the limits of the distribution of authority, which is generally mandatory (unlike in the less rigid limited liability company legislation), especially for the management board, and the principles of established court practice relating to the foundation's "supervisory board-like" advisory board; see Section 3.2.2.3.

3.3.1.3 Establishment and tasks of the advisory board established under the law of obligations

The advisory board may be established by the shareholders on the basis of the articles of association or on the basis of the law of obligations.[87] The latter means that the advisory board is based merely on a decision taken by the shareholders, the management, a reciprocal arrangement between the shareholders (e.g., consortium agreement), an agreement between the shareholders and the management or an

---

81 See already *Reich-Rohrwig*, ÖJZ 1981, 509 (513).
82 Cf. *Reich-Rohrwig*, GmbH-Recht I² Rz 4/513; *Kalss/Probst*, Familienunternehmen Rz 13/169.
83 OGH 21.12.2017, 6 Ob 104/17p.
84 *Reich-Rohrwig*, GmbH-Recht I² Rz 4/514; *Kalss/Probst*, Familienunternehmen Rz 13/169.
85 *Fritz*, Der Beirat in der Gesellschafterpraxis, SWK 2005, 164 (165 et seq.).
86 *Kalss* in Kalss/Probst, Handbuch Aufsichtsrat² Rz 39/49.
87 *Reich-Rohrwig*, ÖJZ 1981, 509 (509 et seq.); *Reich-Rohrwig*, GmbH-Recht I² Rz 4/493 et seq.; *A. Heidinger* in Gruber/Harrer, GmbHG² § 29 Rz 57; *Kalss/Probst*, Familienunternehmen Rz 13/150.

agreement between the company and third parties (e.g., investors or lenders) with or without the shareholders joining.[88] The establishment of an advisory board under the law of obligations may also be laid down in the articles of association, although this is not mandatory.[89] The rules applying to the advisory board established under the law of obligations are solely determined by the agreement under the law of obligations.[90] The contract partners cannot confer on each other more rights than they are entitled to themselves: Therefore, lenders and investors usually demand that the borrower's shareholders be bound to the advisory board agreement so that they must use their shareholder rights for the best possible implementation of the authority of the advisory board.

Unlike an advisory board established on the basis of the articles of association, an advisory board based on the law of obligations cannot have body status and use any relevant powers under corporate law (supervision, control, the right of action or appeal, etc.); providing advice is thus the only activity typically left for the advisory board established under the law of obligations.[91] The managing directors or the shareholders may very well be obligated in the contractual (consulting) agreements under the law of obligations with the members of the advisory board to inform the advisory board, get its opinion or refrain from taking a decision against its advice.[92] But the only consequences incurred from a contravention are consequences under the law of obligations and never any sanctions under corporate law.[93] Thus, the advisory board established solely under the law of obligations is a highly flexible but also a less binding instrument.[94] In view of its lack of authority the advisory board established solely under the law of obligations does not carry the risk of "similarity to a supervisory board" and the associated application of the relevant provisions, e.g., on employee participation.[95]

---

88 *Kalss/Probst*, Familienunternehmen Rz 13/150.

89 *A. Heidinger* in Gruber/Harrer, GmbHG[2] § 29 Rz 57.

90 *Aburumieh/Hoppel* in Foglar-Deinhardstein/Aburumieh/Hoffenscher-Summer, GmbHG § 29 Rz 79.

91 *A. Heidinger* in Gruber/Harrer, GmbHG[2] § 29 Rz 57; *Aburumieh/Hoppel* in Foglar-Deinhardstein/Aburumieh/Hoffenscher-Summer, GmbHG § 29 Rz 76; *Reich-Rohrwig*, ÖJZ 1981, 509 (510); *Reich-Rohrwig*, GmbH-Recht I[2] Rz 4/494.

92 *Reich-Rohrwig*, ÖJZ 1981, 509 (510); id, GmbH-Recht I[2] Rz 4/494.

93 *A. Heidinger* in Gruber/Harrer, GmbHG[2] § 29 Rz 57; *Reich-Rohrwig*, ÖJZ 1981, 509 (510); *Reich-Rohrwig*, GmbH-Recht I[2] Rz 4/494; *M. Heidinger*, Aufgaben 371.

94 See *Aburumieh/Hoppel* in Foglar-Deinhardstein/Aburumieh/Hoffenscher-Summer, GmbHG § 29 Rz 79.

95 The relevant established court practice and the literature quoted there speak only of advisory boards established on the basis of articles of association (OGH 9 ObA 130/05s, DRdA 2008/15 [*Putzer*] with further references). More cautious in contrast are *Aburumieh/Hoppel* in Foglar-Deinhardstein/Aburumieh/Hoffenscher-Summer, GmbHG § 29 Rz 80, who affirm the similarity to supervisory boards "from a circumvention standpoint" when body quality is "de facto" implemented and the responsibilities are (likely also "de facto") supervisory board-like.

For an advisory board established under the law of obligations the GmbHG provides no rules on organisational structure – neither directly nor mutatis mutandis, because it does not qualify as a body. Any potential restrictions applying to the advisory board laid down in the articles of association (incompatibilities) are irrelevant here. On the other hand, this means that there is no predefined general system of regulations like for bodies established under corporate law (appointment, appointment of substitutes, term of office, dismissal, commitment to duties, liability, rights to inspection, etc.), so that the contractual arrangements must provide for all these aspects. In any event arrangements must be made for the following: appointment, removal/resignation, term of office, qualification requirements, incompatibilities, meeting frequency, use of electronic media, flow of information to and from bodies, confidentiality, chairing of meetings, taking minutes, quorum, weighting of votes, calling of meetings, chairmanship, remuneration, insurance, ways to reduce the workload and sanctions for disregard of the advisory board commitment.[96]

3.3.2 Operating method/internal organisation

The basic structures of the advisory board are laid down in the articles of association or qua agreement under the law of obligations. The details of how the advisory board works are usually defined in rules of procedure either by the shareholders' meeting or – if relevant authority is granted – by the advisory board itself.[97] It is customary to be guided by the legal provisions on the internal organisation of the supervisory board (§§ 30g to 30i GmbHG; §§ 92 et seq. AktG [Stock Corporation Act]).[98] The rules of procedure usually define the internal organisation (chairperson, deputy chairperson and their tasks), majority required for resolutions, quorum, organisation of meetings (mandatory physical presence or support provided by electronic forms of communication), participation rights of persons who are not members of the advisory board (shareholders, members of other bodies, experts), arrangements for convening meetings, creating and communicating the meeting agenda and keeping of the minutes.[99]

The decisions of the advisory board are generally taken in the form of resolutions. The provisions on the required majority for resolutions must balance the elements consensus and acceptance (speaks for unanimity) and flexibility and decision-making

---

96 Instructive *Aburumieh/Hoppel* in Foglar-Deinhardstein/Aburumieh/Hoffenscher-Summer, GmbHG § 29 Rz 81.

97 *Kalss/Probst*, Familienunternehmen Rz 3/180.

98 See already *M. Heidinger*, Aufgaben 383 et seq.; *A. Heidinger* in Gruber/Harrer, GmbHG² § 29 Rz 68; *Aburumieh/Hoppel* in Foglar-Deinhardstein/Aburumieh/Hoffenscher-Summer, GmbHG § 29 Rz 70. In our view unfounded: the concerns in *Fritz*, remarks on 9 ObA 130/05s, AR aktuell 2007, 13 (14).

99 Cf. the recommendations in Österreichischer Governance Kodex für Familienunternehmen (2017) Chapter 3.2.2; *Kalss/Probst*, Familienunternehmen Rz 13/181.

capability (principle of majority rule); usually not a general majority requirement but a graduated system based on significance and risk weight of the subjects of resolutions is favoured.[100]

In voting, one vote per member is usually adopted as standard. In many cases the capital interest of a member of the advisory board or multiple voting rights are used, especially in family owned companies. Also rights to rule in favour of somebody or something in the event of a voting tie or veto rights for certain advisory board members are possible.[101] Any interference with the rights of minority shareholders via the advisory board organisation must be excluded, however.[102]

Careful arrangements as to the flow of relevant information are key to ensure the effective functioning of the advisory board, which should be able to receive and demand at least the information the management is otherwise required to deliver to the supervisory board (see § 28a GmbHG: quarterly reports, annual reports and special reports, where applicable).[103] To the extent the assignment of tasks is admissible in terms of the risk of "similarity to a supervisory board" granting the information rights to which otherwise a supervisory board is entitled must be unproblematic.[104]

3.4 Members, breach of duty and liability

3.4.1 Members

3.4.1.1 Size

Basically, the shareholders are at discretion to choose the structure and size of the advisory board. The size of the advisory board depends on the enterprise and its significance and interests;[105] in Austria, family owned companies typically have advisory boards with three to six members.[106] As to the number of members, the question whether the body should be able to operate more flexibly than the supervisory board or the general meeting of shareholders should be taken into account: Inertia

---

100 *Kalss/Probst*, Familienunternehmen Rz 13/183 et seq.
101 *Kalss/Probst*, Familienunternehmen Rz 13/184.
102 *Kalss/Probst*, Familienunternehmen Rz 13/184.
103 *Kalss* in Kalss/Kunz, Handbuch Aufsichtsrat² Rz 39/79; *Kalss/Probst*, Familienunternehmen Rz 13/179; cf. Österreichischer Governance Kodex für Familienunternehmen (2017) Chapter 3.1.2.
104 Along these lines *A. Heidinger* in Gruber/Harrer, GmbHG² § 29 Rz 62.
105 Cf. Österreichischer Governance Kodex für Familienunternehmen (2017) Chapter 3.2.
106 See *Josef Fritz* in Die Presse of 17.03.2018, at https://www.diepresse.com/5390081/der-beirat-der-neue-berater (last accessed: 25.10.2019); cf. also *Kalss/Probst*, Familienunternehmen Rz 13/175: Typically four to six members.

naturally increases with an increasing membership figure.[107] Generally, the number of members of the board should be an odd number to avoid tie votes.[108]

There is no mandatory requirement for an advisory board to be organised as a collegial body. If the advisory board is only charged with the tasks of a sharehold-ers' committee and/or an advisor to the managing directors, it may also consist of only one person. This was established recently by case-law[109] with regard to advi-sory boards in private foundations, with the decisive argument – the absence of any standards of membership figures for non-mandatory bodies established under corporate law – basically also applying to the advisory board of a limited liability company.[110] This does not apply to supervisory board-like advisory boards, which must have a minimum of three members (including employee representatives, where applicable), as defined by § 30 GmbHG § 86 AktG and § 23 PSG.[111]

3.4.1.2 Eligibility

Only (natural) persons having full legal capacity who have the necessary expertise for the specific tasks of the advisory board are eligible to be members of the advi-sory board.[112] Like supervisory board members they must provide evidence of spe-cific qualifications at regular intervals and must be able to discuss matters with the management on an equal footing. Technical and personal requirements include pro-fessional expertise, successful management experience, social skills in the sense of assertiveness but also conflict-solving capacity, analytical power, creativity and an appropriate personal reputation.[113]

Naturally, experts with special know-how and relevant experience are especially suitable.[114] When the advisory board is set up, requirements – depending on the area of responsibilities – concerning the professional and personal characteristics of its members may be defined – for example, a specific combination of persons close to the company and technical experts. In practice, a special understanding of the (family owned) enterprise and/or its history, dynamics and focus is expected.[115]

---

107 *Kalss/Probst*, Familienunternehmen Rz 13/175.
108 *Reich-Rohrwig*, ÖJZ 1981, 509 (514).
109 OGH 6 Ob 42/13i, ZfS 2013, 116 (*Karollus*).
110 *A. Heidinger* in Gruber/Harrer, GmbHG² § 29 Rz 68.
111 Cf. *Kalss* in Kalss/Kunz, Handbuch Aufsichtsrat Rz 39/44; *A. Heidinger* in Gruber/Harrer, GmbHG² § 29 Rz 68; *Hasch* in Hasch, PSG² § 14 Rz 63.
112 See e.g. Österreichischer Governance Kodex für Familienunternehmen (2017) Chapter 3.2.2; *Fritz*, Der Beirat in der Gesellschafterpraxis, SWK 2005, 164 (167).
113 Cf. *Fritz*, SWK 2005, 164 (167).
114 See *Fritz*, SWK 2005, 164 (167).
115 *Kalss/Probst*, Familienunternehmen Rz 13/173.

Attention should be paid to any potential conflicts of interest that may arise in connection with the appointment of business partners, customers or advisers closely associated with the enterprise, e.g., lawyers, public accountants or bank representatives.[116] Predefining certain incompatibilities but also the required positive qualities (e.g., professional experience, education, family membership) is helpful.

3.4.1.3 Incompatibilities

Attention must be paid to the specific role of the advisory board: If the advisory board is expected to supervise the management or principally exercise some of the powers reserved to the shareholders, appointment by the management is excluded.[117] If the advisory board must be classified as "supervisory board-like", the legal incompatibility provisions of § 30a (limitation on the number of supervisory board mandates) and § 30e GmbHG (supervisory board members cannot be managers or permanent representatives of managing directors of the company or its subsidiaries at the same time) apply also to the members of the advisory board.[118] If the organisation of an advisory board is similar to that of a shareholders' committee, a managing director and a member of the advisory board in a limited liability company may be one and the same person; likewise, a managing director may be a shareholder at the same time.[119] As to the strict incompatibility provisions in the law on private foundations, see Section 3.2.2.3.

A person eligible for supervisory board membership may also be a member of a "supervisory board-like advisory board"; the same applies also to shareholders, of course. The fact that in such a case the shareholder issues instructions to the managing directors and supervises them simultaneously is generally unproblematic and also admissible in the relationship between the members of the supervisory board and the members of the advisory board, because an advisory board existing alongside the supervisory board usually performs duties of the general meeting of shareholders.[120]

3.4.1.4 Appointment

Members may be appointed by individual shareholders (this may also be laid down as a special shareholder's privilege [*Sonderrecht*] in the articles of association) or

---

116 Cf. *Kalss/Probst*, Familienunternehmen Rz 13/174.
117 *Reich-Rohrwig*, ÖJZ 1981, 509 (514).
118 Cf. *Kalss* in Kalss/Kunz, Handbuch Aufsichtsrat² Rz 39/33, 42.
119 E.g. *Kalss* in Kalss/Kunz, Handbuch Aufsichtsrat² Rz 39/41.
120 See *A. Heidinger* in Gruber/Harrer, GmbHG² § 29 Rz 66.

elected by the general meeting of shareholders[121] or appointed using a specific appointment procedure – also with third-party involvement. In the case of family owned companies it may be useful to define a mandatory decision-making process for appointments in a family tree.[122] Where the members are elected, at least the majority required for adopting a valid resolution should be laid down. Jurisprudence also proposes a combination of both – especially for family owned companies: For example, each family tree holding a specific share in the company may be entitled to appoint one member to the advisory board, whereupon the members thus appointed shall co-opt more members.[123] The appointment may also be assigned to unrelated third parties – an advisory board may, for example, attend to the interests of contract partners of a limited liability company, such as creditors, limited partners, silent partners or know-how providers.[124] In the absence of any explicit arrangements on how to choose members, recruiting members is the duty of the shareholders.[125] An appointment of members of the advisory board by a court is not possible.[126] Therefore, it makes sense to make arrangements for appointing a (temporary) substitute in case appointment rights cannot be exercised or are not exercised in time or if no appointment resolution can be obtained; typically, such an arrangement is temporary co-opting by the other advisory board members until the resolution primarily intended is obtained.

3.4.1.5 Are the members independent or bound by instructions?

The members are generally bound to act in the company's best interest as set out in detail in the articles of association; this follows from the character of an advisory board as a body established under articles of association. Depending on the task assigned to the advisory board the members may be independent or bound by instructions to a varying degree. The latter is basically admissible if the advisory board performs tasks that are normally assigned to the shareholders' meeting or if it is expected to make other managerial decisions.[127] The right to issue instructions may be vested either in the shareholders' meeting or – for individual advisory board members – in the appointing shareholder and/or company/family tree.[128]

---

121 *Fritz*, SWK 2005, 164 (166).
122 *Kalss/Probst*, Familienunternehmen Rz 13/176.
123 Cf. *Kalss/Probst*, Familienunternehmen Rz 13/176.
124 *Reich-Rohrwig*, ÖJZ 1981, 509 (514).
125 *A. Heidinger* in Gruber/Harrer, GmbHG² § 29 Rz 66.
126 *Fritz*, SWK 2005, 164 (167).
127 Cf. *M. Heidinger*, Aufgaben 395; *Reich-Rohrwig*, ÖJZ 1981, 509 (512); *Kalss/Probst*, Familienunternehmen Rz 13/152 et seq.; *Nowotny*, RdW 2008, 699 (699 et seq.); *Schneiderbauer/Krebs*, GesRZ 2018, 285 (289 et seq.); critical *Kastner*, RdW 1983, (98) 101.
128 See *Kalss/Probst*, Familienunternehmen Rz 13/188.

However, an advisory board acting as arbitrator cannot be organised in such a way that it is bound by instructions in this respect,[129] and also an advisory board with powers close to those of a supervisory board will have to act independently according to § 30j para 6 GmbHG.[130] In the context of control and advisory functions any obligation to comply with instructions is self-defeating, of course.[131] If the advisory board is organised in such a way that it is not bound by instructions, the possibility of removals at any time is of particular significance (see Section 3.5.1).[132]

3.4.1.6 Reimbursement of expenses, compensation and insurance

Members of an advisory board are entitled to be reimbursed – according to the principles of contract law – for expenses.[133] As to compensation, there is unlimited freedom to agree on any compensation plan. The amount of compensation will be calculated mainly according to the responsibilities/function of the advisory board and should be governed by explicit agreement.[134] On the other hand, if no compensation is to be paid, this should also be clarified contractually,[135] failing which the right to a reasonable compensation according to general civil law principles could give rise to a dispute in which the compensation eventually would have to be determined by an expert.

To ensure (external) long-term expertise and the commitment the pursuit of the interests of the company deserves, at least external advisory board members who are not members of or close to the group of shareholders should get paid according to their qualification, expected time commitment, responsibility and liability risk.[136] Moreover, increasingly directors' and officers' liability insurance (D&O insurance) is also taken out for the activities of members of an advisory board – at any rate in case of a high-risk propensity corresponding to the activity. This practice has proved to be definitely beneficial to the necessary culture of risk taking.[137]

---

129 *Kalss/Probst*, Familienunternehmen Rz 13/189.
130 Cf. *Kalss* in Kalss/Kunz, Handbuch Aufsichtsrat² Rz 39/83.
131 Cf. *Kalss* in Kalss/Kunz, Handbuch Aufsichtsrat² Rz 39/82 et seq.
132 *Kalss/Probst*, Familienunternehmen Rz 13/190.
133 Cf. *Kalss/Probst*, Familienunternehmen Rz 13/191.
134 See Österreichischer Governance Kodex für Familienunternehmen (2017) Chapter 3.3.1.
135 Cf. *Kalss* in Kalss/Kunz, Handbuch Aufsichtsrat² Rz 39/86.
136 See Österreichischer Governance Kodex für Familienunternehmen (2017) Chapter 3.3.1; *Kalss* in Kalss/Kunz, Handbuch Aufsichtsrat² Rz 39/88.
137 *Kalss/Probst*, Familienunternehmen Rz 13/184; *Kalss* in Kalss/Kunz, Handbuch Aufsichtsrat² Rz 39/87.

3.4.2 Rights and obligations of the members of an advisory board

3.4.2.1 Voting

As to the voting right, see Section 3.3.2. Besides voting the members of the advisory board have a number of other rights and obligations.

3.4.2.2 The right to participate

Participation in a supervisory board meeting is reserved to members of the supervisory board – with the exception of the management board members in a stock corporation – unless the chairman of the supervisory board invites other persons to participate as experts or providers of information for individual items of the agenda (§ 30h GmbHG; § 93 AktG). For an advisory board, the participation rights are freely definable, by contrast.[138] This does not apply to a supervisory board-like advisory board; see Section 3.2.2.2 et seq.

3.4.2.3 The duty of personal participation/right of representation

Members of a supervisory board may only be represented under the quite narrow conditions provided by law – for a limited liability company in § 30j para 6 GmbHG and for a stock corporation in § 95 para 7 AktG: Generally, members are required to fulfil their obligations personally, and all the articles of association may allow is that a member of the supervisory board may designate another member of the supervisory board in writing to represent him at an individual meeting (but not to chair the meeting).

In advisory boards – unless they are supervisory board-like and the relevant rules apply from the outset – the right of representation is freely definable. Clear rules should be laid down as to whether and in what form representation is admissible.[139] In the absence of an explicit clause it is inevitable that in case of divergence there will be proxy disputes involving lawyers and controversies about the admissibility and consequences of potential inadmissibility of the resolutions adopted or prevented; the absence of a means of legal redress analogous to an appeal against a resolution creates legal uncertainty, which may quickly lead to inertia of the advisory board.

---

138 *Kalss* in Kalss/Kunz, Handbuch Aufsichtsrat[2] Rz 39/80.
139 *Kalss* in Kalss/Kunz, Handbuch Aufsichtsrat[2] Rz 39/81, 85.

3.4.2.4 Fiduciary duty

Usually a contractual relationship under the law of obligations exists between the company and the members of the advisory board;[140] if the advisory board was set up in the articles of association, the members of the advisory board are additionally subject to the general obligations under corporate law.

The members of an advisory board, whether established under the law of obligations or under corporate law, have a fiduciary duty to act on behalf of the interests of the company. This duty arises in any event from the civil law contractual relationship to the company or from the obligations as a body established on the basis of articles of association.[141] Thus, the members of the advisory board are required to protect the company's well-being and/or best interests at all times, even if they were only appointed by individual shareholders or groups of shareholders.[142]

3.4.2.5 Confidentiality

The fiduciary duty gives rise to the confidentiality obligation, again regardless of the basis on which the advisory board was established.[143] Thus, the advisory board members are obligated to protect internal business and trade secrets.

3.4.2.6 Prohibition of insider trading

A member of an advisory board shall not use any inside knowledge gained in the advisory board in his own interest. The prohibition to utilise any business opportunities of the company that the advisory board member gains knowledge of due to his membership in the advisory board for his own benefit stems from the fiduciary

---

140 See espcially *Kalss/Probst*, Familienunternehmen Rz 13/193.
141 *A. Heidinger* in Gruber/Harrer, GmbHG² § 29 Rz 69; *Kalss/Probst*, Familienunternehmen Rz 13/194.
142 See *Reich-Rohrwig*, ÖJZ 1981, 509 (515); *Reich-Rohrwig*, GmbH-Recht I² Rz 4/525; *M. Heidinger*, Aufgaben 403 (at any rate for advisory boards established under corporate law); cf. also *Kalss/Probst*, Familienunternehmen Rz 13/194. This applies to advisory boards established under the law of obligations and advisory boards established under corporate law alike: In case of advisory boards established under corporate law it follows from the articles of association, in case of advisory boards established under the law of obligations from the respective relationship under the law of obligations, whose protection will usually aim at the whole company; a commitment to the interests of individual groups of shareholders is considered possible by *M. Heidinger*, Aufgaben 403 in case of advisory boards established under the law of obligations.
143 Fundamentally *M. Heidinger*, Aufgaben 408; *A. Heidinger* in Gruber/Harrer, GmbHG² § 29 Rz 69; *Kalss/Probst*, Familienunternehmen Rz 13/143 and/or 193.

duty the members of the advisory board owe to the company.[144] For example, insider trading may occur in connection with upcoming real estate acquisitions and/or sales or other investment opportunities.[145]

3.4.2.7 Prohibition of competition

In Austria, a general prohibition on competition under corporate law does not exist for shareholders (who are not members of the management) or for members of a supervisory board and thus cannot be based on corporate law for members of an advisory board either. A different situation may arise expressly or by implication from the relationship under the law of obligations between a member of the advisory board and his principal; if the principal is a shareholder, a prohibition of competition resulting from the contractual relationship may also operate to the benefit of the company. It is recommended to lay down a clarifying provision to avoid legal uncertainties.

3.4.3 Liability

The legal basis of liability depends primarily on whether the advisory board was established under the law of obligations or under corporate law.

3.4.3.1 Liability of advisory boards established under corporate law

For advisory boards established in the articles of association jurisprudence draws an analogy in law between § 25 (liability of the managing director) and § 33 GmbHG (liability of the supervisory board) and/or the relevant parallel provisions in the AktG (§§ 84, 99 AktG).[146] Thus, irrespective of the structure and the concrete tasks at least the standardised (objective) standard of due diligence as defined by § 25 para 1 GmbHG including the Business Judgment Rule (§ 25 para 1a GmbHG)[147] is the

---

144 This applies both to advisory boards established by provisions in the articles of association and advisory boards established on the basis of the law of obligations.

145 Cf. *Kalss/Probst*, Familienunternehmen Rz 13/193 and 143.

146 See *Kalss/Probst*, Familienunternehmen Rz 13/194; cf. *A. Heidinger* in Gruber/Harrer, GmbHG[2] § 29 Rz 69; *Spindler* in MüKoGmbHG[3] (2019) § 52 Rz 762 with further references to the German prevailing view.

147 § 25 para 1a GmbHG: "A managing director acts in accordance with the due diligence of a prudent businessman, if in an entrepreneurial decision he is not guided by irrelevant interests and may expect, based on reasonable information, to act for the benefit of the company."

minimum standard applied to the diligence of a prudent advisory board member,[148] with the burden of proof lying with the member of the advisory board, and the statute of limitations regulation (five years) being applied. The general obligations are defined more specifically by the tasks and responsibilities assigned to the advisory board in the articles of association. If the advisory board performs additional tasks, it shall be measured by them – provided that it is acting in agreement with the shareholders. If it performs such tasks arbitrarily it is acting fundamentally against the law.[149] If the advisory board was granted supervisory and control rights, the principles applying to the liability of members of the supervisory board are applicable.[150] Generally, the articles of association may also provide for a different standard of diligence for the limited liability company – e.g., the liability (to the limited liability company) could be limited, in derogation from the statutory basic principle, to intent or gross negligence.[151] If the advisory board is to a certain extent bound by instructions, and if it acts within the framework of such instructions, it is exempt from liability to the company in this respect.[152] The company may waive the advisory board's liability, which may be expressed in the form of an approval of the actions of the advisory board under certain circumstances, provided that the shareholders already know the facts giving rise to liability by that time.[153] Third parties, including, but not limited to, the company's creditors, remain unaffected by such a liability waiver; the question to what extent admissible liability limits under corporate law apply to third parties is a debatable point.

This applies generally also to the liability of advisory boards in private foundations, where the general (and mandatory) liability regime is laid down as standard in § 29 PSG.[154] Also in this case the actual duty of care depends on the qualifications of the advisory board and its defined tasks and responsibilities.[155] Unlike in corporate law the foundation cannot waive the claims – at most a release from liability

---

148 See *A. Heidinger* in Gruber/Harrer, GmbHG[2] § 29 Rz 69; from the German literature on GmbH *Spindler* in MüKoGmbHG[3] (2019) § 52 Rz 762; *Bayer* in FS Schneider 75 (83).
149 *Kalss/Probst*, Familienunternehmen Rz 13/197.
150 E.g. *Kalss/Probst*, Familienunternehmen Rz 13/197; probably less far-reaching, *A. Heidinger* in Gruber/Harrer, GmbHG[2] § 29 Rz 71, states this only for the supervisory board-like advisory board. Regarding the liability of the supervisory board, see for the AG *Eckert/Schopper* in Artmann/Karollus, AktG II[6] § 99 Rz 8 et seq. and for the GmbH *Rauter* in Straube, WK GmbHG § 33 Rz 16 et seq.
151 See *Kalss/Probst*, Familienunternehmen Rz 13/202 also in connection with Bayer in FS Schneider 75 (85).
152 *Kalss/Probst*, Familienunternehmen Rz 13/202; *Altmeppen* in Roth/Altmeppen, GmbHG[9] (2019) § 52 Rz 94 with further references.
153 Cf. *Kalss/Probst*, Familienunternehmen Rz 13/203 for Austria and *Altmeppen* in Roth/Altmeppen, GmbHG[9] (2019) § 52 Rz 94 for Germany.
154 § 29 PSG: "[. . .] each member of a body of the foundation is liable to the private foundation for any damage suffered because of a culpable breach of duty committed by him or her."
155 *Arnold*, PSG[3] § 29 Rz 4 with further references.

agreement by internal arrangement between the bodies and the founder of a foundation is possible.[156]

3.4.3.2 Liability of advisory boards established under the law of obligations

In case of an advisory board established under the law of obligations the legal relationship is to a significant extent determined by the contractual relationship between the company and the member of the advisory board. The general rules of the Austrian civil law for contractual liability (§§ 1293 et seq. ABGB [General Civil Code]) apply. This liability generally requires a culpable breach of the duty of care. For advisory board members an increased standard of due diligence as defined by § 1299 ABGB applies:[157] They are considered experts and must not only meet the average skills and performance standards of an average person but also apply the due diligence that is adequate to their special activity.[158] In this objective-abstract analysis the legitimate expectation of the group of persons affected is decisive. If the member of the advisory board has been appointed exactly because of his (for example, technical or legal) know-how, he must demonstrate such specific skills to the extent expected.[159] With regard to the liability exposure of a member of the advisory board it must be checked whether he has the skills and know-how required for the tasks assigned and complies with the relevant duty of care requirements. The standards of liability resulting from general civil law can of course be modified by contract, however; reduced liability standards and other limits to liability may be agreed upon.

3.4.3.3 Third-party liability

The standards of §§ 25, 33 GmbHG (and/or §§ 83, 99 AktG) used in jurisprudence dictate that the advisory board members are only liable to the company (internal liability). Nevertheless, the general civil damages law remains applicable, and thus a liability (for pecuniary loss) of the members of an advisory board to third parties (external liability), in particular shareholders and creditors, according to the general civil law rules should be considered, especially in case of breaches of protective legislation according to § 1311 ABGB, which includes in many cases criminal law standards (more details are given below), and in cases of intentional unethical damage (e.g., to creditors).[160]

---

156 *Arnold*, PSG³ § 29 Rz 8 with further references; also *Kalss/Probst*, Familienunternehmen Rz 13/215.
157 Also *Kalss/Probst*, Familienunternehmen Rz 13/193.
158 Generally *Schacherreiter* in Kletečka/Schauer, ABGB-ON¹·⁰⁷ § 1299 Rz 1 with further references.
159 *Kalss/Probst*, Familienunternehmen Rz 13/193.
160 In detail on the constellations of third-party liability (there: of the managing director) *Reich-Rohrwig* in Straube/Ratka/Rauter, WK GmbHG § 25 Rz 262 et seq. and 266 et seq.

3.4.3.4 Criminal liability

If the advisory board established under corporate law takes on tasks that are otherwise the responsibility of the supervisory board or the management, a criminal liability for its conduct may also be applied. In addition to the general criminal provisions (e.g., on bankruptcy offenses)[161] especially the increased occurrence of charges of embezzlement (§ 153 StGB [Penal Code]) should be pointed out, which may apply in case of a variety of breaches of corporate law obligations.[162] The advisory board members' – and supervisory board members' – acting as accessories to an act of management misconduct would be most relevant, although their acting as direct perpetrators cannot be ruled out.[163] A criminal liability (as direct perpetrator) for negligent impairment of creditors' interests was generally rejected in the case of an advisory board established under the law of obligations without any authority to issue instructions to the management,[164] which is likely to still apply today, despite various amendments to legislation relating to criminal law. According to recent judgments[165] members of an advisory board are not considered "executive staff" or "managing directors, members of the executive board or the supervisory board and authorised officers of the company" according to § 74 para 3 StGB (Penal Code) or persons treated as such. In this respect direct culpability as defined by § 161 (provisions on the accountability of executive staff) in conjunction with § 156 (fraudulent bankruptcy offenses), § 158 (preference of a creditor), § 159 (grossly negligent impairment of a creditor's interests), § 160 para 2 (activities during court-supervised management or insolvency proceedings) and § 162 (enforcement thwarting) StGB is excluded, unless the advisory board members themselves are creditors or debtors.

---

161 See e.g. *Arnold*, Strafrechtliche Verantwortlichkeit der Mitglieder des Aufsichtsrates, AR aktuell 0/2004, 7 (7 et seq.) and *Reich-Rohrwig* in Straube/Ratka/Rauter, WK GmbHG § 25 Rz 266 et seq.
162 Cf. *Rauter* in Straube, WK GmbHG § 33 Rz 66.
163 See *Kühteubl*, Der Arbeitnehmervertreter im Aufsichtsrat als Beitragstäter bei Straftaten der Geschäftsführung, RdA 2012, 244 et seq.
164 OGH 11 Os 75/89, JBl 1991, 465; in agreement *Reich-Rohrwig*, GmbH-Recht I² Rz 4/526. According to OGH 12 Os 39/18d, RdW 2020, 847, direct perpetration of embezzlement (§ 153 StGB) by members of an supervisory board can only be affirmed in those cases in which the supervisory board has an independent competence to represent the company externally. This case-law concerning supervisory boards of Limited Liability Companies should also apply to adivsory boards (which typically do not represent the company externally).
165 OGH 17 Os 23/17m.

3.5 Termination

As to termination, a distinction should be made between the removal of one member/more than one/all member(s) of the advisory board and the dissolution of the advisory board itself. In doing that a distinction should also be made between the status of the advisory board under corporate law and the associated obligation relationship to the company. The latter may be terminated both by the company as principal and by the advisory board as power holder according to general civil law (§§ 1020, 1021 ABGB where a contractual relationship exists) or labour regulations (where an employment relationship exists).

3.5.1 Removal

There are no legal requirements regarding the implementation, and hence arrangements must be laid down in the articles of association (or for the advisory board established on the basis of the law of obligations: in the civil law agreement).[166] Generally, the body that elected/appointed the members of the advisory board also has the power to remove the members. Where no arrangements have been made, members of the advisory board may be removed at any time on the basis of a resolution passed by a simple majority.[167] As with other continuing obligation agreements, terminating/removing a member of the advisory board who was appointed for an indefinite period of time is generally possible at all times. In case of doubt this should also apply to members of the advisory board who were appointed for a definite period of time;[168] in that case claims for compensation arising from the agreements with the members of the advisory board on grounds of untimely (but effective under corporate law) termination may be raised.[169] If the members of the advisory board (or only some of them) are to be granted a stronger legal position, it would have to be laid down in the articles of association. The appointment of a life member and also limiting the removal power to removal for cause are considered admissible.[170] A member may be removed for cause at any time in case of gross breach of duty or incapacity for proper participation in the advisory board; this may happen also to a shareholder who was granted a special shareholder's privilege

---

166 See Österreichischer Governance Kodex für Familienunternehmen (2017) Chapter 3.2.2.
167 See *Enzinger* in Straube, WK GmbHG § 35 Rz 125 referring to BGH WM 1973, 101; *A. Heidinger* in Gruber/Harrer, GmbHG² § 29 Rz 67.
168 *Reich-Rohrwig*, GmbH-Recht I² Rz 4/521; *A. Heidinger* in Gruber/Harrer, GmbHG² § 29 Rz 67; not unambiguous, however, *Koppensteiner/Rüffler*, GmbHG³ § 35 Rz 57 cited by *Heidinger*.
169 Cf. *Reich-Rohrwig*, GmbH-Recht I² Rz 4/521.
170 Cf. *Heermann* in Habersack/Löbbe/Casper, GmbHG-Gesetz II₃ (2020) § 52 Rz 339.

(*Sonderrecht*) to become a member of the advisory board based on an analogy to § 16 para 2 and § 30b para 5 GmbHG.[171]

3.5.2 Resignation

Resignation and withdrawal from advisory board membership are not regulated by law either. In the German jurisprudence[172] the fiduciary duty of the advisory board gives rise to the obligation not to resign the mandate at an inopportune moment (restructuring, takeover, etc.). Legal certainty on deadlines is provided by an arrangement in the articles of association[173] on resignation subject to a defined notice, also without giving any reason. A member may resign for good reason in any event.[174] If a member of the advisory board steps down, it will usually also include, at least by implication (§ 863 ABGB), a termination of the contractual relationship under the law of obligations with the company.

3.5.3 Removal from office on grounds of incompetence or death

In many cases an age limit[175] for members of an advisory board is provided for. When a member reaches that age, his advisory board membership ends automatically. Appropriate arrangements are recommended to deal with cases of a member's incapacity to contract or inability to act, which is not only temporary, to prevent unexpected vacancies.

When a member of the advisory board dies, his advisory board membership, which is personal in nature, ends; the same applies to any existing contractual or employment relationship. Upon the death of a member of the advisory board his personal position is not hereditary, although family owned companies sometimes provide for an automatic succession to the board by a specified other family member upon the departure of an advisory board member assigned to a family tree.

---

171 *Koppensteiner/Rüffler*, GmbHG[3] § 35 Rz 57; *Reich-Rohrwig*, GmbH-Recht I[2] Rz 4/521; *A. Heidinger* in Gruber/Harrer, GmbHG[2] § 29 Rz 67.
172 See *Spindler* in MüKoGmbHG (2019) § 52 Rz 739 with reference to *Wiedemann* in FS Lutter (2000) 801 (814).
173 Cf. Österreichischer Governance Kodex für Familienunternehmen (2017) Chapter 3.2.2.
174 See *Reich-Rohrwig*, GmbH-Recht I[2] Rz 4/522.
175 Cf. Österreichischer Governance Kodex für Familienunternehmen (2017) Chapter 3.2.4.

3.5.4 Dissolution of the advisory board

3.5.4.1 General

The advisory board has no right to dissolve itself. The modalities by which the shareholders may dissolve the advisory board generally depend on the rules that apply to its formation: For the dissolution of an advisory board directly based on corporate law, an amendment to the articles of association is required; for an advisory board established on the basis of corporate law by means of a shareholders' resolution, a resolution of the shareholders to dissolve the advisory board is required. A resolution taken by a majority of the shareholders – which does not achieve the quorum to dissolve the advisory board – may under certain circumstances be interpreted as removal of all the current members (where this is possible by a simple majority according to the procedure in place).[176] In the case of an advisory board established under the law of obligations, an actus contrarius is necessary unless other contractual arrangements are in place.

3.5.4.2 Incapacity or idleness of the advisory board

It may happen that an advisory board loses capacity to act through resignations, member absenteeism due to illness, serious conflicts of interest or unsolvable stalemate. Provisions for such cases should already be made when the advisory board is set up; for example, by defining a quorum that does not require the presence of all the members and the appointment of a sufficient odd number of members – to prevent tie votes – and by granting special members of the advisory board the right to cast the tie-breaking vote (see also Section 3.3.2). If the advisory board is generally capable but unwilling to act, however, it is a breach of duty that may lead to removal for cause without notice and, under certain circumstances, also to claims for damages by the company against the members of the advisory board who are unwilling to act.[177]

Years of inaction or inoperativeness of the advisory board do not lead to an automatic dissolution of the advisory board.[178] In this context the prevailing view[179]

---

176 Cf. *Voorman*, Beirat im Gesellschaftsrecht[2], 171 on the comparable German legal situation.

177 See Section 3.4.3.1 et seq.

178 *Voorman*, Beirat im Gesellschaftsrecht[2], 171 with reference to BGH II ZR 67/82, WM 1983, 835, 836 on optional supervisory boards; see also *Schnorbus* in Rowedder/Schmidt-Leithoff, GmbH-Gesetz[6] (2017) § 53 Rz 38.

179 For Austria see *Reich-Rohrwig*, GmbH-Recht I[2] Rz 4/523 and, following that, *Koppensteiner/Rüffler*, GmbHG[3] § 35 Rz 60; for Germany BGH NJW 1954, 799 (799 et seq.); OLG Brandenburg NZG 2000, 143 (144); *Ganzer* in Rowedder/Schmidt-Leithoff, GmbH-Gesetz[6] (2017) § 45 Rz 19; *Schindler* in

advocates a so-called fallback competence of the general meeting of shareholders – i.e., during the period the advisory board is not operational (in its form as an optional body established under corporate law) the powers otherwise vested in the advisory board revert to the shareholders.

3.5.4.3 The advisory board in a dissolved company

If a company is dissolved (e.g., by a shareholders' resolution) (§§ 84 et seq. GmbHG, §§ 203 et seq. AktG), the company moves from the stage of normal exercise of its activity to the liquidation phase. Its legal personality and all legal relationships remain unaffected thereby.[180] The dissolution of the company is followed by its liquidation (winding up the affairs of the dissolved company with a view to deleting it from the commercial register). Thus, dissolution does not mean that the company ceases to exist; this does not happen until all assets and property of the company have been redistributed and its deletion has been entered in the commercial register.[181] Thus, the dissolution of the company has no immediate direct effect on the advisory board (and any contracts between the members of the advisory board and the company), although from then on the advisory board is required to align its activities with the purpose of liquidation. The advisory board ceases to exist when the company ceases to exist.

3.5.4.4 The advisory board in a crisis or insolvency

A crisis or insolvency does not lead to the dissolution of the advisory board or termination of the activities of the members of the advisory board, but it does have an impact on the advisory board's responsibilities. Unlike the management or the board of directors the insolvency administrator is not subject to the supervisory board's control and approval[182] and even less so to an advisory board's control and approval. The members of the advisory board must comply with the relevant rules and above all make sure they are not involved in any unnecessary protraction of the insolvency process, which could lead to liability.[183] The advisory board itself will not be obligated to file for bankruptcy, however. Any claims for payment, reimbursement of expenses or any compensation on the part of members of the advisory board qualify as claims against the insolvent company; claims arising from an

BeckOK GmbHG (2020) § 45 Rz 39 et seq. with further references to the critical jurisprudence; opposing fallback competence: especially *Voorman*, Beirat im Gesellschaftsrecht², 172 et seq.
180 OGH 8 ObA 46/06g; RIS-Justiz RS0106409; *Rieder/Huemer*, Gesellschaftsrecht⁵, 334.
181 OGH 8 ObA 46/06g; *Rieder/Huemer*, Gesellschaftsrecht⁵, 334.
182 *Kalls/Oelkers*, Der Aufsichtsrat in der Insolvenz, AR aktuell 1/2007, 11 (16).
183 See Section 3.4.3.

employment contract may be secured under the IESG (Insolvency Remuneration Guarantee Act). If insolvency proceedings are not instituted, e.g., because the company does not possess sufficient assets, the company will be dissolved (§ 84 para 1 subpara 4 GmbHG; § 203 para 1 subpara 4 AktG) and the advisory board will cease to exist as soon as the company eventually ceases to exist; see Section 3.5.4.3.

References

Arnold, Nikolaus, Strafrechtliche Verantwortlichkeit der Mitglieder des Aufsichtsrates, Aufsichtsrat aktuell 0/2004, 7.

Arnold, Nikolaus, Der Beirat einer Privatstiftung, Aufsichtsrat aktuell 5/2005, 4.

Arnold, Nikolaus, Einschränkungen für begünstigtendominierte Beiräte und Stifter, GesRZ 2009, 348.

Arnold, Nikolaus, Kommentar zum Privatstiftungsgesetz[3] (2013); cited: *Arnold*, PSG[3] (§ Rz).

Artmann, Evelin/Karollus, Martin (eds), Kommentar zum AktG, Volume II[6] (2018); cited: *Author* in Artmann/Karollus, AktG II[6] (§ Rz).

Auer, Martin, Zum GmbH-Beirat, der ein fakultativer Aufsichtsrat sein soll, GeS 2007, 183.

Bankhaus Carl Spängler/INTES Akademie für Familienunternehmen (eds), Österreichischer Governance Kodex für Familienunternehmen (2017); cited: Österreichischer Governance Kodex für Familienunternehmen (2017) (Chapter).

Bayer, Walter, Die Haftung des Beirats im Recht der GmbH und der GmbH & Co. KG, in Burgard, Ulrich/Hadding, Walther/Mülbert, Peter/Nietsch, Michael/Welter, Reinhard (eds), Festschrift für Uwe H. Schneider zum 70. Geburtstag (2011) 75; cited: *Bayer* in FS Schneider (2011).

Briem, Robert, remarks on OGH 6 Ob 139/13d, GesRZ 2014, 63.

Csoklich, Peter, remarks on OGH 6 Ob 139/13d, PSR 2013, 175.

Doralt, Peter/Nowotny, Christian/Kalss, Susanne (eds), Kommentar zum PSG (1995); cited: *Author* in Doralt/Nowotny/Kalss, PSG (§ Rz).

Doralt, Peter/Nowotny, Christian/Kalss, Susanne (eds), Kommentar zum AktG[2] (2012); cited: *Author* in Doralt/Nowotny/Kalss, AktG[2] (§ Rz).

Feltl, Christian, remarks on OGH 9 ObA 130/05s, GesRZ 2007, 197.

Fleischer, Holger/Goette, Wulf (eds), Münchener Kommentar zum GmbHG, Volume II[3] (2019); cited: *Author* in MüKoGmbHG[3] (2019) (§ Rz).

Foglar-Deinhardstein, Heinrich/Aburumieh, Nora/Hoffenscher-Summer, Alexandra (eds), Kommentar zum GmbHG (2017); cited: *Author* in Foglar-Deinhardstein/Aburumieh/Hoffenscher-Summer, GmbHG (§ Rz).

Fritz, Josef, Der Beirat in der Gesellschafterpraxis, SWK 2005, 164.

Fritz, Josef, remarks on OGH 9 Ob A 130/05s, Aufsichtsrat aktuell 2/2007, 13.

Gruber, Michael/Harrer, Friedrich (eds), Kommentar zum GmbHG[2] (2018); cited: *Author* in Gruber/Harrer, GmbHG[2] (§ Rz).

Habersack, Mathias/Löbbe, Marc/Casper, Matthias (eds), Großkommentar zum GmbH-Gesetz, Volume II[3] (2020); cited: *Author* in Habersack/Löbbe/Casper, GmbH-Gesetz II[3] (2020) (§ Rz).

Hartlieb, Franz/Zollner, Johannes, Der fehlerhafte Beirat, PSR 2019, 4.

Hasch & Partner (ed), Kurzkommentar zum Privatstiftungsgesetz[2] (2014); cited: *Author* in Hasch, PSG[2] (§ Rz).

Heidinger, Markus, Aufgaben und Verantwortlichkeit von Aufsichtsrat und Beirat der GmbH (1989); cited: *M. Heidinger*, Aufgaben.

Hochedlinger, Gerhard, Zulässige und unzulässige Regelungen zur Vorstandsvergütung, PSR 2014, 4.

Huber, Peter, Fakultativer Aufsichtsrat, Beirat und Arbeitnehmermitwirkung in der GmbH, ecolex 1995, 807.

Kalls, Susanne/Oelkers, Janine, Der Aufsichtsrat in der Insolvenz, Aufsichtsrat aktuell 1/2007, 11.

Kalss, Susanne/Probst, Stephan, Familienunternehmen. Gesellschafts- und zivilrechtliche Fragen (2013); cited: *Kalls/Probst*, Familienunternehmen (Rz).

Kalss, Susanne/Kunz, Peter (eds), Handbuch für den Aufsichtsrat² (2016); cited: *Author* in Kalls/Kunz, Handbuch Aufsichtsrat² (Rz).

Karollus, Martin, remarks on OGH 6 Ob 195/10k, JBl 2011, 329.

Karollus, Martin, remarks on OGH 6 Ob 230/13m, ZFS 2014, 111.

Kastner, Walther, Aufsichtsrat und Realität, in Schwarz, Walter/Spielbüchler, Karl/Martinek, Oswin/Grillberger, Konrad/Jabornegg, Peter (eds), Möglichkeiten und Grenzen der Rechtsordnung. Festschrift für Rudolf Strasser zum 60 Geburtstag (1983) 843; cited: *Kastner* in FS Strasser (1983).

Kastner, Walther, Beiräte im österreichischen Gesellschaftsrecht, RdW 1983, 98.

Kletečka, Andreas/Schauer, Martin (eds), Onlinekommentar zum ABGB, version 1.07 from 01.05.2020 (rdb.at); cited: *Author* in Kletečka/Schauer, ABGB-ON$^{1.06}$ (§ Rz).

Koppensteiner, Hans-Georg/Rüffler, Friedrich, Kommentar zum GmbHG³ (2007).

Kühteubl, Stefan, Der Arbeitnehmervertreter im Aufsichtsrat als Beitragstäter bei Straftaten der Geschäftsführung, RdA 2012, 244.

Löschnigg, Günther, Die Entsendung der Betriebsräte in den Aufsichtsrat – organisationsrechtliche Probleme des § 110 ArbVG (1985).

Nowotny, Christian, Beirat – Aufsichtsrat – Ausschuss, RdW 2008, 699.

Nowotny, Christian, Privatstiftungen "in troubles", RdW 2009, 834.

Pittl, Raimund, Der Stifter einer Privatstiftung und die ihm zustehenden Rechte, NZ 1999, 197.

Reichert, Jochen, Der Beirat als Element der Organisationsverfassung einer Familiengesellschaft, in Grunewald, Barbara/Westermann, Peter (eds), Festschrift für Georg Maier-Reimer zum 70. Geburtstag (2010) 543; cited: *Reichert* in FS Maier-Reimer (2010).

Reich-Rohrwig, Johannes, Der Beirat der GmbH, ÖJZ 1981, 509.

Reich-Rohrwig, Johannes, Das österreichische GmbH-Recht, Band I² (1993); cited: *Reich-Rohrwig*, GmbH-Recht I² (Rz).

Rieder, Bernhard/Huemer, Daniela, Gesellschaftsrecht⁵ (2019).

Roth, Günther/Altmeppen, Holger *(eds)*, Kommentar zum GmbHG⁹ (2019); cited: *Author* in Roth/Altmeppen, GmbHG⁹ (2019) (§ Rz).

Rowedder, Heinz/Schmidt-Leithoff, Christian (eds), Kommentar zum Gesetz betreffend die Gesellschaften mit beschränkter Haftung: GmbHG⁶ (2017); cited: *Author* in Rowedder/Schmidt-Leithoff, GmbH-Gesetz⁶ (2017) (§ Rz).

Schneiderbauer, Bernd/Krebs, Viola-Katharina, Die Reichweite der Delegierbarkeit von Gesellschafterkompetenzen an einen Beirat, GesRZ 2018, 285.

Straube, Manfred (ed), Wiener Kommentar zum GmbHG (2013); cited: *Author* in Straube, WK GmbHG (§ Rz).

Straube, Manfred/Ratka, Thomas/Rauter, Roman (eds), Wiener Kommentar zum GmbHG (2014–2020); cited: *Author* in Straube/Ratka/Rauter, WK GmbHG (§ Rz).

Torggler, Hellwig, remarks on OGH 6 Ob 42/09h, JBl 2010, 336.

Voorman, Volker, Beirat im Gesellschaftsrecht² (1990).

Wenger, Thomas, Beirat als Aufsichtsrat, RWZ 2006, 356.

Wiedemann, Herbert, Beiratsverfassung in der GmbH, in Schneider, Uwe/Hommelhoff, Peter (eds), Festschrift für Marcus Lutter zum 70. Geburtstag (2000) 801; cited: *Wiedemann* in FS Lutter (2000).

Ziemons, Hildegard/Jaeger, Carsten/Pöschke, Moritz (eds), Beck'scher Online-Kommentar GmbHG, 46. Edition (2020); cited: *Author* in Ziemons/Jaeger/Pöschke, BeckOK GmbHG (2020) (§ Rz).

Zollner, Johannes, Grenzen der Gestaltungsmöglichkeiten für Beiräte einer Privatstiftung, JBl 2009, 22.

Paulo Penna and Luisa Shinzato
Chapter 4
Brazil

4.1 Introduction

In Brazil, medium-sized enterprises are generally organised as limited liability companies (*sociedades limitadas*) or closely held corporations (*sociedades anônimas fechadas* or *companhias fechadas*). The choice of one corporate structure over the other will take into account different factors, specially the level of complexity of the relationship among the shareholders. Since the law applicable to corporations is more equipped to deal with conflicts that may arise among shareholders, enterprises with a higher number of shareholders or a complex organisation concerning shareholders' rights and obligations tend to be organised as corporations. Limited liability companies, on the other hand, are typically employed for enterprises that require a simpler corporate structure. These predispositions, however, are not always followed. Limited liabilities can be tailored to address the needs of enterprises with complex shareholders' relations, while sometimes simpler enterprises will be organised as corporations.

Corporations can have a two-tier or a single-tier management structure. Corporations with a two-tier management structure will have two management bodies: the board of directors (*conselho de administração*) and the board of officers (*diretoria*). The two-tier structure is only mandatory in publicly held and government-controlled corporations. In other corporations, the existence of a board of directors is not required by law. Despite being optional, many medium-sized enterprises organised as corporations have a board of directors. Some will also have an operating overseeing board (*conselho fiscal*) or a consulting board (*conselho consultivo*), which, strictly speaking, are not considered management bodies.

Limited liability companies will more often than not have just a one-tier management structure and it is usually a simple structure, with the officers not necessarily being organised as a board. The law applicable to limited liability companies does not contain any provision about a supervisory or advisory board and this type of corporate entity is mostly adopted because of its simpler structure. However, there are instances where a limited liability company is attributed a more complex structure. Those that adopt this more complex structure will sometimes have an overseeing board, which is regulated but not required by law. Finally, a few limited liability companies will also adopt some kind of supervisory or advisory board.

We examine below the differences, organisation and roles of these boards.

https://doi.org/10.1515/9783110666182-004

4.2 Concept and definition, delimitation from other corporate bodies

4.2.1 Medium-sized enterprises in Brazil

Before examining the types of boards that apply to medium-sized enterprises and, more specifically, advisory boards, it will be useful to understand what is considered a medium-sized enterprise in Brazil. Although there is no specific legal definition of a medium-sized enterprise, we can infer which companies fall into such a range from certain laws, regulations and business practices.

Brazilian law provides tax benefits to certain small-sized enterprises. According to Federal Law 123/2006, small-sized enterprises consist of companies with an annual gross revenue of up to BRL 4,800,000. Any company with revenues exceeding such threshold is automatically excluded from the beneficial tax regime applicable to small-sized enterprises. Accordingly, from a Brazilian tax standpoint, the range of medium-sized enterprises will start with companies that have an annual gross revenue of BRL 4,800,000.

Brazilian corporate law does not define what will be considered a medium-sized enterprise. It does, however, circumscribe what will be considered a large-sized enterprise for accounting purposes. All large-sized enterprises, whether organised as a corporation or not, must follow the more detailed rules applicable to corporations concerning the preparation of their financial statements and must be audited by independent auditors. According to Brazilian corporate law, a company will be considered a large-sized enterprise if its total assets exceed BRL 240,000,000 or if it has annual gross revenues exceeding BRL 300,000,000. If the company belongs to an economic group and is therefore under the same control as other companies, such thresholds will be calculated considering the assets and revenues of all companies under the same control.

In line with the criteria referred to above, Brazil's main development bank, BNDES – Banco Nacional do Desenvolvimento Econômico e Social – considers that a medium-sized enterprise will have an annual gross revenue between BRL 4,800,000 and BRL 300,000,000.

These same criteria are adopted in the Brazilian Securities and Exchange Commission (Comissão de Valores Mobiliários (CVM)) rule on private equity funds (Instrução CVM 578/2016, which applies to *fundos de investimento em participações*). Under such rule, a fund will be classified according to the companies in which it invests. A private equity fund focusing on emerging companies – which would be another name attributed to medium-sized enterprises with a high growth potential – may invest in companies that have annual revenues of up to BRL 300,000,000.

On a different approach, the IBGE – the Brazilian Institute of Geography and Statistics – the agency responsible for official collection of statistical, geographic and other information in Brazil, classifies enterprises according to the number of employees they have. An industrial enterprise will be considered medium-sized if it has 100 to 499 employees. A service provider, on the other hand, will be considered medium-sized if it has 50 to 99 employees.

In this text, we will follow the definition of medium-sized enterprises used by the BNDES. It is wide ranging and encompasses varying companies, including family owned companies, venture capital or private equity invested companies, subsidiaries of multinational groups and joint venture companies.

Some important observations on corporations and limited liability companies
Closely held corporations, as well as publicly held corporations, are regulated by the Brazilian Law of Corporations (Federal Law 6,404/1976, as amended). They are governed by their bylaws (*estatuto social*), approved by and amended only by the corporation's shareholders.

Limited liability companies, on the other hand, are regulated by the Brazilian Civil Code (Federal Law 10,406/2002, as amended). They are governed by their articles of association (*contrato social*), approved by and amended only by the company's shareholders. Shareholders in limited liability companies are often also referred to in English as quotaholders, since in Brazil they are known as *quotistas*.

Throughout this text, when referring specifically to "limited liability companies", we will use their full denomination in English. When referring to both closely held corporations and limited liability companies, we will use the generic term "companies". Finally, we will refer to the *quotistas* of limited liability companies as "shareholders", even though the term "quotaholders" could also apply.

4.2.2 Corporate structure of medium-sized enterprises and the board of officers

As previously emphasised, medium-sized enterprises will be generally organised as a limited liability company or a closely held corporation. Neither of such corporate entities is required to have a supervisory or advisory board. What is required of them is to have officers (*diretores*).

Officers will be responsible for carrying out the company's activities and managing its operations. They are a mandatory presence in all Brazilian companies, no matter the size or nature. They represent the company in all dealings with third parties. Brazilian companies may only undertake obligations through their officers; shareholders and directors may not act on behalf of a company, unless they are also officers (or are appointed as attorneys-in-fact by the company, through the officers).

The definition and general roles of the officers are set forth by the Brazilian Civil Code with respect to limited liability companies and by the Brazilian Law of Corporations with respect to corporations.

Limited liability companies are required to have only one officer. They may of course have more than one, which is what usually occurs as the company's activities expand and managerial tasks become more complex. Corporations, on the other hand, must have at least two officers. The company's articles of association or the corporation's bylaws will establish if the entity will undertake obligations based on the signature of only one officer or by the joint signature of two or more officers.

Supervisory and advisory boards, on the other hand, do not represent the company, nor do they directly carry out the company's activities. Supervisory and advisory boards normally have powers to set forth general guidelines to be followed by the officers of the company or are entrusted with an advisory role.

According to the law, the officers will act individually and will not necessarily function as a board. However, the company's articles of association or bylaws may establish that the officers will hold regular meetings and will pass decisions concerning the company's affairs on such meetings. They will, in such a case, function as a board of officers.

> **Some clarifications on the designation of officers and directors in Brazil**
> In Brazil, officers are designated *diretores*. As a group or if organised as a board of officers, they are referred to as *diretoria*. They should not be confused with what is known in English-speaking countries as a board of directors. In Brazil, a board of directors is designated *conselho de administração* and their members are often referred to as *conselheiros*, even though the term *conselheiro* may also apply to members of other boards, such as the overseeing board (*conselho fiscal*) and the consulting board (*conselho consultivo*).
>
> Accordingly, in companies with more than one officer, customarily one of them is designated chief executive officer or, in Portuguese, *diretor presidente*. The other officers may be designated chief financial officer (in Portuguese, *diretor financeiro*), chief commercial officer (in Portuguese, *diretor comercial*) and so on. They may also be designated simply as officer without any specific designation (*diretor sem designação específica*).
>
> Throughout this article, we will refer to *diretores* as "officers" and to members of the *conselho de administração* as "directors".

4.2.3 Advisory and supervisory boards in Brazil: Concept, the consulting board and the board of directors

The term advisory or consulting board (*conselho consultivo*) in Brazil designates a voluntary board with purely advisory services. The Law of Corporations only contains one article about this board (article 160) and it simply establishes that the rules regarding the duties and liabilities of officers and directors will also apply to members of a consulting board. The Civil Code does not contain any regulation concerning the advisory or consulting board in limited liability companies.

Even though some corporations and limited liability companies have advisory or consulting boards, there is not much literature on this corporate body and no significant judicial precedent on them.

As we have learned by reading a draft of Daniel Graewe's chapter on advisory boards in Germany, which was provided to us as a guide to write this chapter on Brazil, in Germany the term "advisory board" is generally used as a generic term for the various forms of advisory bodies, including supervisory boards, administrative boards with management powers or shareholders' committees. Although that is not the case in Brazil, if we were to apply the German broader term of advisory board to Brazilian companies, it would include what we refer to as board of directors (*conselho de administração*) and other boards or committees.

A board of directors in Brazil would better fall under the concept of supervisory board, considering that it has powers to appoint the officers and also to set forth the general guidelines for the company's business activities. It is a controlling body. Although it may also "advise" the officers on business matters, its authority goes beyond merely giving advice. According to Brazilian law, the board of directors is responsible for defining the company's strategy and deliberating on relevant decisions. They stand in between the shareholders and the officers.

As indicated in the introduction to this chapter, a board of directors will only be mandatory in publicly held and government-controlled corporations, which are typically all large-sized enterprises. It is thus fair to say that in all medium-sized enterprises the existence of a board of directors is voluntary.

Thus, in light of the above and also considering the lack of literature and legal precedents on consulting boards, in this text we will address both the voluntary board of directors and the consulting board (*conselho consultivo*) in medium-sized enterprises organised as closely held corporations and limited liability companies. The element that unites both of these bodies is that they are voluntary, not imposed or required by law. It further makes sense to address both the board of directors and the consulting board because in corporations, as set forth by the Law of Corporations, the rules regarding the duties and liabilities of directors apply to the consulting board members.

4.2.4 The overseeing board (*conselho fiscal*): A specific advisory board

Another important corporate body is the overseeing board (*conselho fiscal*). The overseeing board is a mandatory board in all corporations, but it will generally only be operational upon the request of the shareholders. The bylaws of the corporation may establish that it will function on a permanent basis, but that is usually not the case. In limited liability companies, the overseeing board is not mandatory.

The role of the overseeing board is to oversee the company's financial situation and assess the compliance by them of the applicable duties under the law and the company's bylaws or articles of association. The overseeing board is required to review the company's financial statements and express its opinion on them. It will also give an opinion on proposals to be submitted by officers or directors to the shareholders' meeting on certain corporate restructuring transactions and investments. It has the power to request information from the officers and directors and may denounce them for errors, frauds and crimes and present its recommendation on the necessary measures that the company should take to address such issues. The overseeing board will also call the annual shareholders' meeting if the management bodies fail to do so for more than a month or, in cases of urgency, call special shareholders' meetings.

As set forth both in the Law of Corporations and the Civil Code, the attributions and powers of the overseeing board may not be granted to another body of the company.

The overseeing board answers to the shareholders and its members will be elected by the shareholders. In corporations, the overseeing board must have from three to five members. In limited liability companies it must have at least three members, but no maximum number is established. Minority shareholders will have the right to appoint at least one member of the overseeing board. Officers and directors may not be members of the overseeing board, in order to try to ensure the board's independence and impartiality.

To a certain extent, the overseeing board can be considered an advisory board with a very specific focus: the company's financial condition. Indeed, under the broader German concept of advisory board, the overseeing board would be considered an advisory board, especially since its role is essentially to advise and report to the shareholders on the company's financial statements and the activities of the officers and directors. It will generally be incumbent upon the shareholders to decide to act on what is advised and reported by the overseeing board.

Considering the many peculiarities of the overseeing board in Brazilian law and, furthermore, that in closely held corporations it is not a voluntary board (it is only voluntary in limited liability companies), in this text we will not address the overseeing board, focusing only on the board of directors and the consulting board.

Overseeing board is not the only translation of *conselho fiscal*

There is no perfect translation into English of *conselho fiscal*. It is sometimes referred to as overseeing board, overseeing committee, supervisory board, fiscal council, fiscal committee or audit committee.

In the past, *conselho fiscal* was commonly translated as audit committee (a popular translation of the Law of Corporations made available by the Brazilian SEC referred to it on its website as the audit committee). However, after the US Sarbanes–Oxley Act of 2002, some Brazilian publicly held corporations listed in the US adopted the audit committee used in US publicly held companies, which, differently from the *conselho fiscal*, reports to the board of directors. In some Brazilian publicly held corporations, there is now both an audit committee and a *conselho fiscal*. Accordingly, in our view the term "audit committee" ceased to be a good translation for *conselho fiscal*.

For the lack of a better translation, we will refer to the *conselho fiscal* as the "overseeing board".

4.3 Establishment, organisation and operation

The Law of Corporations regulates the board of directors in corporations. However, such law only contains a very simple rule concerning consulting boards. The Brazilian Civil Code, applicable to limited liability companies, does not contain any provision regarding boards of directors or consulting boards. We will therefore examine the establishment and functions of each of these corporate bodies in corporations and limited liability companies separately. We will also discuss the possibility of establishing non-statutory consulting boards. We will afterwards examine the organisation and operation of these bodies.

4.3.1 Board of directors in closely held corporations

The board of directors in corporations is specifically regulated by articles 140, 141 and 142 of the Brazilian Law of Corporations. In closely held corporations the board of directors in principle is optional. The board will only be mandatory in a closely held corporation if it has an authorised capital (*capital autorizado*), by which the board – hence the need for this management body – has authority to issue shares.

In closely held corporations, the board of directors can be established at the time in which the company is incorporated or can be included in the bylaws at any time after its incorporation through a resolution taken at a shareholders' meeting. Such resolution will depend on the majority vote of the shareholders present at the meeting, unless a supermajority or even unanimous vote is required by the bylaws (or a shareholders' agreement).

According to article 140 of the Law of Corporations, the board will have at least three members. It is common for closely held corporations to have a three-member board or a five-member board, although some will have larger boards. Boards with more than fifteen members are rare though, due to the difficulties in the operation of a board with so many participants. Directors will be elected and dismissed by the shareholders' meeting. In Section 4.4 we examine who may serve as director of a corporation.

The bylaws of the corporation must establish: (i) the number of members of the board or the maximum and minimum number of members (the law allows the board to operate without a set number of members); (ii) the process of nomination and replacement of the chairperson of the board (we discuss the functions of the chairperson in Section 4.3.7.3); (iii) the manner through which the directors will be replaced; (iv) the term of office of the directors, which must not exceed three years; and (v) the rules concerning the way through which board meetings will be convened and installed, and how the board will function.

The bylaws may set forth that the employees of the company will have the right to appoint a member of the board. The inclusion of this rule in the bylaws is optional and rarely practiced by medium-sized enterprises in Brazil. When included, such member of the board will be elected through a voting process held among the employees, organised by the company jointly with the unions that represent the company's employees.

The members of the board will be appointed by the shareholders' meeting, usually through the affirmative vote of the majority of the voting shares represented at the meeting.

Closely held corporations may issue different classes of voting shares, by which each class will have the right to separately elect a certain number of directors. This arrangement can be useful, for instance, to accommodate the interests of different family branches in family owned enterprises: a different class of shares (common shares A, common shares B and so on) can be attributed to each family branch, each class having the right to elect a certain number of directors.

The Law of Corporations grants to shareholders holding 10 per cent or more of the voting shares the right to call for the cumulative voting procedure. According to this procedure, each share will entitle its shareholders to cast a number of votes corresponding to the vacant seats and the votes can all be cast on one or just a few members of the board. The procedure allows minority shareholders to concentrate their votes on a few members of the board and thereby increase their chances of electing one or more directors.

As set forth in article 142 of the Law of Corporations, the board of directors will supervise, direct and oversee the business and activities of the corporation. The board will establish the corporation's general policies and business strategies, as well as appoint and remove officers and oversee and evaluate their performance. If the company is not performing well because of the officers, the board should take action and replace the officers.

The board of directors also has the power to call shareholders' meetings. It will call the annual shareholders' meeting as well as special meetings that are required throughout the year.

The board of directors may also have the power to approve certain material or sensitive transactions such as the sale of fixed assets, the establishment of liens and the rendering of guarantees. It is common to grant to the board the power to approve material contracts and material loans.

In essence, the board of directors has a supervisory, rather than an advisory, role.

The bylaws may assign additional tasks and authority to the board, but may not transfer to the board functions of the officers or the overseeing board.

4.3.2 Consulting boards in closely held corporations

Article 160 of the Law of Corporations establishes that the provisions of the law concerning the duties and liabilities of officers and directors also apply to members of any bodies set forth in the bylaws having technical or advisory functions. This is the only provision set forth in law specifically concerning statutory consulting boards.

Therefore, shareholders are free to set forth in the bylaws the rules regarding the establishment, composition and roles of consulting boards that they seem fit. So long as the consulting board is a statutory body, governed by the company's bylaws, its members will have to observe the duties and liabilities applicable to officers and directors. We discuss such duties and liabilities in Section 4.4.

A consulting board can be created at any time through an amendment to the bylaws, approved by a resolution of the shareholders' meeting.

Consulting boards in closely held corporations can be set up to advise the officers or the board of directors. A consulting board could also be set up to advise the shareholders directly, even though article 160 of the Law of Corporations does not refer to such a possibility. They will often be called committees (*comitês*), instead of boards (*conselho*), to differentiate themselves from the board of directors and the overseeing board.

The consulting board may provide advice on a broad spectrum of matters or may have a more limited scope of activity, the latter being more common. For instance, a closely held corporation may set up a search advisory committee that will advise the board of directors on potential candidates for the roles of officers. The committee will review the résumé of potential candidates, interview them and present to the board a list of approved candidates, along with a proposed compensation based on a market study. Corporations may also have an audit committee that will advise on financial matters, the role of the audit committee not being confused with that of the overseeing board.

In family owned enterprises that already have a board of directors, the consulting board is sometimes occupied by important family members that were left out of the board of directors. The board of directors will then be required to consult with the consulting board before passing resolutions on important business matters. Consulting boards are also used in corporations that do not yet have a board of directors, where important decisions are taken by the officers. In this case, consulting boards are used as a "test-drive" or as a transition for a board of directors. At first the members of the consulting board take on merely advisory functions. The board will meet from time to time to discuss the company's activities with the officers and advise on certain matters. As the company develops, the consulting board is then converted into an effective board of directors and takes on a supervisory role with powers to approve or disapprove important business matters.

Another possibility in family owned enterprises is to establish in the bylaws that the advisory board will become effective after the corporation reaches a certain number of shareholders. As one generation succeeds the other and the shares are dispersed among more family members, at some point the threshold will be reached and the consulting board will be implemented.

In Brazil, private equity vehicles are customarily structured as funds; they can, though, be structured as closely held corporations. Some private equity vehicles organised as closely held corporations set up a consulting board composed of private equity investors to provide their opinion on investment opportunities.

The consulting board may also take on a more technical role, advising the directors or officers on technical matters. For instance, if the company has had an accident with serious environmental consequences, the shareholders may wish to set up a technical consulting board to advise on how to deal with the accident and help monitor the clean-up.

Typically, the consulting board will have merely advisory functions. It will not have ultimate decision-making powers. It can be established, however, that the board of directors or the board of officers may only pass certain resolutions or take certain measures if the consulting board is previously consulted on the matter. For instance, it can be determined that the board of directors in principle will only appoint as officers individuals who have been previously interviewed and approved by the search advisory committee. Although the board of directors will have the final say on who will be the next officers, the opinion of the consulting board on the matter will be relevant.

The consulting board will not represent the company before third parties. The only persons that have the authority to represent and bind the company are its officers and attorneys-in-fact. In order for members of the consulting board to have powers of representation, they would have to be appointed as attorneys-in-fact. Therefore, the consulting board will not have powers to, for instance, retain service providers or order a specific study. If the consulting board needs to hire the services of a specialised consultant to help in its functions, it will have to request the officers to do so.

It is also important to point out that the consulting board may not take on the functions attributed by law to the officers, board of directors and overseeing board. This prohibition is set forth in article 139 and paragraph 7 of article 163 of the Law of Corporations.

A company may, of course, have more than one consulting board, each with a different set of functions and a different set of rules.

The rules regarding the functions, the composition and the operation of the consulting board can be set forth in the bylaws. The bylaws can also lay out the basic functions of the consulting board and delegate to the board of directors or the board of officers the power to determine the rest of the rules applicable to the consulting board, including its composition and operation. Finally, the bylaws can also determine that the rules concerning specially the operation of the consulting board will be construed by the consulting board itself. In this case, the consulting board will approve its *regimento interno* or internal rules.

Given the great flexibility in establishing the rules applicable to a consulting board, there is no minimum or maximum number of members, nor a fixed or maximum term of office. This will vary depending on the needs of the company and the interests of the shareholders. Albeit rare, the consulting board may even have just one sole member.

The appointment of the members of the consulting board may vary depending on the shareholders' interest. The bylaws may set forth that they will be elected by the shareholders. If the consulting board is set up to advise the board of directors or the board of officers, it can also be established that the members of the board will be appointed respectively by the directors or the officers. It would also be possible to set up a self-appointing consulting board in which the members (except for the first members, of course) are appointed by the consulting board itself: In case of vacancy of a seat in the board, the rest of the members would meet and select a new member.

4.3.3 Board of directors in limited liability companies

There has been some discussion in Brazilian legal literature as to whether limited liability companies may have a board of directors, with the same functions attributed to such board in a corporation, given that the Brazilian Civil Code is silent on such matter.

Despite the lack of provisions in the law explicitly allowing limited liability companies to have a board of directors, it is generally understood that such type of company may have a board of directors based on two arguments. First, the law does not prohibit the implementation of a board of directors. Second, the sole paragraph of article 1,053 of the Civil Code allows the shareholders to establish that the limited liability company's articles of association will be governed, on a supplementary basis, by the Law of Corporations. Naturally, the Law of Corporations will not apply in full to a limited liability company, since there are many provisions that are incompatible with it. The provisions relating to the board of directors, though, are in general not incompatible with a limited liability company. Thus, limited liability companies may have a board of directors with similar functions to that of a corporation, but with some important caveats.

In a corporation, one of the most important functions of the board of directors is to appoint the officers. The Civil Code, however, expressly sets forth that the appointment of officers in a limited liability company is incumbent upon the shareholders. Therefore, the board of directors in a limited liability company will not be able to appoint officers; even if the company has a board, the officers will continue to be appointed by the shareholders.

The board of directors of a corporation may also have the authority to decide on the issuance of shares if the corporation has an authorised capital stock. Since limited liability companies do not issue shares (their capital stock is represented by quotas) and may not have an authorised capital stock, such function will not apply to their boards of directors.

Aside from such important limitations, a board of directors in a limited liability company can be set up similarly to a board of directors in a corporation.

The members of the board of directors will be appointed by the shareholders. The articles of association must indicate the number of members of the board, which may not be less than three. In limited liability companies, managers (directors and officers) will be nominated in the articles of association itself or separately by the shareholders' meeting, depending on what is established in the articles of association. The nomination of the directors in the articles of association requires the approval of shareholders representing 75 per cent of the capital stock, which is the required quorum for amending the articles of association. On the other hand, the appointment of the directors in a shareholders' meeting only requires the approval of shareholders holding the majority of the capital stock.

4.3.4 Consulting boards in limited liability companies

The Brazilian Civil Code, applicable to limited liability companies, does not contain any rule on consulting boards. Therefore, the shareholders may freely decide whether the company will have a consulting board and what rules will apply to it. The shareholders are only prevented from transferring to the consulting boards the functions attributed by the Civil Code to the overseeing board.

Accordingly, the same considerations made in Section 4.3.2 with respect to the consulting board in a corporation also apply to the consulting board in a limited liability company.

4.3.5 Non-statutory consulting boards

So far, we have addressed consulting boards that are set forth in the corporation's bylaws or in the limited liability company's articles of association. A consulting board could, though, be established outside the company's internal corporate structure, either by a resolution of the shareholders, the board of directors or the board of officers, or even by a decision of the officers. It would be a non-statutory consulting board.

Again, there is great flexibility in establishing the rules applicable to such non-statutory consulting boards. They will frequently have a shorter lifespan, being used in specific temporary situations.

A non-statutory consulting board would resemble more a service provider than an actual management body. In principle, the duties and liabilities of the management bodies, which are applicable to statutory consulting boards, would not apply directly to non-statutory consulting boards.

4.3.6 Compensation of the members of the board

According to article 152 of the Law of Corporations, the shareholders' meeting will establish the compensation to be paid to directors and officers of the company. The shareholders' meeting may determine the individual compensation to be paid to each member or set forth a global compensation to be allocated by the board of directors among the company's directors and officers.

In corporations that have a mandatory dividend rule corresponding to 25 per cent or more of the profits, the bylaws may grant to the directors and managers a participation in the profits, provided that it does not exceed their annual compensation or 10 per cent of the profits, whichever is lower.

In closely held corporations the compensation paid to each director is oftentimes the same, since they perform the same roles. There are many instances, however, in which the compensation will vary among board members, due to the seniority of the members, his experience and professional reputation. Sometimes the chairperson of the board is entitled to a higher compensation, seeing that he will customarily have to dedicate more time to the board.

Members of the consulting board will not necessarily be paid. For instance, in family owned enterprises, where the seats of the consulting board are occupied by family members, it is common to establish that they will not receive compensation. Nevertheless, it is customary to at least reimburse members of consulting boards for expenses in connection with their functions in the board. Naturally, in family owned companies with higher levels of professionalisation or where the time dedicated by the members of the consulting board to their functions increases, the tendency is for the company to pay some compensation to them. Details of the remuneration can be provided in the bylaws or articles of association, by a shareholder resolution or by some other means set forth in the bylaws or articles of association.

4.3.7 Operation of the board

The board of directors is a collegiate body – which means that it will operate through the collective decision of its members. Resolutions passed by the board will depend on the approval of the members of the board taken at a board meeting.

Directors, as well as officers, are bound by the duties of care and loyalty to the company, not to the shareholders that appointed them. This means that they should always vote on board meetings having in mind what is best for the company, not for themselves or the shareholder or group of shareholders who elected them.

Although there is no specific rule applicable to the board of directors of limited liability companies or consulting boards, they will normally follow the rules applicable to the board of directors with regard to the operation of the board.

The bylaws or, in limited liability companies, the articles of association will establish how the board will operate. Details of the operation of the board may also be set out in internal rules approved by the shareholders or the board itself.

4.3.7.1 Meetings of the board

The Law of Corporations does not establish how the board of directors will meet. The bylaws should set forth the rules concerning such matter.

Under most bylaws, the meetings will be called by chairperson of the board. It is also common to provide that any member – or a certain number of members – may call a board meeting. Sometimes the bylaws also allow the chief executive officer or other officers to call board of directors' meetings.

Meetings will be called with a certain number of days in advance. The call notice will indicate the agenda of the meeting.

Meetings will habitually be held at the company's head office, but the bylaws may establish that they can be done through videoconference or other means through which the board members are able to communicate with one another and cast their votes. The bylaws may also establish that the board members may provide their written vote in advance and thus be considered present at a meeting. Board members may not appoint an attorney-in-fact to represent them at meetings.

It is also common for bylaws to establish that there will be a minimum number of board meetings per year. The establishment of a certain regularity to the meetings allows board members to monitor the company more closely than an occasional advisor. In any event, bylaws will customarily leave room for extraordinary meetings, called whenever the interests of the company so require.

The bylaws may also require the attendance of a minimum number of members in order for a meeting to be installed. Oftentimes, a meeting may only be installed if the majority of the board members are present. Naturally, all members of the board must have been duly invited in order for a meeting to be considered valid.

Meetings will customarily be presided by the chairperson of the board. This is one of the main functions of the chairperson. The bylaws will usually also establish that the chairperson will appoint a secretary of the meeting, who will be responsible for preparing the minutes of the meeting. In the position of presiding director, the chairperson of the board will organise the meeting observing the agenda set forth in the invitation. The chairperson will also take the votes and declare whether a resolution was approved or not. Under article 118 of the Law of Corporations, the chairperson will not count the vote cast by a board member in violation of a shareholders' agreement filed with the company.

At the end of the meeting, the secretary will draw up the minutes of the meeting, which will be signed by the attending directors.

Again, there is no rule in the law concerning meetings of consulting boards. Such rules will have to be determined in the bylaws, articles of association or some internal regulation and will by and large follow the guidelines set forth above.

4.3.7.2 Resolutions of the board

According to item IV of article 140 of the Law of Corporations, resolutions of the board of directors will be taken by the majority vote of the directors. The bylaws may establish, however, that certain matters (normally relevant matters) will require a supermajority vote. The bylaws may attribute to the chairperson of the board a second or casting vote if the directors are equally divided on a matter.

The shareholders' agreement can also establish a supermajority vote or a qualified vote for certain decisions. For instance, in joint ventures composed of two partners, it is common for them to establish in a shareholders' agreement that relevant matters of the board be approved by a majority vote, provided that at least one director appointed by each partner casts a favourable vote. This voting structure can also be used in family owned enterprises, to accommodate the interests of different family branches. As previously mentioned, the chairperson of the meeting must not take into account any vote cast by a director in breach of a shareholders' agreement. It will, instead, grant such vote to the directors appointed by the non-breaching party of the shareholders' agreement so that they may cast the vote on behalf of the breaching director.

As we have seen, there is no specific rule for the board of directors in limited liability companies and for consulting boards. The bylaws or articles of association will normally provide that resolutions be taken by the majority vote, with certain more sensitive decisions depending on a supermajority or even unanimous vote. Note that typically such resolutions will actually just reflect the recommendation of the board members, given that the consulting board will not have actual decision-making powers.

If the board of directors approves resolutions that will have an effect on third parties (for instance, the election of the officers of the corporation), then the minutes of the meeting must be registered with the Registry of Commerce and published. Generally, minutes of the meetings of a consulting board will not need to be registered with the Registry of Commerce.

4.3.7.3 Chairperson of the board

The Law of Corporations sets forth that the bylaws must determine how the chairperson of the board of directors will be appointed and replaced. His appointment may be incumbent upon the shareholders of the board of directors itself. When the choice falls upon the shareholders, usually the shareholders will indicate, among the elected directors for a new mandate, who will serve as chairperson and who will replace the chairperson in his absence. When the choice falls upon the board of directors itself, after the board members are elected, they will hold a first meeting and vote on who will be the next chairperson.

The functions of the chairperson of the board will be set in the bylaws and also sometimes in the board's internal rules. Typically, the chairperson of the board will have the power to individually convene board meetings, preside over such meetings and appoint the secretary of the meeting. As previously mentioned, some bylaws attribute to the chairperson a second or casting vote in the event of a deadlock. Some bylaws also assign to the chairperson powers to take certain actions on urgent matters (for instance, in the event of resignation of the chief executive officer, appoint one of the other officers to act in his place until the board of directors decides on who will be the new chief executive officer).

Given that there is no rule concerning the structure of consulting boards, they may have a chairperson or not. If they have a chairperson, the process of appointing and replacing the chairperson may be similar to the one used for the board of directors.

Bylaws and articles of association can also set forth the role of a vice or deputy chairperson, who will perform the tasks of the chairperson in his absence.

4.4 Members, breach of duty and liability

We examine below who may be a member of the board of directors and of a consulting board, their duties and the consequences of a breach of duty.

4.4.1 Members and eligibility requirements

Under the Law of Corporations, the members of the board of directors must all be individuals. A legal entity may not hold a seat in the board of directors. The law previously required that the directors also be shareholders, but such requirement has been revoked.

Only one-third of the directors may also be officers of the corporation. Since the board of directors supervises the actions of the officers, it would not make sense for the officers to hold the majority of seats in the board of directors. The Law of Corporations establishes the limit of one-third of the seats.

The Law of Corporations also sets forth in its article 147 that an individual may not be appointed as director if he (i) occupies any position in a competing company, especially in consulting boards, board of directors or overseeing boards; and (ii) has a conflicting interest with the corporation.

The Law of Corporations further states that a person will not be eligible for a seat in the board if he has been condemned for bankruptcy crimes, prevarication, bribery, concussion, embezzlement or against the popular economics, against the national financial system, against anti-trust rules, consumer relations, public faith or property, or for any other crime that bars the person from taking a public office. He must also not be prevented from taking on the role of director under any special laws (for instance, some government officials are not allowed under law to work for private enterprises).

The Brazilian Civil Code contains a similar rule with respect to the appointment of managers of a limited liability company. Since a director of a limited liability company is considered a manager, he will also be subject to such rules.

It is not clear whether the requisites detailed above would apply to members of a consulting board, given that they are not, strictly speaking, managers of the company.

The bylaws and articles of association may also establish additional requisites in order for a person to be appointed a member of the board of directors or of a consulting board. For instance, it may be required that the board members have a certain level of education, certain years of professional experience or be a certain age.

It is usually interesting to have members in the board with different backgrounds and expertise (such as in finance, accounting, marketing, law and of the company's business sector), due to the strategic role they play.

On larger enterprises or those with a higher number of shareholders, it may also be convenient to have independent members – individuals not related to the majority shareholders, bound by shareholders' agreements or with business relations with the company or its shareholders. This could ensure impartial insights in board meetings and decisions.

4.4.2 Rights and duties

The basic right of any board member is to attend and vote in board meetings. Naturally, in connection with such a basic right, the board member will have the right to be called to meetings, to speak at meetings and to request documents and information available to all board members.

As previously mentioned, the Law of Corporations establishes in article 160 that the rules concerning the duties of directors and officers will also apply to members of consulting boards. In closely held corporations such duties are: (i) to act with diligence and care; (ii) to act within their powers, observing the purposes of the entity; (iii) to be loyal towards the corporation; and (iv) to avoid conflicts of interest.

The duty of diligence and care requires board members to exercise the same diligence, care and skills that a sound businessperson would exercise in dealing with his personal assets in comparable circumstances.

To fulfil the duty to act within their powers and purposes of the corporation, board members must consider the interests of the corporation and of shareholders as a whole in their actions and decisions, without privileging the shareholders responsible for their appointment, and while observing the corporation's social function. As such, a board member may not receive from third parties any type of personal benefit, whether direct or indirect, due to his position in the board, without prior statutory or shareholders' approval. Any amounts received in breach of such rule will belong to the corporation.

The duty of loyalty translates mainly into the obligation to preserve confidentiality and not to use privileged or sensitive information relating to the corporation for personal benefit or the benefit of third parties. Accordingly, a board member may not use for his personal benefit any commercial opportunity to which he comes across due to the position occupied in the board, whether or not causing harm to the corporation. A board member may also not fail to act in order to protect the corporation's interests or fail to take advantage of business opportunities for the company in order to reap personal benefits for himself. A board member may also not acquire a certain asset or right that he knows is necessary for the company or that the company is thinking of acquiring, to later resell with a profit.

With respect to the duty to avoid conflicts of interest, board members may not take part in transactions or resolutions in which they have a personal conflicting interest. They must also inform the other officers or directors about the nature and relevance of their personal interest and indicate such interest in the minutes of the corresponding board meeting. In this sense, paragraph 1 of article 156 of the Law of Corporation establishes that a member of a management body may only enter into a contract with the corporation on such terms that would exist if the transaction had been negotiated between unrelated parties. Any business transaction that is done in violation of this rule may be annulled and the board member will be required to transfer to the company any benefit he may have obtained.

The Brazilian Civil Code does not contain detailed rules concerning the duties of the members of management bodies, yet does set forth the broad general duty to act with diligence and care. As we have previously mentioned, the articles of association of limited liability companies with a board of directors normally set out that the company will be governed, on a supplementary basis, by the Law of Corporations. In this case, the duties spelled out above will also apply to the directors of the limited liability company.

4.4.3 Breach of duty

As a general rule, the members of management bodies will be liable for damages that he may cause to the company or third parties when acting with negligence or fraud, or in violation of the law or the company's bylaws or articles of association.

Accordingly, a board member who violates any of the duties set forth in Section 4.4.2 and, by such action or inaction, causes damages to the company or third parties may be held personally liable. This does not mean that a board member will be personally responsible for a decision that proves to be harmful for the company from a business perspective. Indeed, Brazilian courts have embraced the business judgement rule.

According to such standard, if the board made a decision in good faith, considering the company's best interests and in accordance with the fiduciary duties set forth by the law, its members should not be held personally liable, even if, when examining the circumstances, there could be a better business decision. The obligation of the board members is to take an informed, weighted and impartial decision, abiding to the duty of diligence and care. The outcome of the decision itself – even if disastrous – will not be the element that will determine the personal liability of the board member. There are risks in any business decision, as there are risks in business overall, and the members of a management body will not be held personally liable if a decision ends up being detrimental to the business, unless acting in violation of the duties spelled out above.

To take an informed decision, the board member must inform himself on the matter, based on a reasonable amount of information. Depending on the matter, he should consider prior assessments and studies on the subject, prepared by other managers, employees or third parties. The decision should be weighted, meaning that it should be made taking into consideration other alternatives, consequences and effects. Finally, the decision should be impartial. It should not produce a personal gain to the board member, be it direct or indirect.

Paragraph 6 of article 159 of the Law of Corporations further states that the courts may exempt members of management bodies from the obligation to indemnify the company if proven that he acted in good faith and was seeking the company's best interests.

Differently from directors, typical consulting boards do not take decisions that are binding on the company. They will normally issue advice and thereby influence the decisions taken by the shareholders, directors or officers, but not directly cause the company to take any action or inaction. Accordingly, they are less likely to bring damage to the company.

This does not mean that they are immune to liability. As previously mentioned, the rules concerning the duties and liabilities of officers and managers also apply to members of consulting boards of corporations. Therefore, if the consulting board breaches his duties and, in doing so, causes harm to the company or third parties, he may be held personally liable.

The Law of Corporations sets forth that a member of the management body will not be held responsible for unlawful acts of other members unless he is complicit with such acts, does not take action to discover such acts or, being aware of them, does not take the necessary measures to block them.

It is important to bear in mind that in collective bodies such as board of directors and consulting boards, decisions are taken collectively, mostly by the majority vote. If a specific member is against the decision that is being taken by the majority because he believes it violates a duty of the board, he must set out a dissenting vote in the minutes of the meeting and give immediate and written notice of the matter to the shareholders, the board of directors or the overseeing board.

Finally, note that in a corporation shareholders can seek enforcement against directors and members of a consulting body through a derivative or direct claim. It is generally incumbent upon the corporation, previously authorised by the shareholders' meeting, to bring an enforcement action against members of management bodies (and consulting bodies) for losses caused by them to the corporations. If the shareholders' meeting decides to pursue such action but the corporation fails to do so, any shareholder may bring a derivative claim against members of the board of directors of a consulting body on the corporation's behalf. However, even if the shareholders' meeting decides not to pursue such action, shareholders jointly holding 5 per cent of the corporation's shares may initiate a derivative claim. Any proceeds of a successful derivative claim are awarded to the corporation, which must reimburse the shareholders that initiated the action for litigation expenses.

A shareholder of a corporation or a limited liability company may also bring a direct claim against directors and members of the consulting board when directly affected by their action or negligence (i.e., when the damage is not a result of the loss of value of the investment made in the corporation).

It is becoming more common in Brazil for directors to request for a directors' and officers' liability insurance (D&O insurance) to be put in place in order to become a member of the board.

4.5 Termination

We examine below the termination of the appointment of a member of the board of directors and of the consulting board, and the termination of the board itself.

4.5.1 Termination with regard to a certain member

4.5.1.1 Automatic termination at the end of the term

According to the Law of Corporations, the term of office of the members of the board of directors will not exceed three years. Terms of office of one or two years are common. Members of the board of directors may not be appointed for life or even for an indefinite term. The term of office of members of consulting boards will usually be determined by the company's articles of association or bylaws or even the shareholders' meeting.

Once the term expires, the shareholders will convene in a shareholders' meeting and elect the new members of the board of directors, or re-elect existing members, and the individuals that were not re-elected will cease to hold such function. Their mandate will automatically terminate. A similar procedure can be used with regard to consulting boards, taking into account who has the powers to appoint them.

Note that article 150, paragraph 4, of the Law of Corporations establishes that the term of office of the board members will be extended up to the date in which the new elected directors take office. Therefore, the triggering event for termination of a board members' term of office is not actually the expiration of its period of duration, but actually the date in which the new members take office.

4.5.1.2 Automatic termination of a member of a consulting board upon completion of a task

Since the law does not establish any rule concerning the term of office of members of consulting boards, in theory a member of such board could be appointed to complete a certain task. In this case, it could be established that the term of office of such member will automatically terminate upon completion of the task.

4.5.1.3 Automatic termination due to failure to continue to fulfill appointment requirements

As previously mentioned, the Law of Corporations contains certain requirements that must be fulfilled in order for an individual to be appointed member of the board of directors. The company's bylaws or articles of association may also establish additional requirements.

If the member of the board ceases to fulfil such a requirement, then he will cease to be a board member. For example, the Law of Corporations establishes that a person may not be appointed to the board if he is condemned for crimes under the bankruptcy law. It is required that the person have a clean record with regard to such crimes. If a person is condemned for such a crime during his term of office, then he will cease to fulfil such requirement and thus not be able to continue to be a member of the board. It is recommended, in this case, to hold a shareholders' meeting acknowledging that such individual ceased to be a member of the board of directors and to subsequently register the minutes of such meeting with the Registry of Commerce and publish them, thereby letting third parties know of the change in the board.

4.5.1.4 Resignation

A member of the board of directors can resign at any time. According to article 151 of the Law of Corporations, the resignation of a board member will become effective with regard to the company at the time in which he presents his resignation letter. The resignation must be presented in writing.

With regard to third parties, the resignation will become effective after evidence of the resignation is registered with the Registry of Commerce and published. Normally the company will register and publish the minutes of the shareholders' meeting in which the shareholders acknowledge the resignation of a board member and elect his substitute. However, the resigning director does not have to depend on the company and can register and publish the resignation letter himself, thus letting third parties know that he is no longer a member of the board.

The same principles will apply to the resignation of a member of a consulting board, with observance of any specific rule set forth in the company's bylaws or articles of association.

4.5.1.5 Dismissal

Regardless of the term of office set forth in the company's bylaws or articles of association, the shareholders may at any time dismiss the directors. In corporations, dismissal of a board member will take place in a shareholders' meeting by a majority vote of the attending shareholders or another higher quorum set forth in the bylaws. In limited liability companies, dismissal will require the vote of shareholders representing the majority of the capital stock. The dismissal will only be effective before third parties after the minutes of the shareholders' meetings are registered with the Registry of Commerce.

The same principles will apply to the dismissal of a member of a consulting board. For instance, if the members of the consulting board are elected by the board of directors, then it is generally established that they can be dismissed at any time by the board of directors.

As we have examined, the Law of Corporations establishes that the members of the board of directors may be elected through cumulative voting. If this procedure is adopted, then the dismissal of one member of the board will automatically entail the dismissal of the remaining members, with a new election of all board members. This is the rule established in article 141, paragraph 3, of the Law of Corporations. The purpose of this rule is to prevent the majority shareholders of unfairly removing a director appointed by a group of minority shareholders. Since there will be a new election, such group of minority shareholders will in theory be able to request the adoption of the cumulative voting procedure and once more appoint a member of the board to their liking.

4.5.2 Termination of the board itself

4.5.2.1 Elimination of the board

Seeing that the board of directors and the consulting board are not mandatory in closely held corporations and limited liability companies, they may at any time be eliminated through a decision of the shareholders, just like they were created. In this case the shareholders' meeting will pass a resolution terminating the board and removing the provisions of the bylaws or articles of association relating to the board.

Instead of eliminating the board, the shareholders may also change the rules applicable to the board at any time.

In closely held corporations, the resolution concerning the elimination of the board will be taken by the majority vote of the shareholders present at the meeting, unless a higher quorum is set forth in the bylaws. In limited liability companies, any change to the articles of association requires the vote of shareholders representing at least 75 per cent of the capital stock. Therefore, the elimination of a board of directors or a consulting board regulated by the articles of association will require the vote of shareholders representing 75 per cent of the capital stock.

The elimination of the board of directors will not affect the resolutions previously taken by the board. Such resolutions will continue to be effective until otherwise revoked by the shareholders' meeting or otherwise supplanted by a new resolution taken by whoever the shareholders attribute the corresponding powers of the board.

4.5.2.2 Temporary consulting board

Even though not usual, a consulting board could be structured to last for a certain period of time or until completion of a task or achievement of a goal. For instance, after a merger the company could set up a consulting board to provide support in the integration process for a couple of years or until full integration of the merged companies is completed.

4.5.2.3 Non-acting board

A non-acting board would be a board that is capable of acting yet fails to do so due to the omission of its members, or at least the majority of its members. In other words, the board is set forth in the bylaws or articles of association, its members are appointed and take office, but nothing happens. The board members fail to show up at meetings or fail to even convene meetings.

In such a scenario, the natural consequence would be for the shareholders to hold a meeting and dismiss all board members, replacing them with diligent individuals. The previous board members that failed to fulfil their duties could be held liable for damages caused to the company.

4.5.2.4 Boards in companies in judicial recovery and bankruptcy

The undergoing by the company of a financial crisis does not immediately affect the existence of the board of directors or a consulting board. They will continue to function normally and, of course, should try to take measures within their powers to try to resolve the crisis.

According to Brazilian law, it is up to the shareholders to file for judicial recovery or bankruptcy. The board of directors or the consulting board, depending on its purpose, may recommend the shareholders to go forward with such filing, but it is ultimately up to the shareholders to take such a decision.

If the company files for judicial recovery, article 51 of the Brazilian Insolvency Law (Federal Law 11,101/2005) establishes that such request will be accompanied by a list of personal assets held by all the company's officers and directors. This provision has been very criticised since it exposes personal property that in principle should not be affected by the company's debts. Note that it does not encompass members of consulting boards, as they in principle are not strictly speaking considered to be managers of the company.

During the judicial recovery, the company's activity and its financial situation will be supervised by a court-appointed administrator. The board of directors will still continue to function normally, jointly with the board of officers. Nevertheless, a director may be removed from office if there is strong support that he committed a crime under the Insolvency Law, has acted in fraud against the interest of the creditors of the company, has had personal expenditures that clearly exceeded his financial situation or denies to provide information requested by the court-appointed administrator, among other situations set forth in the Insolvency Law.

The bankruptcy of the company has a different effect. It will remove the company from the hands of its directors and officers. The company's management in a bankruptcy proceeding will be taken over by the court-appointed administrator. The company will therefore cease to have a board of directors. Although there is no specific rule concerning consulting boards, the same should apply to them.

If the company is not able to pay its debts in the bankruptcy proceeding and there is proof that such circumstance was caused by the actions of officers and directors in breach of their fiduciary duties, they may be held personally liable for the company's debts. They may also be condemned for certain crimes set forth in the Insolvency Law.

4.5.2.5 Boards in dissolved companies

A company that is dissolved will enter into liquidation. In liquidation, the officers of the company are replaced by a liquidator, who will have the powers to finish all of the business activities of the company, collect and sell the company's assets and pay all of its debts, costs and expenses and distribute any surplus to the shareholders.

The Law of Corporations sets forth in its article 208, paragraph 1, that if the company has a board of directors it may keep such board functioning during the liquidation. In this case, it will be incumbent upon the board to appoint the company's liquidator. In other cases, the liquidator will be appointed by the shareholders.

The law does not contain any rules concerning the functioning of consulting boards during liquidation. Since the focus of the company will be on the liquidator's activities, it does not seem to make sense to maintain consulting boards in operation during a liquidation. However, in theory a consulting board that advises the board of directors could continue to function as long as the board of directors is kept in place.

Upon conclusion of the liquidation, the company will then be terminated.

Jan Holthuis and Li Jiao
Chapter 5
China

5.1 Introduction

5.1.1 The concept of advisory boards in China

Before probing into advisory boards in China, it is important to first clarify that the advisory board is not a prescribed body or concept under the current legal framework related to Chinese enterprise governance. However, the advisory board, although not prescribed and mandated under the existing legal framework, is functioning de facto through existing bodies established in Chinese enterprises. This section will elucidate the advisory board under the context of Chinese law from the functional perspectives.

As a new concept of enterprise governance, the advisory board is not meant to only exercise certain fixed and limited functions like an institution that has existed for a long time and been regulated perfectly; it may vary among different enterprises. In general, as an internal body set up by shareholders or partners on a voluntary basis, one of the most important features of the advisory board is its flexibility. However, from comparative law perspectives, the advisory board usually possesses four typical functions.

The first and most obvious function is the consulting and supporting function, including but not limited to the advisory of management, the consulting of shareholders, the coaching of successors and supporting the company in the absence of management.

The second function is the monitoring and controlling function, concerning controlling management and board approval of transactions. This function is intended to ensure the legality and compliance of companies' actions and to assume part of the function of a supervisory board. To some extent, in respect of the monitoring function, the delineation between the advisory board and the supervisory board is not clear cut, especially in China. Thus, it is important to mention the supervisory board in Chinese limited liability corporations when discussing the advisory board.

The third function is the arbitral function, which includes managing disputes among family lines, management and shareholders.

The last function is the personnel competence function, under which the board can supervise the management and find a successor.

In China, functions of the advisory board can be exercised by several separate bodies in different types of enterprises. Therefore, the following section will make a brief introduction of the classification of the types of Chinese enterprises and their enterprise structure.

https://doi.org/10.1515/9783110666182-005

5.1.2 The classification of enterprises and governance structure in China

To address advisory boards existing in Chinese enterprises, it is vital to have a basic idea about the classification of the types of Chinese enterprises and their governance structure.

5.1.2.1 The limited liability company

The limited liability company (LLC) is the main sub-form of limited liability corporation in China,[1] which are, in the majority, medium- and small-sized enterprises. The essential nature of the LLC is that its equity is not divided into equal shares but represented by the capital subscribed and contributed by the shareholders. Each shareholder is liable for the LLC limited to the amount and portion of his subscribed capital.

Incorporation of an LLC shall satisfy the following requirements:[2]
(1) The number of shareholders meets the quorum (i.e., no more 50).
(2) There is capital of the company subscribed by all shareholders in accordance with articles of association.[3]
(3) Articles of association of the company are jointly formulated by all shareholders of the company.
(4) A company name shall exist and the organisation shall satisfy the requirements of a limited liability company.
(5) A company address shall exist.

The corporate governance mechanism in the LLC is composed of a shareholders' meeting (or sole shareholder), a board of directors (or an executive director) and a supervisory board (or one or two supervisors).

The shareholders' meeting shall exercise the following duties and powers:[4]
(1) decide on the business direction and investment plans of the company
(2) elect and remove directors and supervisors who are not representatives of the employees and decide on the remuneration of directors and supervisors
(3) review and approve reports of the board of directors
(4) review and approve reports of the supervisors or the board of supervisors

---

1 According to Article 2 of the Company Law, the classification of limited liability corporation in China follows the dual classification model of companies in traditional civil law countries. "Company" can be divided into Limited Liability Companies (LLCs) and Companies Limited by Shares (CLSs).
2 Articles 23 and 24 of PRC Company Law.
3 The capital of LLC can only be contributed by the fund of incorporators but cannot be publicly raised from the public.
4 Article 37 of PRC Company Law.

(5) review and approve the annual financial budget and financial accounting plan of the company
(6) review and approve the profit distribution plan and loss recovery plan of the company
(7) resolve on increase or reduction of registered capital of the company
(8) resolve on the issue of corporate bonds
(9) resolve on merger, division, dissolution, liquidation or change of company structure
(10) amend the articles of association of the company and
(11) other duties and powers stipulated in the articles of association of the company

The board of directors shall be accountable to the shareholders' meeting and shall exercise the following duties and powers:[5]
(1) convene shareholders' meetings and report to the shareholders' meeting
(2) execute the resolutions passed by the shareholders' meeting
(3) decide on the business plans and investment schemes of the company
(4) formulate the annual financial budget and financial accounting plan of the company
(5) formulate the profit distribution plan and loss recovery plan of the company
(6) formulate the plan for increase or reduction of registered capital and issue of corporate bonds
(7) formulate the plan for merger, division, dissolution or change of company structure
(8) decide on the set-up of the internal management organisation of the company
(9) decide on appointment or dismissal of company managers and their remuneration, and decide on appointment or dismissal of deputy managers and finance controller of the company based on the nomination by the managers
(10) formulate the basic management system of the company and
(11) other duties and powers stipulated by the articles of association of the company

Article 53 of PRC Company Law provides that a board of supervisors or a supervisor (in the case of companies that have not established a board of supervisors) shall exercise the following duties and powers:
(1) inspect the company finances
(2) supervise the performance of duties by directors and senior management personnel and propose to remove a director or senior management personnel who violates the provision of the laws and administrative regulations and the articles of association of the company or the resolutions of the shareholders' meeting

---

5 Article 46 of PRC Company Law.

(3) require a director or senior management personnel who acts against the interests of the company to make a correction
(4) propose to convene an interim shareholders' meeting, convene and chair a
shareholders' meeting when the board of directors fails to convene and chair a
shareholders' meeting in accordance with the provisions of this law
(5) make proposals at shareholders' meetings
(6) file a lawsuit against a director or senior management personnel and
(7) other duties and powers stipulated in the articles of association of the company

Besides the above generally understood modern corporate bodies, it is important to
note that Article 19 of PRC Company Law provides that the company shall provide
the requisite conditions for Chinese Communist Party (CCP) organisation activities,
which has paved a way for the establishment of CCP organisation in LLC. Although
there are an increasing number of party committees established in private enterprises, in the current corporate governance of LLCs only in the case of the state-
owned enterprises (SOEs) that are restructured into LLCs is it legally compulsory to
formulate and adopt internal regulations on the functions and operations of CCP
committees, whose functions are, to some extent, quite similar to those of the advisory board indicated above. We will elaborate on CCP committees in the Chinese
enterprises in Section 5.5.

5.1.2.2 The company limited by shares

The company limited by shares (CLS) is the other sub-form of a limited liability corporation. Establishment of a CLS may be through promotion or by share floating.[6]
    Article 76 of PRC Company Law regulates that a CLS shall satisfy the following
requirements:
(1) The number of promoters satisfies the quorum (i.e., more than 2 but less than
200, of which half shall have domiciles in PRC).[7]
(2) There is total capital subscribed by all promoters[8] or total paid-in capital publicly raised in accordance with the company's articles of association.
(3) Share issues and preparatory matters satisfy the provisions of the law.
(4) The articles of association of the company shall be formulated by the promoters
and if the company is established through share floating, it shall be further
adopted by the founding meeting.
(5) There are name, address and qualified governance structure of the company.

---

6 Article 77 of PRC Company Law.
7 Article 78 of PRC Company Law.
8 If a CLS is incorporated through share floating, the total capital subscribed by the promoters
shall not be less than 35 per cent of the total capital of the company.

The corporate governance mechanism of LLCs and the powers and duties of each body explained above shall also apply to CLS.

The difference between CLS and LLC mainly lies in the scale of capital, the number of shareholders, the restriction on equity transfer and corporate governance. Compared with CLS, LLC is smaller in scale and more closed ended. As previously mentioned, the total equity of LLC does not need to be divided into equal shares and transfer of equity by a shareholder to an external third party is more restricted (e.g., consent of at least half of shareholders shall be obtained). By comparison, the equity of a CLS is divided into and represented by equal shares that are freely transferable internally and externally. Furthermore, CLS is mandatorily required to establish a board of director and supervisory board[9] while LLC may only have one executive director and one or two supervisors.

In brief, the corporate governance structure of the LLC (established with board of directors and supervisory board) and the CLS can be referred to as in Figure 5.1.

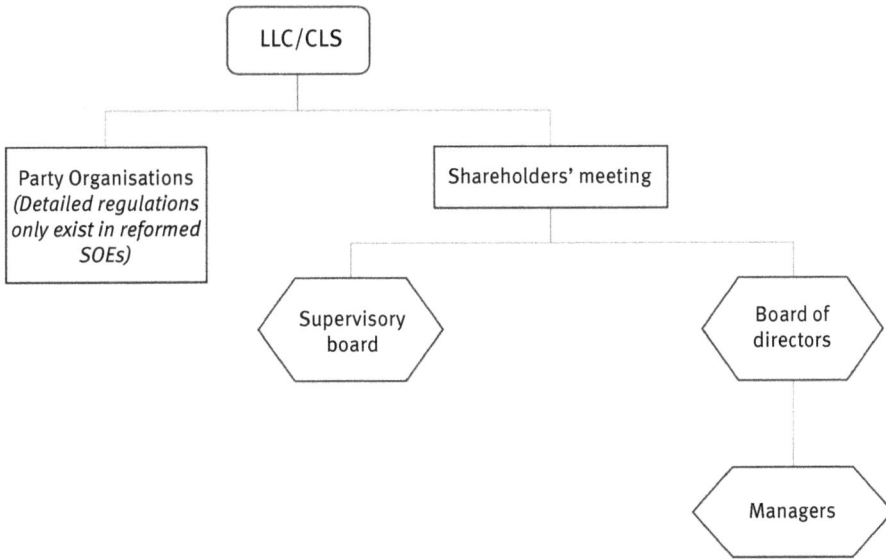

Figure 5.1: Corporate governance structure of the LLC and the CLS.

5.1.2.3 Listed companies

In China, a listed company refers to a CLS whose shares are publicly listed and transferable on the stock exchange with the approval of the State Council or the securities administration department authorised by the State Council (i.e., China

---

9 There are at least three members in the board of directors and supervisory board.

Securities Regulatory Commission [CSRC]). A listed company does not change the limited liability nature of the company. Given its open-ended nature, which involves the interests of the majority of small and medium investors in the public, the CSRC has issued special pieces of law governing the listed companies (e.g., the Code of Corporate Governance for Listed Companies, the Measures for the Administration of Information Disclosure of Listed Companies and the Measures for the Administration of Securities Issuance of Listed Companies).

At the same time, since the PRC Company Law has been enacted for a short period of time and is still in continuous development, listed companies are viewed as a model for the future corporate governance reform and development.

It is important to mention that the Code of Corporate Governance for Listed Companies requires that the listed company shall set up special committees of the board of directors whose functions are similar to those of the advisory board previously indicated. Article 38 of the Code of Corporate Governance of Listed Companies stipulates that the listed company's board of directors shall set up an audit committee and may set up other committees like the nomination committee, the strategy committee and the remuneration and assessment committee by following the decisions of the general meeting of shareholders. The special committee is a permanent internal body of a listed company established by the board of directors, whose members are consisted of directors and is to exercise partial powers of the board of directors or provide assistance to the board of directors in operating the company. Section 5.4 will provide a more detailed analysis of the special committees of the board of directors (Figure 5.2).

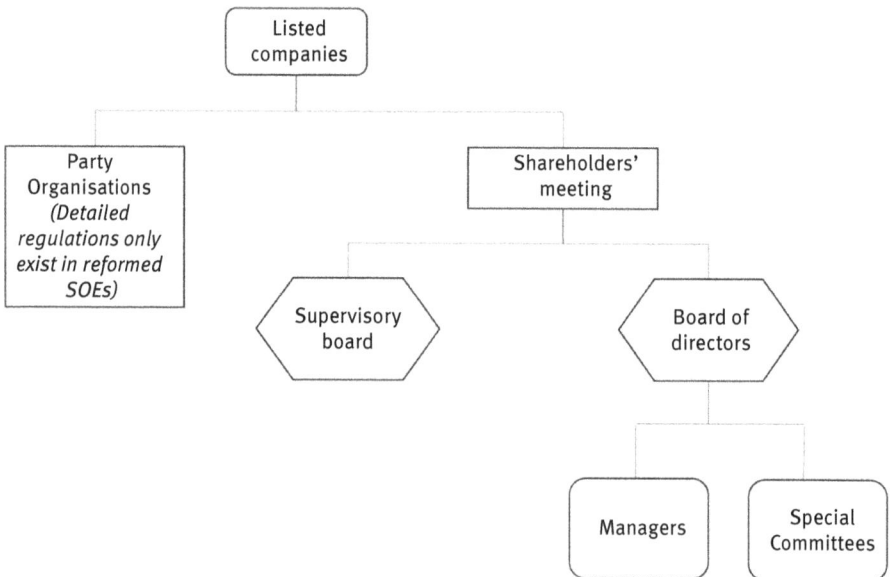

Figure 5.2: Listed Companies.

5.1.2.4 Other forms of enterprises in China

The partnership enterprise

The partnership enterprise includes the general partnership enterprise and the limited liability partnership enterprise. The establishment of a general partnership enterprise shall have at least two partners who shall conclude a written partnership agreement.[10] The limited partnership enterprise shall be established by at least two but not more than 50 partners and shall have at least one general partner.[11]

The general partnership enterprise is established by limited numbers of natural persons, legal persons or other organisations with the characteristic of person cooperation.

The governance structure of the limited liability partnership enterprise is different. The limited liability partnership enterprise's partnership affairs shall be executed by the general partners.[12] The limited partners may not involve in the execution of the partnership affairs, nor may they represent the limited partnership enterprise before external parities.[13] They only have the rights to put forward a proposal on the business management of the enterprise, review the relevant financial materials, participate in choosing an accounting firm, etc. However, no matter by law or in practice, the limited liability partnership enterprise's governance structure does not include any permanent body like the advisory board.

Publicly owned enterprise in the traditional form

Publicly owned enterprises in the traditional form are typically established and operated under PRC Law of Industrial Enterprises Owned by the Whole People and the Regulation of the People's Republic of China on Urban Collectively Owned Enterprises. There are some unique internal bodies, such as the employees' assembly, the factory director and the party committee as opposed to a shareholders' meeting, a board of directors and a supervisory board, as these are existing in the publicly owned enterprises transformed into limited liability corporations.

For publicly owned enterprises in the traditional form that adopt a manager (factory director) responsibility system, the general manager (in most cases also serving as party secretary) is the person in charge of the enterprise (legal representative).

---

10 Article 14 of the Partnership Enterprise Law of China.
11 Article 61 of the Partnership Enterprise Law of China.
12 Article 66 of the Partnership Enterprise Law of China.
13 Article 67 of the Partnership Enterprise Law of China.

5.1.3 Structure forms of advisory board in medium-sized enterprises in China

Since the reform and opening up in 1979, China's corporate governance has been groping forward in practice and has not yet formed a solid foundation. Under current practice, there is not a single and unified body to exercise the functions of advisory board in corporate governance, but they are scattered in various organisations in different enterprises. In the following sections, we will first go through the broad context of such Chinese enterprises and then go deep into various organisational bodies carrying out the functions of an advisory board.

Based on the functions of the advisory board revealed above, existing prescribed bodies set up internally in the medium-sized enterprises that are closely related to the advisory board are: the board of supervisors in limited liability corporation (Section 5.3), the special committees of the board of directors in the listed companies[14] (Section 5.4) and the party committee in various enterprises (Section 5.5).

Moreover, according to the principle of corporate autonomy, a limited liability corporation may introduce an advisory board in its corporate governance structure, provided that such introduction does not violate compulsory rules of Chinese law, which will be discussed in Section 5.6 below.

5.2 The context of advisory boards: Chinese corporate governance

5.2.1 The history of the Chinese corporation

PRC Company Law is in the process of transitioning from chaos to unification, which is shown in the development of enterprises owned by different players. Divided by the control and ownership of a Chinese enterprise, there are three major players, namely publicly owned enterprises, domestic privately owned enterprises and foreign-invested enterprises (FIEs) (Figure 5.3).

Domestic privately owned enterprises, which take the typical forms of modern enterprises such as limited liability corporation and partnership, only emerged after the reform and opening up policy was rolled out in 1978, introducing the market economy in China.

In contrast, China's publicly owned enterprises have a long history dating back to the establishment of PRC in 1949. At that time, the country had been devastated

---

14 Although the listed company is not a medium-sized enterprise, scholars in China often analyse corporate governance based on the structure of listed companies with the most comprehensive and complete regulations, which can indicate the development direction of corporate governance in China.

State-owned Enterprises — PRC Law of industrial Enterprises Owned by the Whole People Law
Public-ownership Enterprises — Private ownership reform

Collectively owned Enterprises — Regulation of the People's Republic of China on Urban Collectively owned
MSEs — Private ownership reform

Private-ownership Enterprises — LLC
CLS
Partnership

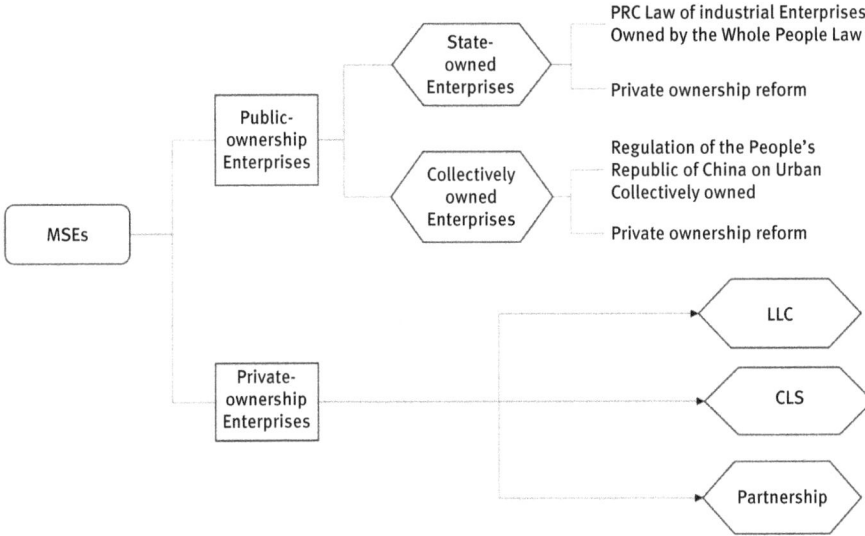

Figure 5.3: Public and Private Owned Enterprises.

by a long period of war and underdevelopment. It was the publicly owned enterprises that gradually undertook all the nation-building tasks, and provided for the livelihood of many people. The publicly owned enterprises include state-owned enterprises (SOEs) and collectively owned enterprises (COEs). Before 1978 when the planned economy was dominating the economy, SOEs and COEs had covered all cross-business sectors and industries in the market. Since the economic reform and opening up policies began in 1978, China's publicly owned enterprises have undergone a long process of gradual and progressive transformation, from a traditional form to the modern limited liability corporation, due to decreased profitability and inefficiency that emerged in the publicly owned enterprises before the market economics era. Nowadays, both the traditional and the transformed publicly owned enterprises exist in parallel in China.

FIEs used to be subject to the regulation of a separate and special legal regime independent from domestic enterprises, i.e., in the legal form of a wholly foreign-owned enterprise (WFOE), an equity joint venture enterprise (EJV) and a cooperative joint venture enterprise (CJV). Since the implementation of the Foreign Investment Law as of 1 January 2020, the legal forms of FIE have majorly coincided with those of domestic privately owned enterprises, i.e., either the limited liability corporation or partnership.

In the past 30 years, China has continuously developed into a modern corporate governance structure for the enterprises "with Chinese characteristics". Different governance systems are gradually moving towards unification, and this process has also affected the current corporate governance structure, which will be discussed in the next section.

5.2.2 Corporate bodies in Chinese corporations

Under PRC Company Law, it seems that a shareholders' meeting has emerged more to the front and centre. PRC Company Law endows the shareholders' meeting with powers normally reserved for boards in the United Kingdom and the United States. The shareholders in China, for instance, are required to develop and formulate the company's annual budget and business plan, not just review and approve the budget and plan, as is common in the Anglo-American world. However, given that those attending the shareholders' meeting cannot effectively exercise discretionary power due to the relatively low frequency of meetings and convenience, most of the real decision-making power remains in the hands of the directors and managers.

We note that the board of directors and general manager who have the power to operate the company appear even more powerful in the SOEs having been reformed into limited liability corporations. Publicly owned enterprises have established a modern corporate governance system in the process of modern corporate restructuring. However, owing to the "separation of ownership and operation" in modern companies, shareholders in state-owned enterprises in general do not intervene and have no control over the operation of the company, which makes the board of directors and general manager become overly powerful without necessary supervision and constraints. This is the reason why Chinese SOEs can easily fall into "insider control", and develop serious issues such as corruption and inefficiency.

Against such a background, in the process of modernisation reform there is an imminent need to establish a mechanism to exercise the supervisory functions in SOEs. Due to the historical reason that led to the establishment and existence of a large number of SOEs in China, the subsequent widespread modern corporation restructuring of SOEs at the same time exerted strong force on shaping the current corporate governance structure of limited liability corporations by incorporating a mandatory supervisory board designed to exercise the supervising functions over the management.

The supervisory board originates from Germany and is primarily established to oversee the board of directors. Such a two-tier system in Germany embodies the hierarchical relationship between the two boards. By contrast, the Chinese supervisory board is not superior over but parallel with the board of directors and is only endowed with the supervisory function. Meanwhile, since the regulations of the supervisory board are too general and the institution design is not reasonable, its supervisory power exists in name only.

At present, supervisory boards are weak and ineffective and the power of the board of directors is still rather unrestricted. The *PRC Company Law, the Guiding Opinions on Establishing Independent Director System in Listed Companies (2001)* and *the Listed Companies Governance Guidelines (2002)* have, however, introduced a "dual-core supervision mechanism" with a supervisory board and an independent board of directors as the main body of internal supervision. This mechanism was introduced to further improve the governance structure of listed companies. Based on the requirement of independent directors, special committees exercising similar functions as advisory boards are set up to assist the board of directors.

However, after nearly 20 years of practice, the effect is not eminent. Independent directors in Chinese listed companies, in practice, can hardly guarantee their independence, and fail to truly supervise the management of the company on behalf of all shareholders in order to act in the overall interests of the company.

Although SOEs are striving towards a modern corporate structure through establishing boards of directors and supervisory boards, in practice, most SOEs, whether SOEs of traditional or reformed form, still retain certain Chinese characteristics, for example, the incorporation of a party committee for the purpose of upholding and strengthening the Chinese Communist Party's (CCP's) political leading position as further discussed below.

In general, the structure of corporate governance in China is still not well-established and coherent after 30 years of reform and development, and the divisions of functions of different corporate bodies in the company are not clear. Advisory board functions are scattered in various bodies and they are cross-exercised over several bodies. The following sections will further introduce these different bodies.

5.3 Supervisory board

The system of supervisory boards, which originated from the public stock companies, has been continuously improved with the development of the latter. It can be said that the origin, function and mission of the supervisory board are closely related to public stock companies.

However, in Mainland China, the supervisory board is not limited to public stock companies; by contrast, the supervisory board or supervisor(s) is a mandatory mechanism in limited liability corporations.

5.3.1 Concept and functions

5.3.1.1 Concept

Before the enactment of PRC Company Law (1993), relevant administrative regulations promulgated by the State Council provided a legal definition of a supervisory board. In China's first departmental regulation of the State Council on CLS, "Standard Opinions on Company Limited by Shares" (promulgated on 15 May 1992), the legislator made it clear that a public stock company may set up a board of supervisors as its internal organ, whose duty is to "supervise the board of directors and its members and managers" (Article 63). In December of the following year, the National People's Congress passed the first Company Law in the history of PRC, which officially confirmed the status of the supervisory board, and stipulated that the supervisory board was a mandatory organ (Article 124), specialising in the company's supervisory authority, including the company's financial and business execution. The persons under its supervision involve the board of directors and its members, managers and other management personnel (Article 126). Since then, although PRC Company Law has been revised three times in 2005, 2013 and 2018 respectively, the functions and powers of the supervisory board have not been substantially revised in the law.

From the angle of organisational structure and power allocation of corporate governance, the supervision and check-and-balance mechanism stipulated in PRC Company Law is similar to the "two-tier system" model as stipulated in German company law. The similarities encompass that the board of directors and the board of supervisors under the shareholders' meeting are both mandatory organs, and the board of supervisors has the exclusive supervisory power. However, differences remain between the "two-tier system" structure model in Germany and the Chinese model. Under the Chinese model, the legal status of the board of directors and the supervisory board of Chinese companies are equal and independent from each other, which are both parallel organs under and elected by the shareholders' meeting. However, the power of supervisory boards in Chinese companies is relatively weaker than that of the board of supervisors of companies in Germany, Japan and other jurisdictions. For example, Germany's supervisory board has the veto right on important decisions and the power to elect and remove the directors, which, however, is not the case for China's supervisory board. Compared with Japan, which gives each individual supervisor full power to monitor the manager, the Chinese supervisory board is operated in commune and acts by resolution. That is, to exercise regulatory power, supervisory boards in China must adopt a resolution on certain issues before taking any action.

5.3.1.2 Functions

The monitoring and controlling functions of the advisory board are similar to the responsibilities of the supervisory board. It is also possible to empower other duties and powers in the articles of association to the supervisory board, which may include other functions of the advisory board, such as consulting and supporting functions.

The duties and powers exercised by a supervisory board or supervisors under PRC Company Law have already been introduced in the first section of this chapter. We will now further examine these functions.

Inspecting the company finances

The supervisory board exercises the power of financial supervision. According to PRC Company Law, it has the power to consult the company's financial and accounting statements and be informed on the company's scheme for surplus or loss, its investment plan and so on. However, concerning this most important function, in practice, the voice from the supervisory board can hardly be heard inside or outside the company.

The first reason is that the legal provisions are not clear and specific enough. Article 53 (1) of PRC Company Law stipulates that the supervisory board shall enjoy the power of financial supervision. However, the key contents, methods, means, procedures, guarantees and other requirements of the inspection are not further clarified in the Company Law. Although the legislator's intention may be that the company's articles of association should refine this power, in most cases the articles of association either passively repeat the Company Law or do not address it at all.

Second, with respect to financial supervision there is a lack of ability in the Chinese supervisory boards. The purpose of financial supervision is to confirm the status of the company's assets through analysing the company's audit reports and other financial information, to evaluate the performance of the board of directors and the management team, which requires supervisors to be well equipped to perform their duties. They should not only be equipped with general management knowledge, but also possess special knowledge of financial accounting management and supervision. However, without specific requirements in the PRC Company Law, most supervisors of Chinese companies lack specialised training in financial knowledge and experience.

Third, there is a lack of a guarantee system for the implementation of financial supervision. Practice shows that there are obvious defects in the following three aspects:

A. Whether the board of supervisors has, and how to entrust professional institutions to help implement, the power of financial supervision. Considering the busy affairs of supervisors and the lack of knowledge and ability, company law in some countries directly stipulates that supervisors may entrust experts to assist them. PRC Company Law stipulates that "when the supervisory board exercises its functions and powers, it may engage law firms, accounting firms and other professional institutions to help where necessary, and the expenses incurred therefrom shall be borne by the company".[15] However, "where necessary" is a vague condition lacking specific measurement standards and can easily cause controversy. Therefore, once the supervisory board decides to entrust professionals or institutions to assist in financial supervision, the management team can easily stop the actions of the supervisory board under the pretext of this clause, so that this power cannot be properly implemented.

---

15 Article 54 of PRC Company Law.

B. The establishment of the internal audit institutions of the company. To improve the internal check and balance mechanism, some companies also set up audit institutions to supervise the operation of the company's finance. These internal institutions play the role of financial supervision of the supervisory board, but they are under the leadership of the board of directors, such as the special committees in the board of directors that will be introduced in the next section. If the supervisory matters that should be organised, led and engaged by the board of supervisors are managed by the board of directors, it is easy to lead to the circumstance that the board of directors also controls the supervisory power, which leaves division of powers and responsibilities in the corporate governance structure vague.

C. PRC Company Law and its ancillary implementing regulations do not stipulate the remedies and mechanisms available to supervisors if the board of directors or managers refuses, obstructs or interferes with the board of supervisors' exercise of financial supervision power. It is inexplicit whether the supervisory board has the means to eliminate the above obstacles and the means to punish the above conduct.

Supervising the performance of duties by directors and senior managers

Article 53 (2) of PRC Company Law stipulates that the supervisory board shall supervise the performance of duties by directors and senior management personnel and propose to remove a director or senior management personnel who violates the provision of the laws and administrative regulations and the articles of association or the resolutions of the shareholders' meeting. Such supervision power of the supervisory board in Chinese companies encompasses all the duties of directors and managers, and includes non-business activities.

According to Article 53 (3) of PRC Company Law, when the conduct of directors and managers harms the interests of the company, the board of supervisors has the right to ask the directors and managers to make corrections. That is to say, there is no requirement for the prevented behaviour to be related to the company's business activities. When the supervisory board believes that the behaviour of directors and managers has damaged or may damage the company's interests, it may request the directors or managers to make correction. If the directors or the managers ignore or reject such a request, the supervisory board can propose to convene an interim shareholders' meeting[16] as well as proposing a motion related to the correction of the behaviours of relevant directors or managers for such a shareholders' meeting.[17] Whether the shareholders' meeting supports the motion of the board of supervisors

---

16 Article 53 (4) and Article 100 of PRC Company Law.
17 Article 53 (5) of PRC Company Law.

depends on whether the opinions and evidence presented by the supervisory board are sufficient. On the other hand, it also depends on the interests of the game among different shareholders. In any case, if the shareholders' meeting does not support the proposal of the board of supervisors, the board of supervisors can file a lawsuit against the board of directors and other management personnel under the instruction by any of the shareholders in an LLC or by shareholder(s) of a CLS individually or jointly holding at least 1 per cent of total shares for 180 consecutive days, which will be discussed in detail in the section titled "Filing a lawsuit against a director or senior management personnel".[18]

Proposing to convene interim shareholders' meeting

Article 53 (4) of PRC Company Law also stipulates when the board of supervisors performs its supervisory power, it may propose to convene an interim shareholders' meeting when the board of directors fails to convene and chair a shareholders' meeting in accordance with the law.

For a CLS, PRC Company Law provides the following statutory circumstances under which the interim shareholders' meeting shall be convened within two months:[19]

(1) the number of directors falls below two-thirds of the quorum stipulated in this law or articles of association of the company
(2) the losses of the company that have not been made good account for one-third of the paid-up capital of the company
(3) requisition of a shareholders' general meeting by shareholder(s) who individually or jointly hold 10 per cent or more of the company's equity
(4) the board of directors deems it necessary to convene a shareholders' general meeting
(5) the supervisory board proposes to convene a shareholders' general meeting or
(6) other events stipulated by the articles of association of the company

Making proposals at shareholders' meetings

The supervisory board may also make proposals at shareholders' meetings.[20] Although there is no detail about the content and operation, this provision makes it possible for the supervisory board to exercise an advising function.

Filing a lawsuit against a director or senior management personnel

The supervisors can file a lawsuit against a director or senior management personnel if a director, supervisor or senior management personnel violates the provisions

---

18 Article 53 (6) and Article 151 of PRC Company Law.
19 Article 100 of PRC Company Law.
20 Article 53 (4) of PRC Company Law.

of laws and administrative regulations or the articles of association in his performance of duties and powers and causes the company to suffer damages.[21] However, there are some restrictions conditioned on exercising such power of supervisors.

First, Article 151 of PRC Company Law further regulates that any of the shareholders in an LLC or shareholder(s) of a CLS individually or jointly holding at least 1 per cent of total shares for 180 consecutive days may submit a request in writing to the supervisory board or the supervisor (in the case of a LLC that has not established a supervisory board) to file a lawsuit before a people's court against the director or senior management personnel involved. It implies that supervisors cannot directly sue and must rely on the written request of shareholder(s) before filing lawsuits on behalf of the company, which limits the exercise of supervisors' supervisory power.

Second, Article 23 of Judicial Interpretation IV of Company Law further clarifies that the lawsuit, although brought by the supervisory board or the supervisor, shall be in the name and on behalf of the company.

Further, according to judicial practice, the object of the lawsuit filed by the supervisory board is limited to directors and senior management personnel. In the case of the *Board of Supervisors of Taizhou Shangyao Pharmaceutical Co., Ltd vs. Shangyao Holding Co., Ltd*, the supervisory board filed a lawsuit against its shareholder Shangyao Holding Co., Ltd according to Article 151 of the Company Law, and the court finally rejected the lawsuit on the grounds that Taizhou Shangyao Pharmaceutical Co., Ltd should be listed as the plaintiff and the chairman of the board of supervisors should conduct the lawsuit on behalf of the company.[22] After that, the chairman of the supervisory board filed a new lawsuit against the shareholder in the name of the company. The Zhejiang High People's Court rejected the lawsuit again on the grounds that "the company should be listed as the plaintiff, and only the chairman or executive director in the board can carry out the lawsuit on behalf of the company according to law".[23]

Other duties and powers stipulated in the articles of association of the company

Article 53 (7) regulates that the supervisory board can also perform other duties and powers stipulated in the articles of association of the company. As mentioned above, the embodiment of the principle of corporate autonomy makes it possible to introduce more functions to the supervisory board in a company.

Attending meetings of the board of directors

According to Article 54 of PRC Company Law, supervisors may attend meetings of the board of directors and query resolutions of the board of directors or give suggestions.

---

21 Article 53 (6) of PRC Company Law.
22 (2017) Zhejiang 10 Minchu No. 882 Civil Ruling.
23 (2018) Zheminzhong No. 588 Civil Ruling.

Similar to functions of making proposals at shareholders' meetings, consulting and supporting functions are empowered to the supervisory board in law.

5.3.2 Establishment, organisation and operations

5.3.2.1 Establishment

A supervisory board is a statutory organ of a company that supervises the company's business management activities and is an important part of the corporate governance structure. Therefore, the supervisory board should be established at the incorporation of the company.

Article 51 of PRC Company Law stipulates that the supervisory board of an LLC shall comprise not less than three members. LLCs with relatively fewer shareholders or of a relatively smaller scale may appoint one or two supervisors instead of establishing a supervisory board.

The supervisory board shall appoint a chairman; the chairman shall be elected by more than half of the board of supervisors. The chairman of the supervisory board shall convene and chair meetings of the supervisory board. When the chairman is unable or fails to perform his duties, a supervisor appointed by more than half of the members in the supervisory board shall convene and chair the meeting(s) of the supervisory board.[24]

Appointment of supervisory board members

The election and dismissal of supervisors is an important process in the supervisor system. It ensures that qualified personnel will be selected and remain in the position of supervisors, while avoiding those who are unqualified and may hinder the fair and efficient exercise of supervision power, thus preventing the supervisory board from losing its power.

The qualifications of supervisors can be legally divided into positive qualifications and negative qualifications. There are detailed and strict restrictions on the negative qualifications of supervisors that refers to the situation that a supervisor cannot have.

First, Article 51 (3) of PRC Company Law stipulates that directors and senior management personnel shall not hold the post of supervisor concurrently.

Second, Article 146 of PRC Company Law regulates five situations where the person shall not act as a supervisor:

(1) a person who has no civil capacity or who has limited civil capacity
(2) a person who has been convicted for corruption, bribery, conversion of property or disruption of the order of a socialist market economy and five years

---

24 Article 51 of PRC Company Law.

have not elapsed since the expiry of the execution period or a person who has been stripped of political rights for being convicted of a crime and five years have not elapsed since the expiry of the execution period

(3) a person who acted as a director, factory manager, manager in a company that has been declared bankrupt or liquidated and who is personally accountable for the bankruptcy or liquidation of the company, and a three-year period has not elapsed since the completion of bankruptcy or liquidation of such company

(4) a person who has acted as a legal representative of a company that has its business licence revoked or being ordered to close down for a breach of law and who is personally accountable, and a three-year period has not elapsed since the revocation of the business licence of such company or

(5) a person who is unable to repay a relatively large amount of personal debts

However, PRC Company Law and its implementing regulations stipulate only one positive qualification for supervisors, that is, supervisors must include shareholders' representatives or employees' representatives of the company. According to Article 52, PRC Company Law stipulates a basic requirement for the proportional relationship of the members of the board of supervisors. The ratio of employees' representatives therein shall not be less than one-third, and such ratio shall be stipulated by the articles of association of the company. For the two different representatives of the board of supervisors, PRC Company Law does not stipulate a unified election and dismissal system but gives the right of appointment and dismissal to the shareholders' meeting and the company's employee organisations respectively.

It stipulates that employees' representatives sitting on the supervisory board shall be appointed by the employees via an employees' representative congress or employees' congress or other forms of a democratic election. By contrast, para 2 of Article 37 regulates the shareholders' meeting shall exercise the duties and powers of electing supervisors who are not representatives of the employees and decide on the remuneration of directors and supervisors. According to Article 43 of PRC Company Law, the rule of procedure and voting procedures of a shareholders' meeting shall be stipulated by the articles of association of the company, unless otherwise provided in PRC Company Law.

PRC Company Law explicitly regulates that only resolutions on an amendment to the articles of association of the company, increase or reduction of registered capital and company merger, division, dissolution or change of company structure shall be passed by shareholders holding two-thirds or more of the voting rights in a shareholders' meeting. The appointment process of supervisors who are not representatives of the employees is controlled by the articles of association.

Except for the rules introduced above, PRC Company Law and related regulations do not provide clear methods and procedures for the election, dismissal and recall of supervisors who are employee representatives.

As to how to nominate the candidates of supervisors and who will submit the name list to the shareholders' meeting for deliberation and voting, PRC Company Law has made neither clear, which leads to a problem of the nomination right of supervisor candidates. The company's personnel right (including nomination right) is one of the core rights. To some extent, it can even be said that the right to nominate supervisors is the key to the success or failure of the supervisor system. Under the current practice in China, the nomination of candidates of supervisors is largely in the hands of the board of directors, and it is difficult to be elected or re-elected as supervisors without the support of the board of directors.

From the legislation point of view, the control over the nomination of supervisors by the board of directors is reflected in the Guidelines for Articles of Association of Listed Companies. Article 67 stipulates that the board of directors has the power to put forward the list of candidates for the supervisory board to the shareholders' meeting, and the résumés and basic information of the candidate supervisors should be provided to the shareholders' meeting. At the same time, Articles 59 and 60 stipulate that the board of directors of the company has the power to examine and finally decide whether to include the proposal in the agenda of the shareholders' meeting.

In general, the legal norms of the appointment and dismissal mechanism of supervisors in China are rather rough. PRC Company Law does not specify in detail the system of selection, nomination and voting of supervisors. Instead, these norms that directly affect the nature and efficiency of the company's power are left to the company's articles of association, while most companies just repeat PRC Company Law and do not make full use of such flexibility. According to a survey conducted in 2014, even among the listed companies with stricter supervision, only 12 per cent of companies, in their articles of association, clearly stipulate that supervisors should have professional knowledge or work experience in law and accounting.[25]

5.3.2.2 Organisation and operation

To examine how the supervisory board exercises its functions and powers is in fact to analyse its way of deliberation and voting procedures. The supervisory board in China adopts the collective resolution system, that is, the members of the supervisory board

---

[25] Zhipo, Zhang and Wang Guo, "Practice of the governance of the board of supervisors of listed companies in China", *Jinling Law Review* (2014) 2: 112.

exercise their supervisory power uniformly and collectively by attending the board meeting. Under the collective resolution system, a supervisor is usually appointed as the chairman of the board of supervisors, who is responsible for convening and presiding over the meetings of the supervisory board. The meetings of the supervisory board should be held regularly. Article 55 of PRC Company Law regulates that the supervisory board shall convene at least one meeting every year. A supervisor may propose to convene an interim meeting of the supervisory board. Supervisors should attend the meetings of the supervisory board when there are no special circumstances, and the resolutions of the meetings must meet the statutory requirements.

Generally speaking, the substantive contents of the supervisory power in China are clearly defined by PRC Company Law, while the procedural rules of how to realise these substantive rights such as discussion methods and voting procedures are mostly determined by the articles of association.[26] In terms of the ways and procedures for the supervisory board to exercise its functions and powers, PRC Company Law only stipulates the number of meetings held each year and the ratio required to pass the resolutions at the meeting. Resolutions shall be passed by a simple majority of votes. Other matters such as the service of the meeting notice and the contents of the notice are not stipulated in the necessary clauses of the company's articles of association, which are arbitrary norms.

5.3.3 Members, breach of duty and liability

5.3.3.1 Members

As mentioned above, a supervisory board is composed of shareholder representatives and employee representatives. However, PRC Company Law does not clearly define the identity of shareholders' representatives and employees' representatives in the supervisory board. PRC Company Law is also silent on whether supervisors are full-time or part-time, and whether they are paid is not.

In practice, supervisors are mostly part-time, and it is not common for supervisors to receive independent remuneration. The role that supervisors can play varies widely. To some extent, it affects the independence and effectiveness of supervisors in performing their duties.

Meanwhile, it is difficult to define the relationship between the company and the supervisor as a labour relationship if it only performs the duties of a supervisor according to PRC Company Law and the articles of association, and has neither served nor worked for the company. If the supervisor himself accepts the

---

26 Article 55 of PRC Company Law.

management of the company's rules and regulations and provides paid labour for the company in specific positions in addition to performing the duties of a supervisor, both parties meet the essential characteristics of establishing labour relations. In this case, the position of "supervisor" becomes another identity of the employee who has labour relations with the company and does not affect the existing labour relations between the employee and the company.

5.3.3.2 Breach of duty and liability

According to Article 147 of PRC Company Law, directors, supervisors and senior management personnel shall comply with the provisions of laws and administrative regulations and the articles of association of the company and bear fiduciary duties towards the company. They shall not abuse their duties and rights to receive bribes or other illegal income and shall not convert company assets.

 If a supervisor violates the provisions of laws and administrative regulations or the articles of association of the company in his performance of duties and powers and causes the company to suffer damages, he shall bear compensation liability.

Fiduciary duties

Fiduciary duties include two aspects of duties: the obligation of loyalty and the obligation of diligence. However, Article 147 of PRC Company Law above-mentioned that regulates the supervisors' obligations is only a principled provision and its scope of application is limited. For example, although supervisors have not violated laws, regulations or the articles of association when performing their duties, they may still be deemed to be violating their diligence obligations. In practice, when there is a dispute over whether supervisors violate the obligation of diligence, the judgment criteria are formed in the following three steps:

 First, the court will investigate whether the supervisors are exercising the supervisory functions. In *Case (2018) Hu 02 Min Zhong No. 1769,* the court dismissed the claim that Mei violated the fiduciary duties of supervisors by misappropriating company funds since misappropriation of company funds is a typical prohibited behaviour of directors and senior managers, rather than the behaviour of supervisors. In practice, the supervisor can participate in the company's business, but, in this case, the corresponding identity has been transformed into the employee's identity participating in the actual operation of the company. If the company's fund is misappropriated in this case, it is a legal relationship in which the company's employee damages the interests of the company, rather than a legal relationship in which the supervisor violates the fiduciary duties.

 Second, the court will distinguish whether there is a legal conflict of interest between the supervisors and relevant decisions or transactions. If the conflict of interest is established, breach of fiduciary duties will be directly determined by the court. If there is absence of conflict of interest, the court will move forward to examine whether the supervisors have collected necessary information for relevant decisions or transactions, and made decisions or transactions on this basis. It is worth noting that the most obvious feature of diligence obligation is measured by the standard of a rational person whose knowledge and intelligence in this context is based on the managers of the company in the market but not the ordinary people in society. Such a standard imposes higher requirements for the management skills of directors, supervisors and senior managers, and requires them to have a cautious attitude under the corresponding management skills. On the other hand, they are exempted from the diligence obligation when commercial risks still occur outside the former, so as to prevent excessive restrictions on their business decisions. If the supervisors do not follow the requirement, the behaviours will be directly determined to constitute a violation of due diligence obligations, and, if so, proceed to the next step.

Finally, the plaintiff can prove that the decision-making or trading behaviour of supervisors is unreasonable. From the theoretical and practical point of view, business judgement rules should be loosely determined: as long as directors, supervisors and senior managers believe that the decision making or trading is reasonable to the company, even if most people think that the risk is too great and unfavourable to the company, provided that a small number of people still believes it is worth taking risks.

However, in general, the cases related to supervisors violating fiduciary duties are limited, which indirectly indicates that a supervisor in practice is a symbolic position.

5.3.4 Termination

Since the supervisory board is a statutory mechanism in Chinese companies, this paragraph will mainly discuss termination concerning a certain member.

Termination occurs when the term of supervisor expires, or the supervisor resigns during the term of office. The statutory term of a supervisor is three years.[27] A supervisor may be re-elected.[28] Since supervisors participate in the supervision of the company and have important responsibilities, in order to investigate and measure whether a person is suitable to serve as a supervisor, it is necessary to set a certain term of office.

---

27 Article 52 of PRC Company Law.
28 Article 52 of PRC Company Law.

However, as the supervisor plays an important role, when the supervisor's term of office expires, or he resigns during the term of office, the supervisor shall postpone the performance of his duties in case of the following circumstances:[29]

(1) if there is no timely re-election.
Upon expiration of the supervisor's term of office, the company shall timely re-elect and elect the next supervisor. However, in practice, due to various reasons, it often happens that supervisors are not re-elected in time when their term expires. Under such circumstances, the former supervisor shall still perform his duties as a supervisor in accordance with the provisions of laws, administrative regulations and the articles of the association until the company elects a new supervisor. The former supervisor cannot refuse to perform his duties as a supervisor on the ground that his term of office expires.

(2) if the number of members of the supervisory board is lower than the quorum.
Upon expiration of the supervisor's term of office or after the resignation, the position of the supervisor will be vacant, and the number of supervisors will possibly be lower than the quorum. In this situation, before the newly elected supervisor takes office, the supervisor shall also still perform his duties as a supervisor.
As for the liabilities of former supervisors who continue to exercise the functions in the two situations above, there are no cases directly related. Only in *case (2020) Gan 01 Min Zhong No. 1715*, the court stated that although the term of office of the supervisor has expired, it still performs the duties of the supervisor of the company, and there is no difference between the specific matters of exercising the functions in these two stages. In other words, based on this judgment, although there is no clear case-law and regulations, only if the supervisor continues to perform the duties, we infer that he remains liable even after his resignation or the expiration of his term of office.

5.3.5 Summary

To sum up, PRC Company Law entitles a wide scope of powers to the supervisory board, but the powers of the supervisory board stipulated are general and principled with large room for flexibility, and its operability is poor. The legal provisions are not clear and specific enough when it comes to the methods and procedures for exercising supervisory power and the qualifications of the supervisors. The lack of detailed regulations about the key contents, methods, members, procedures, guarantees and

---

29 Article 52 of PRC Company Law.

other requirements results in low efficacy of supervising functions exercised by the supervisory board in Chinese companies.

Such large room of flexibility, on the other hand, enables the company to make full use of the principle of autonomy to regulate the monitor power in the articles of association. In this way, if the regulations are implemented in a jurisdiction with a long tradition of commercial companies, it still has significance. However, China is still in the transitional stage from the traditional planned economy model to the modern enterprise system. The power of companies is highly concentrated and extremely unbalanced, and the influence of the traditional enterprise checks and balances mechanism on administration and rule by man are still quite serious. Against this background of corporate governance, the simplification of legislation is tantamount to giving up the perfection and construction of the company checks and balances mechanism. In this way, in order to improve China's supervisory board system, the feasible way is to make the regulations clearer and easier to implement and to guide the reform of the supervisory board.

Nevertheless, although the vague regulations affect the efficacy of the supervisory board, in small and medium-sized enterprises, if the supervisory board system with detailed regulations is forced to be set up, it will also affect the efficiency of the company operation. In this sense, another available option is that enterprises take advantage of the flexibility of corporate autonomy, and refer to the mechanisms of the advisory board to design a more tailor-made supervisory board for each company.

5.4 The special committees of the board of directors

The special committee of the board of directors is an innovation from the team production theory. In a team, the various cooperative inputs do not produce clearly defined independent outputs, so that the sum of the independent outputs equals the total outputs. This cooperative production activity is known as team production.[30] Team production theory breaks through the traditional principal–agent theory or the analytical framework of corporate contract theory that the obligations of the board of directors should also include coordinating and maintaining the balance of interests.[31] The board of directors is the trustee of the company and serves the participants' interest in the company. Therefore, any party in the company needs to be vigilant, and the board of directors for the company's overall interests could even

---

30 Blair, Margaret M. and Lynn A. Stout, "A team production theory of corporate law", *Virginia Law Review* (1999): 247–328.
31 Blair, Margaret M., "Boards of directors as mediating hierarchs", *Seattle UL Rev.* 38 (2014): 297.

sacrifice the interests of shareholders. The special committee of the board of directors was designed to ensure the independence of the director to achieve the "Coordinated Architecture".[32]

5.4.1 Concept

The special committee is a permanent internal body of a company established by the board of directors and consisted of directors to exercise partial powers of the board of directors or assist the board of directors in operating the company.

The functions of the board of directors are mainly to discuss and vote on the proposals that have been formed. Professional and effective proposals usually require extensive and in-depth research and investigation. The functions of the board of directors are related to various aspects of the company's operation, and the professionalism and complexity of the business affairs require the directors to have a relatively high level of professional knowledge. Moreover, when the board of directors exercises certain obligations and functions, such as audit and performance evaluation, it requires the board of directors to regularly monitor and review the subject's performance. For the board of directors, which only holds a few plenary meetings a year, fulfilling their obligations and implementing their functions will be a realistic problem, especially for a listed company. The solution, then, is to enhance the specialisation of the board of directors by establishing several special committees as a permanent body to assist the board of directors in dealing with specific issues and exercising specialised functions. Besides, the special committee as a permanent body could formulate proposals when the board of directors is not in session. Therefore, the establishment of special committees of the board of directors could not only facilitate the efficiency of the board of directors and exert its functions, but also could clarify the obligations and responsibilities of directors. The mechanism of special committees could also facilitate the development of management and specialisation of the modern corporation.

5.4.2 The special committees and the independent director

The Organisation for Economic Co-operation and Development (OECD) Principles of Corporate Governance mentioned that the corporate governance framework should ensure that the board of directors could effectively supervise the company's strategic directions and the senior managers, and the board of directors

---

32 Han, Wen, "Research on optimizing path of board governance: Reconstruction of board committee system", *Law Science Magazine* 40, no. 7 (July 2019): 91–quote from p. 91.

shall be accountable towards the company and shareholders.[33] Supervising the managers to diligently and lawfully operate the company is supposed to be the function of the board of directors. Therefore, the legal framework and operation of the board of directors should ensure the board of directors could effectively exercise their functions, especially the power of supervision. However, the decision-making functions of the board of directors are easily affected by managers in corporate governance. Thus, that the board of directors cannot effectively supervise the senior managers is still a suspended issue.

The establishment of the independent director system is aimed at dealing with this systematic problem. The independent director seems to act as a bridge between the directors and senior managers, which formed a three levels model of principal–supervisor–agent. The agent's work attitudes and performance are unpredictable, and information asymmetry exists between the agent and principal, causing the principal to not hold detailed information about the agent's actions, and therefore, there needs to be a relatively independent supervisor between the principal and agent to collect information about the agent's action and feed this information to the principal. In the corporate governance framework, the independent director is sitting on the supervisor's position.

Meanwhile, the special committees of the board of directors should be introduced to support the functions of the independent director. Since the independent directors were not directly involved in the company's specific business, they might lack accurate control of the company information. To avoid the independent director being treated as a rubber stamp, the special committees should be controlled by the independent director and assist the independent director to fully understand the decision-making processes of the company's essential matters. Meanwhile, to balance the independent director's powers and ensure that the special committees could independently exercise their functions, the special committees shall be fully or mainly formed by the independent directors.

5.4.3 Function

The Code of Corporate Governance of Listed Companies stipulates that the listed company's board of directors shall set up an audit committee and may set up other committees like the nomination committee, the strategy committee and the remuneration and assessment committee by following the decisions of the shareholders' meeting.[34]

---

33 Organisation for Economic Co-operation and Development (OECD), "The OECD principles of corporate governance", *Contaduríay Administración* 216 (2004): 24.
34 Article 38 of the Code of Corporate Governance of Listed Companies (2018 Revision), Announcement No. 29 [2018] of the China Securities Regulatory Commission.

Except for the audit committee, which is mandatory for a listed company, the company could establish other special committees depending on the company's needs and requirements, such as the public policy committee, the investment committee and the environment, health and safety committee.

5.4.3.1 Audit committee

The audit committee is a compulsory organ for a listed company, which shall be completely composed of directors, and the independent directors who shall be in the majority in the committee. Moreover, the convener of the audit committee shall be an accounting professional. The major functions of the audit committee include: 1) supervising and assessing the external audit work and proposing the employment or replacement of an external audit institution; 2) supervising and assessing the internal audit work and being responsible for the coordination of the internal audit and external audit; 3) examining the company's financial information and disclosure thereof; and 4) supervising and assessing the company's internal control.[35] Therefore, the audit committee, as an internal organ of the board of directors, is directly responsible for selecting the audit institution, determining the employment relationship between the audit institution and the company and supervising the audit institution. Moreover, the audit committee has the right to hire independent consultants when it is necessary for the performance of the audit committee's duties.

Since the audit committee's tasks are mainly to supervise the company's senior managers, the board of directors and the chairman, if the board of directors disagrees with the audit committee's proposals, it will be a critical issue for the company. The ideal solution would be for the audit committee and the board of directors to discuss the issues thoroughly. If disagreements cannot be resolved, the audit committee shall have the authority to disclose the disputes to the shareholders in the company's annual report.

5.4.3.2 Nomination committee

To ensure the independence and exercise the supervision function, the nomination committee shall be composed entirely of directors and the independent director shall be part of the majority in the committee. The major duties of the nomination committee are: 1) researching the standards and procedures for the selection of directors and senior executives and offering suggestions; 2) selecting the qualified

---

35 Article 39 of the Code of Corporate Governance of Listed Companies (2018 Revision), Announcement No. 29 [2018] of the China Securities Regulatory Commission.

candidates of directors and senior executives; and 3) examining the candidates for directors and senior executives and offering suggestions.

Nomination of the directors and senior managers is a significant function of the board of directors. The decisions and recommendations made by a nomination committee, mainly consisting of independent directors, could interfere with the independence and quality of nominees. The nomination committee plays an essential role in selecting an appropriate candidate for the company's senior managers and shall establish criteria for selecting senior managers and evaluation of their performance. The nomination committee can also formulate a proposal related to the nomination affairs and submit it to the board of directors.

At the same time, in the state-owned listed companies, *Regulations of the Communist Party of China on the Work of Party Organisations of State-owned Enterprises* specify that the party secretary is also the head of the nomination committee, and the organisation and personnel department is regarded as the daily office of the nomination committee, so as to ensure that the enterprise party organisations supervise the whole process of nominating, inspecting, discussing and deciding the candidates to be appointed.

5.4.3.3 Remuneration and assessment committee

The remuneration and assessment committee is also composed entirely of directors, and the independent director shall be in the majority in the committee. The major duties of the remuneration and assessment committee are researching the standards for the examination of the directors and senior executives, organising examinations and offering suggestions and researching and examining the remuneration policies and plans for the directors and senior executives. The reasonable remuneration policies and plans could motivate directors and senior managers to create considerable value for the company. If the remuneration policies and plans are unjustified, it will not only reduce interests to shareholders and affect the company's profits, but it will also cause the senior managers to focus on the company's short-term performance rather than long-term development. Therefore, the remuneration and assessment committee is also crucial for company governance.

5.4.4 Organisation and operations

As mentioned above, the special committees are the permanent body of the board of directors. Therefore, the special committees shall be composed entirely of directors, and the independent directors shall be in the majority in the committee. The special committees' operations shall follow the operations of the board of directors, which are stipulated in the articles of association and relevant regulations.

5.4.4.1 Organisation

The Code of Corporate Governance of Listed Companies stipulates that the special committee shall be completely composed of directors, and the independent directors shall be in the majority in the audit committee, the nomination committee and the remuneration and assessment committee. The members of a special committee shall be directors with expertise and work experience suitable to the functions of the committee. For example, the members of the audit committee shall have expertise and work experience in finance, audit or accounting, among others. Generally, the head of a special committee should be an independent director, and the heads of different special committees cannot be the same person.

The selection of the special committee members shall be stipulated by the company's articles of association. In general, the members of the special committees shall be nominated by the chairman of the board of directors, or more than half of the independent directors, or one-third of all the directors. The nomination proposal shall be approved by the board of directors.

The term of the special committee members is the same as the director's term, which shall not exceed three years, and could hold a consecutive term upon re-election after the expiry of their term.

5.4.4.2 Operations

The operations of the special committees should also be stipulated by the company's articles of association. Typically, the operation rules follow those applicable to the board of directors. In practice, there is a problem that the authorities of the special committee are purely nominal. Although the company's articles of association or rules of procedure provide that a proposal shall be submitted to the board of directors for consideration only after it has been passed by a special committee, in cases where the members of the board are essential members of the special committees, the aforesaid proposal is usually approved by the board of directors and bypasses the special committees.

5.5 Party committee

5.5.1 Concept, legal basis and functions

5.5.1.1 Concept

One of the unique aspects of corporate governance in China is a body called the party organisation or party committee, which is established by and reports to the Chinese

Communist Party (CCP). Despite its long history, especially in SOEs, the party organisation/committee is perhaps the least understood body of corporate governance with Chinese characteristics.

However, party organisations play a leadership role in SOEs and have also been exerting increasing influence on private enterprises. By the end of 2016, CCP organisations had been established in almost 189,000 publicly owned enterprises, accounting for about 91 per cent of the total number of this type of enterprise, and had been established in almost 1.86 million non-publicly owned enterprises, accounting for almost 70 per cent of the total number of this type of company and having a 16 per cent year-on-year growth rate.[36] With the same proportion, about 70 per cent of all FIEs in China – about 75,000 – had set up party branches. Besides, the policy initiatives over 2010 to 2020 reaffirmed the leadership role of party organisations in SOEs and their status above the board of directors in the business and governance decision-making chain.[37]

These policies offer a different model of corporate governance – they are best understood as an integral part of what the CCP calls the process of "socialist modernization". The preamble to the revised Charter of CCP[38] in October 2017 makes clear that the party remains stoutly opposed to Western liberal values and is still at an early stage of building a "socialist market economy". It is an economy in which "public ownership plays a dominant role", although different forms of corporate ownership can "develop side by side".

Party organisations are also widespread in private firms where they serve as a focal point for party members. According to Article 30 of the charter, private enterprises that have more than three party members should establish party organisations. While at the same time, Article 19 of PRC Company Law clearly regulates that a party organisation in China shall be set up to conduct party activities in a company in accordance with the provisions of the constitution of the Communist Party of China. A company shall provide the party organisation with necessary facilities for its activities. The party organisations in these private enterprises will also organise regular meetings to lay out a road map to the development direction of the company.

In practice, party organisations are regulated more precisely in SOEs, which are the cornerstone of this section.

---

36 *2016 Internal Statistics Communique of the Communist Party of China* (2017). See: http://www.xinhuanet.com/politics/2017-06/30/c_1121242478.htm (accessed 6 December 2020).

37 General Office, CPC Central Committee, "Opinions on Further Improving the Implementation of Decision-Making System of the 'Three Important, One Large' in SOEs", No. 17 (2010); "Constitution of the Communist Party of China" (2017), Article 33; CPC Central Committee and State Council published the "Guiding Opinions on Deepening SOE Reform" (2015); General Office of the State Council, "Guiding Opinions on Further Improving the Legal Person Governance Structure of State-owned Enterprises", No. 36 (2017).

38 A constitution-like and foundation document of CCP rules that binds all CCP members. Since CCP is the ruling party in China, such a charter also greatly influences the national legislation.

5.5.1.2 Legal basis

The basic legal foundation allowing party organisations to be operated in enterprises can be found in the Charter of the CCP. Article 32 of the 2012 version of the Charter of the CCP described the primary-level party organisation as the "political core" of a state-owned enterprise. Article 33 of the latest 2017 version of the Charter of CCP elaborates further and states: "The leading Party members groups or Party committees of state-owned enterprises shall play a leadership role, set the right direction, keep in mind the big picture, ensure the implementation of Party policies and principles, and discuss and decide on the major issues of their enterprise in accordance with the regulations."

Both versions go on to explain that the role of party organisations is to "guarantee and oversee the implementation of the principles and policies of the Party and the State in its own enterprise", and shall "support the meeting of shareholders, the board of directors, supervisory board, and manager (or factory director), in exercising their functions and powers according to the law". The party organisation "participates in making final decisions on major questions in the enterprise" and shall "lead work on political thinking" as well as "efforts towards cultural-ethical progress" in the enterprise.

The legal basis for the party organisations in private enterprises is slightly different.[39] Primary-level party organisations in private entities shall implement the party's principles and policies; guide and oversee their enterprises' observance of state laws and regulations; exercise leadership over trade unions, Communist Youth League organisations and other people's group organisations; promote unity and cohesion among workers and office staff; safeguard the legitimate rights and interests of all parties; and promote the healthy development of their enterprises.

5.5.1.3 Function

In theory, party organisations/committees can participate in the governance of enterprises, while at the same time not directly meddling in their management and operational decision making. From the beginning, party organisations were established to ensure that significant decisions made by enterprises would not deviate from national laws and regulations, party discipline and basic political principles. Indeed, as the CCP Constitution makes clear, Party committees "set the right direction" and "keep in mind the big picture", while ensuring the "implementation of

---

39 As discussed in Section 5.2, since the implementation of the Foreign Investment Law as of 1 January 2020, the legal forms of FIE have majorly coincided with those of domestic privately owned enterprises, i.e., either the limited liability corporation or partnership.

Party policies and principles" and deciding on "major issues".[40] In practice, Party committees have three functions:

A. Making the "Three Important, One Large" decisions: namely, decision making on "important issues", the appointment and dismissal of "important cadres", investment in "important projects" and the use of large amounts of funds.
B. "Double-entry, cross offices": Party committee members can also serve on either the board of directors or supervisory board, and be part of the executive team and vice versa. This helps to make the policies of the party implementable and coordinate communication between the party, the board of directors and executives.
C. Overseeing the system of "Party supervising cadres" and "Party supervising talents". The former is aligned with the appointment of executives by the board of directors and human resource management. In respect of "supervising talents", the party carries out the induction, training and development of professional talent by implementing the "National Plan of Talent Development in Medium and Long Term (2010–2020)".

The functions of party organisations, which are outside the modern company framework with Chinese characteristics, are widespread. Generally speaking, party organisations are even involved in the consulting and supporting function, monitoring and controlling function and personnel competence function of the advisory board.

5.5.2 Establishment

First, although the Charter of CCP and the Company Law stipulate that private enterprises and FIE shall establish party organisations if there are more than three party members, Chinese law and other party regulations do not stipulate the establishment and operation of party organisations in private-owned companies and FIEs, and there is also no systematic practice. By contrast, Regulations of the Communist Party of China on the Work of Party Organizations of State-owned Enterprises ("Party Regulations of SOEs") stipulate most of the rules concerning the party organisations. Therefore, Sections 5.5.2, 5.5.3 and 5.5.4 will focus on the party regulations of SOEs to discuss party organisations in Chinese state-owned enterprises.

Article 4 of the Party Regulations stipulates that different enterprises will establish different types of party organisations. If there are more than 100 party members in a SOE, the party's committees shall be established. If the number of party members is less than 100 and it is really necessary for work, party committees may also be established with the approval of higher-level party organisations. If the number

---

40 Article 33 of Charter of Chinese Communist Party (2017 version).

of party members is more than 50 and less than 100, the party branch committee shall be established. If the number of party members is less than 50, and it is really necessary for work, party branch committees may also be established with the approval of higher-level party organisations. If there are more than three formal party members, a party branch shall be established. Party branches with more than seven regular party members shall establish party branch committees.

According to Article 5 of the party regulations, party committees of SOEs shall be elected by party members' congresses, and each term of office shall generally be five years. The general branch and branch committees of the party are elected by the general meeting of party members, and each term of office is generally three years. At the expiration of the term of office, the general election shall be held on schedule. According to the affiliation of party organisations, the higher-level party organisations should remind them to prepare for the change six months in advance.

The size of the party committee is not fixed. Party committees of SOEs generally consist of five to nine people, with no more than 11 people, including one secretary and one or two deputy secretaries. The standing committee of the party committee generally includes five to seven people, up to no more than nine people, and the party committee includes 15 to 21 people in total. Party committee members should generally have more than three years of party experience. The general party branch of SOEs generally consists of five to seven people, with no more than nine people at most. The party branch committee consists of three to five people, generally no more than seven people. A party branch with fewer than seven full-time members shall have one secretary and one deputy secretary if necessary. The secretary of the party branch (general party branch) should generally have more than one year's party experience.[41] Meanwhile, secretaries and deputy secretaries of SOEs and members of the standing committee of party committees are generally elected by the plenary meetings of the committees at the same levels. The election results should be reported to the higher party organisations for approval.[42]

5.5.3 Members

Members of the party organisations are following the policy of "double entry, cross offices".

In other words, party committee members can also serve on either the board of directors or supervisory board, and be part of the executive team and vice versa. This helps to make the policies of the party implementable and coordinate communication

---

41 Article 6 of Party Regulations.
42 Article 7 of Party Regulations.

between the party, the board of directors and executives. The secretary of the party Committee and chairman is generally one person, and the general manager is the deputy secretary. In an enterprise with no board of directors but only executive directors, the party secretary and executive director are generally held by one person.

5.5.4 Operations

The operation of party organisations is also included in the modern corporate governance. Article 13 regulates that SOEs shall write the requirements of party building work into the articles of association; state the important matters such as the responsibilities and authority, organisation setup, operation mechanism and a basic guarantee of the party organisation; clarify that the research and discussion of the party organisation is the pre-procedure for the decision making of major issues by the board of directors and managers; and implement the legal status of the party organisation in the corporate governance structure.

No matter what role these party organisation members play, the regulations require that party organisations in SOEs implement the system of combining collective leadership with an individual division of responsibilities. Members of party organisations who are also the directors, supervisors and managers are ordered by the party organisations to implement the party policies.

5.5.5 Summary

Although the party committees are ubiquitous in Chinese enterprises, there is no obvious effect in practice. First, for the party organisations of private enterprises, there are no detailed regulations to enable them to exercise their functions. For state-owned enterprises, on the one hand, after the introduction of the new corporate governance structure in SOEs, the board of directors becomes the management decision-making centre, while the set of corporate governance mechanisms under the planned economy system still exists, resulting in the coexistence of two systems. Thus, the board of directors and the party committee overlap in functions. Further, under the "double-entry, cross offices", the party secretary is usually concurrently the chairman of the board of directors, but he often will put the vast majority of his energy into the business and development of enterprises, and ignored social responsibility undertaken by SOEs and the party building work has been marginalised.

On the other hand, the party regulations of the SOEs above are only suggested, instead of mandatory norms, and according to the prevailing PRC Company Law, the political functions of the party organisation are restricted by many factors. For example, the party organisation has no influence in many major issues involving enterprise management. Even if party organisations are not consulted before making the

"Three Important, One Large" decisions, there are no sanctions towards the companies according to related laws or party regulations.

5.6 Advisory boards under corporate governance autonomy

Regulations of corporate governance in PRC Company Law always contain such a clause stating: except for the powers prescribed, the shareholders' meeting/board of directors/supervisory board can exercise other duties and powers as stipulated in the articles of association of the company. Such clauses also appear in the PRC Partnership Enterprise Law.

Enterprises are derived from commercial activities, and the status of civil and commercial legal subjects is equal, so corporate governance naturally has the nature of autonomy of will. The arbitrary provisions in the laws leave a lot of room for party autonomy, and the clauses stated in the above paragraph are generally used to solve the internal legal relationship of companies. From this perspective, the internal corporate governance is highly autonomous, and companies can decide the governance structure that matches their development based on industry characteristics, development stages and scale, among others.

Therefore, although formally there is no advisory board in the practice of corporate governance in China today, the principle of autonomy in PRC Company Law and Partnership Enterprise Law also provides the possibility for the establishment of the advisory board in the future.

5.7 Conclusion

In general, the advisory board is still rather immature under the Chinese corporate governance system. There is no prescribed and specific concept of an advisory board in China. Moreover, after 30 years of development, corporate governance in China is still scattered in different corporate functions that are often not properly exercised. The mandatory supervisory board exists in limited liability corporation of all scales and has a supervising function, but there is no specific implementation method in law and practice, often resulting in that the supervisors exist in name only.

Special established committees mainly consist of independent directors and mainly exist in listed companies and they are substantially controlled by the board of directors. It is also not clear how to divide the functions within companies, especially for the party organisations, which cover a wide range of supervision and overlap with other functions. Chinese laws do not restrict the emergence of functions and operations of the advisory board. At this point, enterprises can take advantage of the flexibility of corporate autonomy and design in the articles of association a detailed supervisory board system. At the same time, the functional transformation of the party organisation in the process of modernisation can also refer to the advisory board to clarify the division of power.

The basic legal foundation for party organisations to be established in Chinese legal entities, and in particular in SOEs, can be found in the Charter of the CCP. The Party organisation is one of the Chinese characteristics of Chinese enterprises, and is in fact as a CCP supervisory board, very secure to supervise the process of "socialist modernisation", which is a CCP policy aim. In October 2017, the party again clarified that it remained stoutly opposed to Western liberal values and the Chinese economy was still at an early stage of building a "socialist market economy". As such, public ownership, that is SOEs, play a dominant role and other private corporate enterprises can develop "side by side".

Antje Luke
Chapter 6
France

6.1 Introduction

In France, corporate law provides for mandatory advisory and controlling bodies only for stock corporations (*société par actions* [*SA*]), limited partnerships by shares (*société en commandite par actions* [*SCA*]) and for Societas Europaea (SE). These bodies are a board of directors (*conseil d'administration*) for one-tier structures (more frequent), or a management board (*directoire*) and a supervisory board (*conseil de surveillance*) for two-tier structures and for the SCA where managing directors have the role of the board of directors. Boards also exist in very specific corporate forms such as mutual insurance companies (*mutuelles*). For the purposes of this article, we will focus on the most current legal forms.

The three most currently used corporate forms are the SA, the company limited by shares (*société à responsabilité limitée* [*Sarl*]) and the simplified stock corporation (*société par actions simplifiée* [*SAS*]). While there is no real flexibility for the creation of other voluntary corporate bodies for SAs and Sarls, the SAS attributes to the shareholders the choice to structure its corporate governance and to establish different corporate bodies. The shareholders may thus create a supervisory or an advisory board. This, among other reasons, is why this latter corporate form is the most used form today, in particular for fully owned subsidiaries within a group of companies, joint ventures and family owned businesses. Medium-sized companies are, since the introduction of the SAS in 1994, more and more organised in the form of an SAS, which is easier to manage than the formal SA.

To better understand French corporate law, we will briefly describe corporate governance for an SA, which is the basic legal form for the SAS. Furthermore, as German entities investing in France often prefer to set up their subsidiary in the legal form of an Sarl, it is interesting to analyse the possibility of setting up an advisory board or a similar committee despite the formal inflexibility in the system of an Sarl for creating other corporate bodies.

6.1.1 SA

According to the French Commercial Code (Code de commerce), the SA is governed by the following corporate bodies: the shareholders' meeting, the board of directors (*conseil d'administration*) with its president of the board, and the general manager.

https://doi.org/10.1515/9783110666182-006

The president and the general manager may be the same person (*président-directeur général* (*PDG*)). Shareholders may also choose to put in place a "two-tier organisation" inspired by the German model of stock corporations with a shareholders' meeting, management board (*directoire*) and a supervisory board (*conseil de surveillance*).

These provisions are stringent, such that the shareholders may not add, either in the bylaws or, for example, by a shareholders' agreement, other formal corporate bodies or committees such as an advisory board. In practise, companies do, however, very frequently have a management organisation with an "executive committee" or a "committee of directors". These committees are composed of employees of the company to support and advise or even control the management. These committees are, however, not to be confused with the "advisory board" as intended here, and should not be considered as corporate bodies, but rather as structural organisations of the company, even though their functions may be similar to those of advisory boards.

The rules regarding these committees are not set out in the articles of association but in internal regulations. Any obstruction to their functioning may constitute behaviour triggering the liability of the president or general manager, but may not invalidate any decisions or actions vis-à-vis third parties. Furthermore, legal obligations to consult the board of directors or supervisory board must, of course, be respected, and an approval granted by such a committee may not replace approval to be granted by law or the articles of association by the formal board.

6.1.2 Sarl

When German companies establish a subsidiary in France, they often tend to choose the form of an Sarl, which they believe to be similar to the German GmbH. Although the Sarl has certain advantages, it diverges from the German GmbH on one very important point: it is much less flexible than the GmbH in terms of organising corporate governance.

An Sarl has two corporate bodies: the shareholders' meeting (Art. L 223-27 subs. Commercial Code) and the managing director(s) (*gérants*) (Art. L 223-18 subs. Commercial Code). The Commercial Code does not foresee the creation of other corporate bodies.

In the relations with shareholders, the powers of the managing director are determined by the articles of association (Art. L. 223-18 3. para Commercial Code). Consequently, limitations (e.g., the obligation of the managing director to request formal approval from other bodies, such as an advisory board) to the managing director's powers may not be inserted into other documents such as shareholders' agreements or internal rules.

Vis-à-vis third parties, even limitations to the powers of the general manager deriving from the articles of association cannot be opposed to them. This is even truer with limitations arising from other documents. On the other hand, according to case-law, confirmed by a recent decision by the French High Court (Cour de Cassation), third parties may invoke the articles of association (or even a shareholder's resolution) that subordinates decisions of the managing directors to prior approval by the shareholders' meeting (Cass. Com., 14 February 2018 No. 16–21.077). In this decision, the High Court even confirmed a judgment that had held as null a filing to court by a managing director without prior consent of the shareholders that was required according to a shareholders' resolution.

An obligation to appoint representatives of the employees of the company (or the group of companies) to the board of directors or the supervisory board (*Mitbestimmung*) known under German law also exists under French law, and has recently been reinforced, extending it also to not-listed companies by the PACTE Law (Action Plan for Business Growth and Transformation) (act No. 2019–486 of 22 May 2019, Art. 184 and 189). However, unlike under German law, this obligation does not trigger an obligation for companies that usually do not have a (supervisory) board to designate such a body. Consequently, the PACTE law does not create a new obligation for Sarls to establish a board.

6.1.3 SAS

The SAS is the corporate form par excellence if shareholders intend to establish an advisory board or other corporate bodies. This legal form was first introduced into French law in 1994, originally solely as a legal form for holding companies or for companies held by other corporations. Driven by the French government's will to offer investors a very flexible form of company, it has, after several reforms, increasingly become a real alternative to the Sarl.

An SAS is a stock corporation. Therefore, many legal provisions applicable to stock corporations apply (Art. L 227-1 3rd para. Commercial Code); e.g., the share capital is divided into shares that can be transferred easily. Corporate governance, however, is very different as the provisions regarding the president and board of directors are not applicable (Art. L 227-1 3rd para. Commercial Code).

By law, SASs have two corporate bodies: the shareholders' meeting (or the sole shareholder) and the president who represents the company vis-à-vis third parties. There can only be one president but one or several general managers may be appointed who may be granted (nearly the same) powers as the president. In terms of governance, the shareholders have an important flexibility particularly in two areas: they may determine how shareholders' meetings are organised and the majorities required for decisions (except for certain provisions set out in the Commercial Code), and they may appoint one or several general managers with (or without) the right to represent the company vis-à-vis third parties, and/or create a board of directors or a supervisory board, or other committees. Lastly, they may also set up an advisory board.

One especially important point to note here is that the Commercial Code only allows shareholders to organise these questions as they intend. As the Commercial Code does not provide rules for corporate governance, aside from certain provisions regarding the president and the shareholders' meeting, and one cannot simply apply by analogy the provisions in force for SAs and SCAs, the shareholders have to set out (all) details in the articles of association. Where the articles of association are not clear, or the shareholders do not fully set out the rules, there is a significant risk that such corporate bodies may not function properly.

As an Sarl may not formally set up an advisory board, and the SAS is a corporate form that is more and more used for commercial companies, the following analysis focuses on (advisory) boards for SASs.

6.2 Concept and definition, delimitation from other corporate bodies

As in German law, there is no legal definition of "advisory board" under French law.

6.2.1 Types of boards

The term "advisory board" appears to be less used in France. The voluntary boards set up in SASs are designated rather as shareholders' committees, executive committees, committees of directors, investment committees and family boards, but also management or supervisory boards. Even though the term "advisory board" appears to be less used in France, we will continue to use this term for the purposes of this publication.

The functions, rights and obligations of these boards vary considerably. They may be limited to pure advice, or have more rights and may be entitled to control, or to exert influence on strategic decisions.

6.2.2 Distinction from board of director and supervisory board

As set out above, the Commercial Code provides for boards of directors and supervisory boards only for SAs, SEs and SCAs (supervisory board) but not for SASs.

A board established for an SAS may be designated as a "board of directors" or as a "supervisory board". However, such denominations would not have as a consequence that all legal terms of the Commercial Code for these boards *automatically* apply. If shareholders intend to organise governance with similar functions, they would need to set out the different provisions in the articles. They can also generally refer to the articles of the Commercial Code regarding these boards, e.g., the management or supervisory board of an SA. However, as the functioning of an SAS is different from an SA, such a general referral may not be properly adapted to the SAS and we would not recommend it.

> **Criminal Chamber of the French High Court, 25 September 2019 n° 18-83.113**
> In this decision, the Criminal Chamber of the French High Court applied certain provisions which normally only apply to SAs (Art. L 225-86 and Art. L 225-88 of the French Commercial Code regarding the so-called "regulated agreements" which are basically provisions for dealing with conflicts of interest, see 3.8.2 below) to an SAS because the articles of the SAS referred generally to the provisions of the SA. For this reason, the president had to follow the system of regulated agreements applicable to SAs, and not just the one applicable to SASs. This decision illustrates how dangerous it can be to make such general referrals in articles of association.

A board in an SAS is consequently always voluntary because it will be set up by decision of the shareholders. This means that shareholders may set the board aside by change of the articles at any time, or change the rules governing such boards. Indeed, such changes and reorganisations of the governance frequently occur when there is a change of control and articles of association are amended.

If one or several shareholders have the specific right to appoint members of the board, shareholders may only abolish such a board with the consent of the shareholder concerned.

Members of management and supervisory boards of a SA, for example, have a number of legal rights and obligations. The obligations include civil and penal liability, obligation of loyalty, etc. Although these rights and obligations do not directly apply, one crucial question is whether the members of the advisory boards are to be considered as *"dirigeants"* (officers) or not. This has an impact on the application of different provisions, as we will see in the course of this analysis.

This question has to be considered on a case-by-case basis.

A person who participates in the management of, and in taking strategic decisions for, the company is considered a *dirigeant*. If the advisory board is rather limited to advice, the members will not be considered as *dirigeants*. If the members have the function of a board of directors, there is a high risk that the members may be qualified as *dirigeants*.

6.3 Establishment, organisation and operations

6.3.1 Establishment solely by the articles of association?

A first question under French law is if there is a difference between setting up such boards in the articles of association or in another document such as a shareholders' agreement, or not.

Art. L 227-1 and 227-5 of the Commercial Code provide for the organisation of the governance of an SAS in the articles of association. Indeed, although such committees or boards are typically set up in the articles of association, a certain practice developed particularly in smaller companies to provide for such committees not in the articles (documents accessible to the public) but in shareholders' agreements or other documents such as internal rules. However, in 2017 the French High Court ruled that corporate bodies may only be organised in the articles of association.

Decision of the French High Court of 25 January 2017 (Cass. Com., 25 January 2017 n° 14-28.792)
This decision has been very largely commented. However, the exact meaning of the role of the articles of association as opposed to other documents for the quality of a person as board member is still not clear in detail, as the French High Court had not to make a decision regarding the responsibility of a board member, but rather about special option rights of one of the shareholders. A stock corporation (SA) had been transformed into a simplified stock corporation (SAS). The former members of the Board of Directors had been granted specific option rights in relation to the shares of the company. The new articles of association of the SAS did not provide for a board. Nonetheless, the Board of Directors continued to be in place and to exercise its functions. Later, an event occurred which would have triggered the right to exercise the option, and one of the board members wanted to exercise this right. The other shareholders/company refused the option right because they held that the board member had lost his quality as board member, lacking provisions in the articles of association. The Cour de Cassation approved this refusal and recalled that in an SAS, in the absence of direct application of the provisions for SAs on board of directors (or supervisory boards) on the one hand, and setting up of a management board in the articles of association, the shareholder concerned could not claim his/her status as member of a management board. The option right was no longer applicable.

This decision has clarified that a board may only formally exist in an SAS if it is set up in the articles of association. The other question is in how far the company itself, the shareholders, the president and the general manager may be bound to the existence of such a board if it is only set up by other documents. In our opinion, shareholders may be committed to set up such a board if they agreed on it in a shareholders' agreement. However, it is questionable if the president may be taken for responsible if he does not ask, for example, for prior approval of a board that is not set up by the articles of association, even if the board is mentioned in his mandate or employment agreement. On the other hand, one cannot conclude from this decision that any and all details regarding the board have to be set out in the articles of association.

6.3.2 Setting up of the board

The shareholders may choose to set up the board from the beginning when the company is set up. They may also let the shareholders decide later by a shareholders' resolution to set up such a board if all the details of the rules are already laid down in the articles of association. In our view, in particular after the afore-mentioned decision of the Cour de Cassation, it is more prudent to leave to the shareholders' meeting only the decision to actually activate the board, but all other details shall already have been provided for in the articles of association.

A board may also be set up by amendment of the articles of association. Majority requirements set out in the articles of association for the amendment of the articles have, of course, to be complied with.

6.3.3 Members of the board

6.3.3.1 Number of members

As boards are a voluntary body of an SAS, there exist no legal provisions regarding the number of members. As set out above, the specific rules about boards, their number and the presence of representatives of employees applicable to an SA or a *société en commandite par actions* do not apply to SASs, even if an SAS voluntarily sets up a board designated as a "board of directors" or "supervisory board". The only exception would be if the articles of association made a full referral to the legal provisions applying to SA.

The articles of association shall therefore determine the number of members. In order to leave more space for the further development of the company, the articles may also provide for a minimum and maximum number of members, e.g., four to six members. There may be an odd or even number of members. If the number is even, it can be advisable to provide for a casting vote, e.g., of the president of the board, unless the company has only two shareholders and the shareholders provide for deadlock provisions either in the articles of association or in the shareholders' agreement (more usual). If the shareholders intend to set up sub-committees, they may provide for a greater number of members. The number of members shall be determined according to the functions of the board, the number of shareholders represented or not by the board members, or the presence or not of other stakeholders who shall be represented.

6.3.3.2 Qualities of members

Natural or legal persons?

It is interesting to note that under French law, legal persons may also be board members of an SAS (and even have the function of president of an SAS), and not only natural persons. If the shareholders want to admit this possibility, the articles of association must expressly grant this choice.

If a board member can also be a legal person, the articles may provide that the legal person shall determine a person to represent the legal person to ensure continuity of personnel. On the other hand, the advantage of the appointment of a legal person is that one may determine that the representative is always the legal representative. In such a case, no new appointments are required.

The director who is a legal person incurs the same liability as natural persons.

In practise, for advisory boards this option may be less interesting if the purpose for setting up the board is, in particular, to receive specific advice for the company from experts.

"Born" and elected members

A further question to decide in setting up the board is if certain persons shall be "born" board members, i.e., if they will automatically be board members due to their position. This can be the president and/or general director of the company, but also a representative of the shareholders or of one shareholder. In practise, if the function of the board is, rather, an executive committee, including the president and/general director may be advantageous because the flow of information may be smoother and it may be easier to keep the board members informed about company matters. It may also be difficult in a small business to find an adequate number of board members representing the various shareholders, if each shareholder has the right to appoint either the president or the director general.

On the other hand, if the function of the board is to control the managers, it only makes sense to include the president and/or director general as board member, if, together, they do not have the majority of the board; otherwise, they may always overrule the other board members.

Employees of the company as members

There is no clear principle as to the question of whether employees of the company may be board members or not. Under French law, managers who have the function of a corporate body are usually not employees (unlike the German *Geschäftsführeranstellungsvertrag*). The conditions for their remuneration and other conditions are determined in a "mandate" (*mandat social*) by shareholder resolution. According to the form of company, such a manager is not an employee within the meaning of employment law, but may be treated as an employee in terms of tax and social security law (at least for certain items). There are, however, some exceptions that have been developed by case-law: it is recognised for an SAS that the president or general director who is not a shareholder, or who is only a minority shareholder and has a distinct function in the company from this function as president (e.g., director of finance, or scientific director), may continue to have an employment agreement and be fully treated as an employee (cumulation of mandate and employee).

As the rules about "cumulation" of the function as officer and employee only apply to officers, the prohibition of cumulation does not apply to board members who are not to be considered as director (*dirigeant*) (see Section 6.2). As set out above, advisory board members who only advise but do not take part in the management of the company are not officers. Therefore, the rules about "cumulation" would not apply to them and they could also have an employment agreement with the company. In practise, it will often also happen that employees of a company assume the function of a board member in a subsidiary. In this case, their employment agreement refers to their functions in the parent company, and the employment agreement may determine that they can take on functions on boards of group companies without a separate remuneration.

In family businesses, where family members are shareholders and at the same time board members, and, as the case may be, even employees, it may happen that the employment agreement be requalified. In such a case, the competence of the labour courts for claims made by the board members on the basis of their employment agreement may even be challenged if the overall circumstances result in the board member not actually being subordinated.

Other qualities

The articles of association may also require other qualities for board members (e.g., certain educational background or knowledge, or being a member of a family) or for the absence of certain characteristics (e.g., not a representative or employee of a competitor). They may also set a limit for age.

When setting up such rules, shareholders shall, however, bear in mind that the articles of association are public. It may therefore be advisable to provide for such qualities, in particular for the absence of certain characteristics, rather in a shareholders' agreement.

Limitations on the number of other mandates

As the provisions regarding boards of a French SA do not apply to a SAS, limitations for the number of mandates that a person may cumulate (Art. L 225-21 Commercial Code) do not apply. It follows that members of advisory boards of a SAS may accept a large number of mandates, although performing diligently with regard to more mandates is not a simple matter and may raise liability issues.

6.3.4 Appointment of the members of the board

Here again, the shareholders have freedom how to organise the appointment of the members but they need to provide clear rules. Members – at least first members – may also be appointed namely in the articles of association. However, to have more flexibility, members are usually appointed by a shareholders' resolution. The articles of association may provide for a specific majority for such a vote, or let it to simple majority.

6.3.5 Publication of board members

The question as to whether the appointment or resignation/dismissal of members of the board may be, or even must be, published in the commercial register cannot be answered in a way applicable to all situations. It is debated in legal literature, and between the French Committee of Coordination of the Commercial Registers (CCRCS) and the Cour de Cassation. Certain authors consider that no board member of an SAS is required to be registered, as the law would request registration and publication only for those board members who are provided for by law (argument derived from Art. R 123-54 Commercial Code, Memento Francis Lefebvre Sociétés Commerciales No. 60339). Others consider that board members of boards that are formally designated in the articles of association of the SAS as "administrative board" or "supervisory board" (such as in a SA) and may thus be considered as *dirigeants* (see Section 6.2 for the distinction) must be registered. Again, others would consider the actual functions of the board: if the board is actively involved in the management of the company and is a *dirigeant*, its members must be registered.

We can observe that the practise of commercial registers diverges and some commercial registers may refuse to register, for example, new articles of association setting up a board if they consider that the board has similar functions as a board of directors and the filing does not request for registration of the board members.

However, if the board is an advisory board within the strict meaning, providing advice only, it is current practise not to register and publish the appointment of the members. We would even advise in such a case not to register them as their registration could suggest to third parties that they are *dirigeants*, which would increase their risk of liability (see Section 6.4.2).

6.3.6 Term of appointment

The term of the function of board members must also be set out in the articles of association. The term can be limited in time or unlimited. If the term is unlimited, the members end their functions only by resignation or dismissal.

The articles of association may set a fixed term or grant the appointing entity the competence to set the term. In practice, a term is often of four years, calculated, e.g., either from appointment on, or from the decision of the shareholders about the annual accounts. This solution is useful because at the end of the term there is no need to call for another shareholders' meeting for the board members. A very short term, e.g., of one year, does not appear to be practicable as new members must be appointed every year, or current members be expressly confirmed. In any event, shareholders must strictly monitor the expiry of mandates so that the board is always in the position to act.

If the articles of association provide for an age limit, it must also expressly set out if the mandate shall automatically expire upon reaching the age, or if the board member may continue until the end of an appointment period.

6.3.7 Remuneration

The articles of association shall set out the basic rules regarding remuneration of board members. Most frequently, the articles of association will entitle the board members only to reimbursement of their costs caused by their membership, and leave it to a shareholders' resolution to set out further remuneration. Remuneration may also be set out in a services agreement, depending on the functions of the board (see for example Cass. Com., 24 November 2015 No. 14–19.685 for a services agreement for a director).

Since the publication of the PACTE Act on 23 May 2019, the members of a board of an SAS may also be granted shares in terms of remuneration with the specific scheme for "creators" of new companies of "BSPCE" (Art 163 bis G CGI – French tax code) if their role is similar to that of an administrative or supervisory board. These are subscription bonds specifically reserved for "creators" of companies, in particular, start-ups. Although advisory board members will usually not be entitled to such subscription bonds, because they are not board members within the narrow meaning, such bonds may be an interesting instrument of remuneration.

6.3.8 Organisation and functioning of the board

First, we would like to point out that the Commercial Code does not provide for any rules as to the organisation and functioning of a board. It is therefore crucial that the articles of association contain all these rules, and that these rules be clearly set out.

It is not clear, though, if the articles of association need to set out all details, or if certain details may be contained in other documents such as management rules, shareholder resolutions or shareholder agreements (see above discussion following the decision of the French High Court, 25 January 2017). In our opinion, the articles of association must, at least provide for the basic rules. Some details may also be left to rules of procedure or a shareholders' agreement.

6.3.8.1 Board meetings and resolutions

Here, again, the articles of association must provide detailed rules for board meetings and resolutions. It is useful to provide for a minimum number of board meetings and the process for calling the meeting. Typically, meetings may be called by the chairman of the board, or also, in his absence, by any other board member, or, if so provided, by the statutory auditor. The president of the company (*président*) may also be entitled to call a board meeting. This can be useful in order to enable the president to initiate a meeting, in particular if the board needs to approve certain actions of the president. The notice period for the calling and requirements for the agenda of meetings shall also be set out.

The articles of association must also contain rules about the notice period for the calling of a meeting, as well as formal requirements for the calling (calling by registered letter, by e-mail, etc.), allowing the proper functioning of the board.

In terms of resolutions, the articles of association must be flexible and allow alternatively physical meetings or the possibility of meetings by telephone or videoconference, and for resolutions in writing, e.g., if all board members agree. This is particularly important where board members are abroad. If the articles do not allow for such alternative forms of meetings, it is questionable if meetings may validly take place in such forms.

Articles should also set out requirements for quorum and majorities. It is possible to provide for a simple majority but with at least one vote of a certain board member (e.g., the representative of the majority or the minority shareholder).

Minutes of board meetings shall be prepared, and be signed by the board members. This is also important in terms of responsibility of board members because such minutes could, for example, prove that the board members, or some of them, refused to approve a certain action by a negative decision.

6.3.8.2 Conflicts of interest

General provisions
There may be a situation where the board has to decide on issues that create a conflict of interest for one or several board members. Such situations are likely to be less frequent for a board whose sole function is to advise the management rather than to control it. However, advice, for example, on the decision of whether to enter into a certain market or not may also be biased if the board member has a personal interest or represents a shareholder having an interest in the outcome of the management decision.

There is no general provision under French law for avoiding conflicts of interest. The reform of the law of contracts of 2016 (Ordonnance No. 2016–131 of 10 February 2016) introduced, in the section about representation, a general rule to avoid conflicts of interest (Art. 1161 Civil Code) similar to the German Sec. 181 BGB, declaring void acts where a person had represented two parties at the same time or one party and themselves, unless it had been authorised by law, or by the persons concerned, or been ratified by those persons. A question had arisen whether this provision would be generally applicable to the representation of companies, whether commercial or civil law companies or not. The Commercial Code provides indeed for a set of specific rules aiming at avoiding conflicts of interest for certain types of companies. Furthermore, these rules vary between different types of companies. As these provisions are part of "special" law provisions, i.e. provisions solely applicable to certain corporations, the question was if they prevail on the general terms of the Civil Code. In the process of ratification of the Ordonnance of 2016 (Act No. 2018–287 of 20 April 2018) by the French Parliament, this provision was narrowed and, since 1 October 2018, applies only to acts entered into by natural persons (representing natural persons).

However, it should be noted that for decisions taken or acts signed between 1 October 2016 and 1 October 2018, Art. 1161 Civil Code applies in its original version, so that the debate is still relevant for those acts. Nevertheless, if the role of the advisory board is solely to give advice, this provision may not apply because no agreement is entered into by the board, and Art. 1161 of the Civil Code concerns rather the rules of representation.

"Regulated agreements"

Another question is if provisions regarding "regulated agreements" (*conventions réglementées*) may apply to (advisory) board members. To avoid conflicts of interest for decisions to be taken by officers, the French Commercial Code provides for detailed rules concerning "regulated agreements". It distinguishes between free agreements, regulated agreements and forbidden agreements. "Regulated agreements" are subject to a procedure of information, authorisation and/or approval. The procedures to be followed differ according to the legal form of the commercial company.

Here again, we focus on the form of an SAS. According to Art. L. 227-10 of the Commercial Code, agreements entered into between the company and, inter alia, one of the "officers" of the company, must be mentioned in a special report from the statutory auditor of the company (or its president if there is no statutory auditor) to be prepared once a year and the shareholders have to approve this report together with the approval of the annual accounts. Consequently, this control only takes place *ex post* and is not an authorisation to be given before entering into the relevant agreement. If the approval is not granted, the agreements remain valid but the president who signed it or the other officers may be held responsible for any negative consequences resulting from such an agreement. This requirement does not apply to "current agreements entered into at usual conditions" (*conventions courantes*, Art. L. 227-11 Commercial Code). A distinction between regulated and free agreements is not easy to draw, but has to be assessed on the basis of case-law and the practise of accountants.

The question here is if the members of an advisory board may qualify as "officers" within the meaning of this provision or not. The distinction must be made on the basis of the criteria we have set out above (see Section 6.2). If the advisory board members qualify as *dirigeants*, then agreements entered into between them and the company shall be subject to this procedure. However, the exclusion of the votes of the member concerned set out in Art. L 225-40 of the Commercial Code does not apply because each form of company has its own system of "regulated agreements", and no such provision exists for SASs.

If the board members are to be qualified as "officers", the prohibition for the company to grant a loan to them or grant securities or collaterals for debt of officers, also applies (Art. L 227-12 and L 225-43 Commercial Code).

> **Criminal Chamber of the French High Court, 25 September 2019 n° 18-83.113**
> According to this decision, the legal system for so-called "regulated agreements" applicable to SA (Art. L 225-86 and Art. L 225-88 of the French Commercial Code, with a prior control of regulated agreements) had to be applied because the articles of association of the SAS referred generally to the provisions of the SA. In such cases, however, the procedure for an SAS must also be respected, because it is a legal and not only statutory obligation.

Statutory provisions or shareholders' agreements

Independently from the legal provisions set out above, articles of associations, by-laws or a shareholders' agreement may provide for other provisions regulating potential conflicts of interest. Particularly in joint ventures, it may be advisable to exclude a board member from the vote or a decision if he is conflicted, or if the decision concerns the shareholder who has appointed the board member, e.g., services or other agreements to be entered into between the company and such a shareholder or a third party linked to the board member.

Articles of association may also put in place a procedure similar to the system of the "regulated agreements" set out in Section 6.3.8.2.

Each shareholder must, however, think carefully before introducing such provisions as they might create blocking situations.

6.3.8.3 Right to information

Board members may only exercise their function if they are provided with adequate information. As the Commercial Code does not provide for any specific provisions regarding boards in an SAS, specific information rights are not set out either. According to Art. L 225-35 para 3 of the Commercial Code, the president and general director of an SA are required to provide members of the board with all documents and information required to perform their duties. As pointed out above, this provision is not directly applicable on boards of an SAS. However, the legal concept underlying it shall also be applicable on other boards of an SAS. As, on the other hand, board members who are not "officers" have no/much less liability, their right to information is, in our opinion, in turn, also less strong. Articles of association may also provide for a right to information and refer, for example, to Art. L 225-35 of the Commercial Code.

6.3.8.4 Committees

It is up to the articles of association to provide for the creation of committees. This only makes sense if the number of board members is sufficient in order to be sub-divided in committees. It must also make sense with respect to the functions of the board.

The question is also as to whether board members may validly create committees if the articles of association do not provide for such committees. In our opinion, the board may establish informal committees to prepare specific types of decisions, but it may not delegate its powers without any basis in the articles of association.

6.4 Members, breach of duty and liability

6.4.1 Duties and obligations of members

There are no specific provisions in the Commercial Code in relation to the duties and obligations of board members of an SAS. According to Art. L 227-8 of the Commercial Code, the provisions regarding the responsibility of the board of directors and of the management board of an SA are applicable to the president of an SAS, as well as to its *dirigeants*.

Consequently, the distinction between a board member who is a *dirigeant*, and one who is not, is again very important. French corporate law has indeed developed specific concepts for the responsibility of *dirigeants* that determines, on the one hand, the types of duties and obligations that board members may have, and the violations for which a board member may be held responsible, and, on the other, who may claim for compensation (the company, shareholders or third parties). Interesting to note, Art. L 227-8 of the Commercial Code does not refer to Art. L 225-257 Commercial Code that stipulates (and limits at the same time) the liability of members of a supervisory board. It is therefore not clear if members of a board of an SAS who have the same functions as a supervisory board incur the same liability. In our opinion, this may be the case, as Art. L 227-1 of the Commercial Code contains the general referral to the provisions applicable to SAs (see also Aubry, Rev soc 2005, p. 793 No. 11).

Furthermore, even though SASs are not subject to codes of good conduct such as the code of governance of AFEP-MEDEF, the Charter of administrators published by the French Institute of Administrators (*Institut français des administrateurs* (IFA)) or the code of governance of MiddleNext, these codes also contain a certain number of duties of good conduct for administrators that give a sense of the standard for an administrator (see Martin/Françon, Actes Pratiques et Ingénierie Sociétaire No. 135 May 2014, dossier 3).

The existence and the extent of such duties will always have to be assessed on a case-by-case basis.

Consequently, a certain number of duties may exist (Martin/Françon, Actes Pratiques et Ingénierie Sociétaire No. 135 May 2014, dossier 3):

a) duty of competency: a board member may be committed to acquire skills necessary for the exercise of his functions. The more the advisory board is set into place for very technical, specific issues, the more one could expect that the members have the competences required for the performance of their functions

b) duty of participation and presence that is certainly the most basic obligation of a board member – the member shall show a minimum interest and presence at board meetings

c) duty of information: board members shall take the initiative to request information they need for the proper performance of their functions, or to ask for clarification if documents are not sufficiently clear

d) duty of opposition/action/resignation: if board members have, for example, to authorise certain actions of the president, they may not authorise actions that are against the social interests of the company. They must document their opposition to such a decision. In the worst case, they may even be led to resign from their position, if that is the only course of action against acts or a strategy contrary to the social interests of the company

e) loyalty duties/non-compete undertaking: board members may have an obligation of loyalty vis-à-vis the company, and even the shareholders. They may therefore be committed to pass on to the company or the shareholders information important for them, or, in any event, they are not allowed to hide such information. They may furthermore have a non-compete obligation if they are qualified as *dirigeants*

6.4.2 Breach of duties and liability

A board member who breaches his obligations may be revoked from his position and incur liability.

A first consequence of the breach of obligations may be the dismissal of the board member, and, according to the situation, the termination for cause of his service agreement or mandate, if applicable.

In terms of liability, civil law liability (obligation to repair damage) must be distinguished from criminal law liability.

As set out in Section 6.4.1, a distinction has to be made between board members who are to be qualified as *dirigeants*, and the others who are not.

6.4.2.1 Liability of a board member who is a *dirigeant*

Civil law liability

Members of the board of directors of a stock corporation or the managing director of a limited liability company incur personal liability and may be committed to pay compensation in the following cases:

– for non-compliance or violation of the law or regulations
– for non-compliance with the articles of association or bylaws and
– more generally, for management error (*faute de gestion*)

This also applies to board members of a board of directors or a management board of an SA (Art. L 225-251 French Commercial Code), and, consequently, to *dirigeants* of an SAS (Art. L 227-8).

In cases where several board members have acted together, the court will determine the portion of responsibility attributable to each of them (Art. L 225-251 para 2 French Commercial Code, applied accordingly).

> **PACTE Act (act n° 2019-486 of 22 May 2019 regarding the growth and transformation of undertakings)**
> Since the PACTE Act went into force, one new issue in terms of potential liability of officers may arise: The PACTE Act has introduced into the general provisions regarding companies (Art. 1833 of the French Civil Code) the obligation to "*manage the company taking into consideration the social and environmental impact of its activity*". The impact of this amendment on the responsibility of an officer is not yet clear, but it cannot be excluded that it could be considered as a management error for said officer to fail to take into account the social and environmental impact of his decisions. In the future, it will therefore be important that the corporate social responsibility (CSR) considerations be documented, e.g. in board decisions.
> Furthermore, in this context, advisory boards may obtain new tasks, as they could monitor or advise the managers in terms of CSR.

a) The categories of fault

As to the three categories of faults (violation of laws and regulations, violation of the articles of association, and management error), the first difficulty for SAS board members, even if they are considered as *dirigeants*, is that they are not *per se* subject to the same functions and thus the same specific legal tasks of a SA board of directors member. It follows that there is no room for sanctioning the violation of specific duties of a SA board of directors member due to the specific organisation of a SA. The above-detailed general obligations (presence, information, protection of the company's interests; see Section 6.4.1) are not related to the specific form of company and are therefore applicable. (see also Aubry, Rev des Sociétés 2005, p. 793 s).

As the Commercial Code provides for few provisions with respect to the management of an SAS, compliance with the articles of association is of particular importance.

A very vast category of fault for *dirigeants* is the "management error". It encompasses all acts or omissions that are not in the interest of the company, and cause harm to it. However, as the board members, such as members of a board of directors or a supervisory board of an SA, do not actively act for the company, behaviour that may trigger their responsibility is often an omission, for example, failure to control the president or other directors, or the lack of interest for the company, or the lack of initiative to ask certain questions or undertake certain controls, but also approving certain actions that cause damage to the company (see in detail Martin/ Françon, Actes Pratiques et Ingénierie Sociétaire No. 135 May 2014, dossier 3).

Furthermore, it is required that the board members have committed a fault, and that this fault has caused a prejudice to the company. As board members generally act collectively, their collective responsibility may often be engaged, for example, if the board approved a harmful act. However, a single board member may be exonerated if he can prove that he voted actively against the decision – a simple abstention would not be sufficient (Cass. Com., 30 March 2010, No. 08–617.841).

Shareholders may not exempt board members from their responsibilities. Even the *quitus*, the formal vote approving the management pronounced on the occasion of the assembly approving the annual accounts, cannot have the effect of exempting board members from their responsibilities.

b) Liability vis-à-vis the Company
Non-compliance by an officer with his obligations or the commission of a fault may cause damage to the company. The company may be entitled to claim for compensation. In such a procedure, the company will be represented by its legal representative (the president for an SAS). If the president or managing director is not willing to act, or fails to do so, the shareholders or one shareholder may act on behalf of the company (action *ut singuli*). In practise, this might be rarer, as the shareholder is not compensated himself but has the burden of the procedure. Indeed, actions against officers are often launched by the administrator following the insolvency of the company.

c) Liability vis-à-vis the Shareholders
The possibility for shareholders to claim for compensation of their own damage is rather limited as shareholders may only do so if they suffered an individual damage that is not just the result of a decrease in the value of the company, and, consequently, their shares. This is rarely the case as most errors committed by managers cause damage to the company in general and concerns all shareholders.

Cass. Com., 18 December 2012 n° 11-24.305 P
According to this decision of the French High Court, a member of a board (*comité de direction*) of an SAS has a duty of loyalty vis-à-vis the shareholders of the company and breaches this duty if he enters personally (or indirectly through a company controlled by him) into a purchase agreement regarding real estate owned by the company and knowing that the shareholders were trying themselves to purchase the same building. The shareholders may then claim for

compensation by the board member. In this case, the breach of loyalty consisted in the fact that the board member failed to act in a transparent manner. This decision applies a very wide concept of the duty of loyalty as the shareholders did not intend to purchase the building for the company, but for themselves (see comment of this decision by Favario Dalloz 2013, p. 288 s).

Cass. Com., 22 May 2019, n° 17-13.565
The duty of loyalty vis-à-vis the (majority) shareholder may also include the obligation for a board member of a subsidiary to vote in favour of a decision which has already been approved at the level of the parent company, unless this decision is not contrary to the interests of the subsidiary (see also comment to the decision, Schmidt, D. 2019, p. 1317 s).

d) Liability vis-à-vis third parties
Compared to German tort law, civil law liability for tort is very far-reaching under French law. In order not to expose managers to extensive liability, the liability of officers vis-à-vis third parties has been limited by case-law. Indeed, officers may only be obliged to indemnify a third party for damages caused by them in the exercise of their functions if they committed a "fault which can be detached from their functions" (Cass. Com., 27 January 1998, D. 1998 somm p. 392). The criteria of what can be "detached" have, however, been widened over the years (see in detail Le Cannu/Dondero, Droit des sociétés No. 484 subs.).

Criminal law liability
Officers may also incur personal criminal law liability in the cases provided by law. The most frequent offences are the abuse of assets of the company (*abus de biens sociaux*), the distribution of fictitious dividends, but also certain offences in labour law or environmental law. The "abuse of assets" constitutes an important risk of responsibility for officers because the constitutive elements of *abus de biens sociaux* are extremely wide-reaching, as is their application by criminal courts: it sanctions the fact of "acting against the interests of the company, for personal purposes or in order to favour another person or entity where the author has a direct or indirect interest" (Art. L 241-3 Commercial Code). Therefore, the perpetrator of this offence does not even need to seek direct, personal enrichment. Entering, for example, into an agreement in favour of another company of a group that is disadvantageous or causes harm to the company may suffice to constitute this type of violation.

Criminal Chamber of the French High Court, 25 September 2019 n° 18-83.113, see comment by B. Dondero JCP E n°46 of 14 November 2019, 1502
This recent decision shows how wide the field of application may be for abuse of assets of the company. A president of an SAS which was apparently organised with a board of directors and a supervisory board signed certain agreements in favour of himself without the prior authorisation of the supervisory board for the signature of these agreements which would have been required according to the reference in the articles to the legal provisions of a French SA. It appears

that solely the lack of prior authorisation led to the qualification as abuse, without further inquiry if indeed the agreements were harmful for the company. This decision is very questionable and has been criticised by commentators, as e.g. by Prof Dondero in his comment.

Case-law, however, recognises the interests of the group even against the interests of the company in clearly defined circumstances (the so-called Rozenblum doctrine following the Rozenblum decision, Cass. Crim., 4 February 1985, No. 84-91.581; Boursier, Le fait justificatif de groupe de sociétés dans l'abus de biens sociaux: entre efficacité et clandestinité, Rev soc 2005, 273 s; more recent decision Cass. Crim., 19 mars 2014, No. 12–83.188, Rev soc 2014, 741 note Boursier): the favoured company must directly or indirectly belong to the group, there must be an overall interest of the group, on the basis of an overall strategy, no lack of counterpart for the company concerned and no exceeding of its financial capacities.

However, as board members usually do not act for the company vis-à-vis third parties, their responsibility is limited to their acts (authorising a harmful action, for example), or their omission of control, according to their concrete functions within the company.

6.4.2.2 Liability of a board member who is not a *dirigeant*

If the functions of the advisory board are truly limited to advice, and the members are not considered as officers, they may only incur liability according to general law principles. If they entered into a services agreement, they may be held responsible for non-compliance with the agreement. If there is no contractual relationship with the company, they may be held responsible on the basis of general civil law liability, Art. 1240 French Civil Code (former Art 1382) that stipulates an obligation to repair damage caused by fault to another person. There is no restriction for tort under French law to damage to body or another absolute right such as in German law. Shareholders may also claim damages based on general civil law liability for violation of contractual obligations, even if the contract is entered into with the company (see for the general principle Cass. ass. plén., 6 October 2006, No. 05–13.255; D. 2006, 2825). The shareholder needs, however, to prove a damage distinct from the damage of the company (Cass. ass. plén., 9 October 2006 No. 06–11.056 D. 2006, 2933). Of course, fault includes intentional action, but also negligence.

6.5 Termination

As to termination, a distinction exists between termination of the function of a single member and of the board as such.

6.5.1 Termination of a single member

The position of a single board member may expire at the conclusion of its term, loss of certain qualities, reaching a maximum age, death, dismissal or, of course, resignation by the board member himself.

6.5.1.1 Automatic termination

The position of a single board member may terminate automatically.

Board members are frequently appointed for a fixed term (e.g., the date of the fourth ordinary shareholders' meeting approving the annual accounts following the year of appointment). In this case, their mandate ends automatically at the conclusion of the term without requiring any further actions by the shareholders or the corporate body competent for the appointment. The corporate bodies competent for the appointment shall monitor the term attentively to avoid that a mandate expire if the corporate body did not want the board member to end his position.

Other grounds for automatic termination of the mandate could be the reaching of a maximum age, if the articles of association provide for such a limit. In such cases, the articles shall also provide for the consequences of reaching the age; otherwise there could be a discussion about what the consequences of the age limit would be. The Commercial Code provides for the SA in such cases that the board member (or director general) be considered as having resigned from his position upon reaching the maximum age. This provision is not directly applicable but could serve as a model for a provision of articles of association.

Another possibility is that the articles of association provide for the automatic termination of the position, e.g., when the shareholder entitled to appoint the member sells or otherwise transfers his shares in the company.

In all these cases, if the articles of association provide for such limits, they must always clearly set out what the consequence of reaching such limits or the occurrence of such events will be.

6.5.1.2 Dismissal by the company

As to dismissal by the company, grounds for dismissal must be distinguished from the procedure of a dismissal, with different consequences in case of non-compliance for both issues. Here again, the Commercial Code does not contain provisions for the board members of an SAS. However, certain principles ruling the dismissal of managers have been developed by case-law and derive from principles of good faith. They shall also apply to managers/board members of an SAS.

Revocability and good cause

The articles of association must, first, determine whether a board member may be revoked at any point in time or not, and whether it may be revoked *ad nutum*, i.e., without cause, or for good cause only. This is a very important distinction. Revocability *ad nutum* would be more usual for board members, but this depends, of course, on the functions of the board and on the level of protection the shareholders wish to grant to board members.

If the articles of association require good cause, the question arises as to whether a dismissal without grounds is void or if it is valid but would entitle the board member to compensation. For other corporate forms where good cause is required by law (e.g., the managing director of an Sarl, Art. L 223-25 Commercial Code, or the director general of an SA, Art. L 225-55 Commercial Code), the dismissal without cause is valid, but the managing director is entitled to indemnification. Therefore, the same principles are likely to apply for the dismissal of a board member of an SAS.

If the articles of association do not contain more details as to the definition of "good cause", case-law developed for the Sarl or the director general of an SA shall be applied. Good cause is, for example, non-compliance with the law or articles of association, but could also be serious conflicts with the shareholders (see Cass. Com., 4 February 2014 No. 13–10.778). The simple "loss of trust" or the change of the majority shareholder is, on the contrary, not considered as good cause (Cass. Com., 4 May 1993 No. 91–14.693).

As to the obligation of compensation for dismissal without good cause see below.

Competence and formal requirements

The body competent for the appointment of the advisory board members is usually the same as for its dismissal. The articles of association must clearly allocate such competence. Frequently, the shareholders' assembly is competent. Competence can also be in the hands of the president or of one shareholder only, or at least require his vote or approval, or even be in the hands of a third party. If the articles of association do not provide for a specific requirement of majority for the dismissal, the general provisions of the articles of association for majority requirements apply.

The right of appointment and dismissal can also be left to specific shareholders by way of a shareholders' agreement. In such cases, the shareholders' party to the shareholders' agreement are committed to vote according to such provisions.

According to case-law, a board member who is also shareholder is not excluded from the vote (Cass. Com., 23 October 2007 No. 06–16.537; Cass. Com., 6 May 2014 No.13–14.960).

Case-law has developed further requirements for dismissals of officers.

If the board member is to be considered as an officer (see Section 6.2), these principles would apply to our opinion. If the board member is not an officer, it is not certain that these principles would protect the board member.

First, even in case of revocability *ad nutum*, the principle of "contradictory process" must be complied with. This means that the director must be heard before the decision and have had the possibility of discussion. This principle is possibly not complied with if the decision is communicated to the board member without any further discussion with him. Furthermore, the circumstances of the dismissal of an officer must not be "brutal" or offensive. This is the case particularly if grounds for dismissal are alleged that do not correspond to reality and are not in the interest of the company.

Indemnification and compensation

Non-compliance with the principles set out above, as well as the lack of "good cause" if such cause is required, may trigger the obligation to indemnify the officer. Both indemnifications must be distinguished (Cass. Com., 22 October 2013, No. 12–24.162).

Indemnification or compensation in case of dismissal may be set out either in the articles of association, which, however, will very rarely be the case, or in the shareholders' agreement, e.g., if the board members are remunerated and have been appointed for a specific period of time.

Compensation for dismissal may also be due on the basis of an agreement with the board member, for example, a service agreement. It must be noted that the compensation to be paid in case of early dismissal must not be so high as to prevent the revocation *ad nutum* (Cass. Com., 6 November 2012 No. 11–20.582 P).

6.5.1.3 Resignation by the board member

Board members may resign from their positions of their own motion. The question here is as to whether a board member may resign at any time, or whether he must respect a notice period.

The problem here, again, is that the Commercial Code does not provide for any specific provisions for board members of an SAS. The question is, therefore, if the provisions or case-law developed for members of other corporate bodies may be transferred.

If the board member is appointed for an indefinite period, it must be possible for the board member to resign at any point. However, general principles of good faith and orderly management shall be applied. The board member must consider the interests of the company, and not resign at an undue time or on such short notice that the resignation would put the company in a difficult situation. This depends on the circumstances. It is, for example, frequent that all board members, or some of them, resign with immediate effect upon closing the transaction when there is a change of control in relation to the company. In such a case, no party could challenge the resignation or claim damages from a board member if he resigns with immediate effect.

If a resignation has been pronounced on too short notice, or in violation of a notice period to be respected according to the articles of association, the general principles of resignation of other corporate bodies will, in our opinion apply: the resignation would not be void, but the board member may have to indemnify the company if the early resignation has caused damage (Cass. Soc., 1 February 2011 No. 10-20.953 P). If the board member has, however, no management functions and the company can handle its current affairs without the board member, it will be very difficult, in practise, for the company to prove damages.

The same principles shall apply if the board member has been appointed for a limited period.

Furthermore, an agreement may oblige a board member to keep his function for a certain period. In such a case, it would be a breach of contract if the board member resigns from his position before its term. In most cases, the consequences are likely to be limited to just the loss of the remuneration of the board member.

In practise, it is recommended that the articles of association provide for a notice period in the case of resignation, with the possibility to waive such notice period by the appointing corporate body. According to the functions of the board, a period of one to three months is usual.

The resignation letter shall be addressed to the company, and if so stipulated in the articles of association, to the shareholders or such other body designated in the articles.

A retroactive resignation is not possible.

6.5.2 Termination of the advisory board as a whole

The advisory board may cease its functions as a whole when the board is abolished. However, the decision to abolish the board cannot be tacit, but must be explicitly taken, i.e., by an amendment of the articles of association.

If, on the contrary, the board is not abolished but the positions are simply vacant, the president shall request that the shareholders appoint new members. This is in the own interest of the president because he may not be capable of acting if, for example, certain acts cannot be approved by the board – as stipulated in the articles of association – if the board is not in the position to act.

Restructuring of the governance and abolition of the board is frequently the case following a change of control of the company, the end of a joint venture, a capital increase and entry into the capital of a new majority shareholder, etc. The mandate of each single member expires automatically when the board is abolished or replaced by another form of board. However, in order to avoid any difficulties, in view of the fore-going, it is also advisable in these cases to inform the board members of the expiry of their mandate before the adoption and effectiveness of the new articles of association.

Board members may, in these cases, only claim for compensation if they had a service agreement or other document in place granting them remuneration for a longer period. However, even if such agreements are in place, it is always advisable to provide for a clause permitting the shareholders to amend the articles and to abolish the board.

The second situation where a board may terminate as a whole is in the event of a merger of the company or change of its legal form. The functions of the board members will automatically expire in such a situation (Cass. Com., 25 January 2017 No. 14–28.792). If there is, for example, a transformation into an SA, the board cannot be automatically considered as becoming the new board of directors (*conseil d'administration*).

6.5.3 The consequences of termination

Following termination, the various rights and obligations of a board member (see Section 4) will end. This also concerns the non-compete obligation, if applicable. There is no non-compete obligation for a board member after expiry of his position, unless this has been agreed with him. However, general restrictions arising from the principle of fair competition as well as the obligation to keep confidential business secrets and general confidentiality obligations continue of course to apply.

If the board member received compensation or remuneration for his functions, these rights also end.

Last but not least, if the board member is a corporation, but has to appoint a permanent representative, it has the obligation to appoint a new one if the permanent representative has left his office.

Francesca Ricci
Chapter 7
Italy

7.1 Introduction

7.1.1 Sources

The primary source for corporate governance regulation in Italy is the Italian Civil Code (ICC), which sets forth the main corporate governance rules for the two most common limited liability corporate vehicles in Italy: *società per azioni* (or SpA, i.e., company limited by stocks) and *società a responsabilità limitata* (or Srl, i.e., limited liability company). As a preliminary remark, it is worth mentioning that both these corporate structures entail a limited liability of the shareholders, a tendency to separation of ownership and managing powers and freely transferable shares. Trends show a well-established tendency to prefer Srl corporate structures rather than SpA ones, especially for mid-sized and smaller companies or for family owned and closely held companies.

Italian company law is subject to a gradual fragmentation process and diversification phenomenon of the legal sources. This phenomenon is called the "privatization of law sources". Notably, self-regulation codes in corporate governance matters, which are a form of private law, are progressively integrating the main sources of public law, such as the Italian Civil Code.

Indeed, there is a trend for medium-sized enterprises and family owned companies to follow the corporate governance organisation and structure of listed companies and companies having a widespread stock ownership, as ruled by the relevant self-regulation codes.

Although decree No. 58 of 24 February 1998 (the Consolidated Financial Act) is the main source of regulation for listed companies, the latter can voluntarily adopt the Self-Regulation Code issued by the Corporate Governance Committee of the Italian Stock Exchange in 2006 and most recently amended in January 2020 (the Corporate Governance Code or the Code).

The current configuration of the Italian Corporate Governance Committee was set up in June 2011 by the issuers and investors associations (ABI, ANIA, Assonime, Confindustria and Assogestioni), as well as the Italian Stock Exchange (Borsa Italiana SpA). The committee's objective is to promote good corporate governance in the financial community by issuing and updating the Corporate Governance Code. The enforcement of the code is based on the "comply or explain" principle, meaning that each company is allowed to decide whether certain provisions are appropriate for it and, in case of non-compliance, it is required to explain the relevant

https://doi.org/10.1515/9783110666182-007

reasons in an annual mandatory report (the so-called Corporate Governance Report). By the end of 2017, more than 90 per cent of Italian companies listed on the Italian regulated market (Mercato Telematico Azionario, MTA), which represented 99 per cent of the market capitalisation, formally declared to have adhered to the latest version of the Code. The choice not to join the Code is limited to a few cases and is generally due to the reduced size of the company.

Notably, self-regulation codes have been published and proposed also to small and medium-sized companies and they contain several provisions that are present in the self-regulation codes for larger and listed companies. The self-regulation codes for unlisted companies are private contributions based on the importance of the corporate governance also in the context of small and medium companies.

AIDAF (Associazione Italiana delle Aziende Familiari, Family Business Network) and Bocconi University published the self-regulation code for family owned non-listed companies in May 2017 (the AIDAF–Bocconi Code). The adhesion to the Code by a family owned company is voluntary. In addition, NEDCommunity, that is the Italian association of non-executive and independent directors, members of corporate governance and control bodies, issued the Corporate Governance Principles for unlisted companies in 2014 (the NED Principles).

In 2018 the Corporate Governance Framework (the "Framework") was issued by Elite – the growth and capital support platform of Borsa Italiana – created in collaboration with Confindustria and Assonime and with the collaboration of Avv. Alessandro Chieffi – addressed to companies that are experiencing growth and that aspire to access the capital market, and in particular to companies participating in the Elite project, the first structured approach to corporate governance, with a more flexible format than existing codes of conduct.

This is in order to offer support also to smaller companies, according to the principle of proportionality, and also to companies operating in a legal and regulatory context different from the Italian one. The Framework stands goes hand in hand with the Code of self-regulation of listed companies, with which it shares some pillars, such as the centrality of the administrative body, the division of tasks within this body and the managerial criterion.

7.1.2 Definition of small and medium company and family company

The presence of advisory boards in small and medium companies as well as in family owned companies is not common in Italy, although recommended.

Italian small and medium-sized companies (SMEs) usually operate mostly in anticyclical sectors with a strong and sustainable competitive position in their niche markets with a significant orientation to exports, especially outside the European Union (EU). According to the definition set forth in article 1, paragraph 1 – quater.1 of the

Consolidated Financial Act SMEs are small and medium listed enterprises, whose sales, even prior to the admission of their own shares to trading, have a volume of less than Euro 300 million, or that have a market capitalisation below Euro 500 million.

In addition to SMEs, family businesses are the backbone of the Italian economy. The latest edition of the AUB Observatory, promoted by AIDAF, UniCredit, the AIDAF Chair – EY of Family Business Strategy in memory of Alberto Falck of Bocconi University and the Milan Chamber of Commerce, depicts the Italian economy as one in which family businesses with a turnover of more than 20 million euros represent 65 per cent of the total of Italian companies, consolidating a total turnover of more than 730 billion euros and employing about 2.4 million workers. Expanding the view to companies with a turnover of less than 20 million euros, it is estimated that the percentage increases to about 85 per cent of all the Italian companies.

7.1.3 Management body

First, it is worth pointing out that, within the Italian system, corporate management bodies may be structured as follows:
- a mandatory sole director;
- a board of directors, a collegiate body – the so called *Consiglio di Amministrazione*;
- a two-tier system, in which both the management board (*consiglio di gestione*) and the supervisory board (*consiglio di sorveglianza*) must be collegiate bodies; the management board must be made up of a minimum of two members, while the supervisory board must be made up of a minimum of three members;
- a one-tier system; generally there is no minimum and maximum number of members for either the board of directors or the management monitoring committee (*comitato per il controllo sulla gestione*).

In SpAs, the management body is structured in one of the following ways:
(1) In the traditional system, in which shareholders appoint:
- a management body (sole director or board of directors) and
- a panel of statutory auditors in charge of ensuring that the company is managed in compliance with the law, the company bylaws and standards of proper management.

If certain conditions are met, the panel of statutory auditors may also be required to carry out accounting control activities. Otherwise, the shareholders must also appoint an external auditing body.
(2) In the two-tier system, in which the shareholders appoint a supervisory board (*consiglio di sorveglianza*), whose task is to ensure that the company is managed in compliance with the law, the company bylaws and standards of proper

management. The supervisory body then appoints the management board (*consiglio di gestione*), which is responsible for the company's day-to-day management. The shareholders must also appoint an external auditing body.

(3) The one-tier system (*sistema monistico*), in which the shareholders appoint a board of directors (*consiglio di amministrazione*), which manages the company. The board of directors then appoints a controlling body (*comitato per il controllo sulla gestione*) among its members. The shareholders must also appoint an external auditing body. In companies adopting the one-tier system, a management supervision committee must be appointed within the board of directors.

If the company's bylaws do not specify the type of management and control system to be adopted, the traditional one applies.

In Srls, the management body can be structured in one of the following ways:
– sole director;
– two or more directors acting jointly or severally in the management of the company, without, however, forming a board of directors;
– a board of directors.

Srl companies are prohibited from adopting the two-tier or the one-tier systems.

The quotaholders must also appoint a controlling body if required by the company bylaws or if the company meets the following specific requirements:
– The Srl is required to draft and approve the consolidated financial statements.
– The Srl controls a company that is required to appoint an external auditing body.
– For two consecutive years, the Srl has exceeded one or two of the economic thresholds provided by section 2435-bis of the Italian Civil Code (total financial statements assets: €2 Mio; revenue from sales and services: €2 Mio; average employees during the financial year: 10 units).

It is quite common for medium-sized enterprises and in particular family owned companies to prefer the appointment of simple corporate governance structures, by way of example preferring the appointment of a sole director rather than a board of directors. Listed companies or companies having a widespread stock ownership usually appoint a board of directors, in compliance with market practice and self-regulation codes. However, this is not mandatory according to the Italian Civil Code, although recommended by self-regulation codes.

The illustration of the corporate governance rules pursuant to the Code constitutes a benchmark in Italy and a model to be taken into account also by small and medium enterprises. It is clear that when making reference to small and medium-sized enterprises it is necessary to make the appropriate adjustments.

According to the Code, the board of directors of listed companies must be made up of executive and non-executive directors with adequate competence and expertise.

The number, competence, authority and time availability of non-executive directors must be such as to ensure that their judgement may have a significant impact on the board's decisions.

An adequate number of non-executive directors, in any case at least two, must be "independent", meaning that they must not have, directly or indirectly or on behalf of third parties, nor have recently had any business relationships with the company, or any persons linked to the same, of such a significance as to influence their autonomous judgement.

Although some criteria are established, the Code provides that the independence of non-executive members has to be evaluated by the board of directors on a substantial – rather than formal – basis.

With regard to their responsibilities, non-executive directors are expected to always provide an independent, unbiased judgement on the proposed resolutions, since they are not directly involved in the executive management of the company.

Independent directors are responsible for monitoring the performance of the executive management, especially with regard to the progress made towards achieving company strategies and objectives.

All directors have a responsibility to carry out their duties without conflict; however, a special responsibility is placed on independent directors to ensure that all decisions are taken in the best interests of the shareholders.

The independence requirements of the directors of listed companies can be used to define the requirements that the members of the advisory board must possess.

7.2 Concept and definition, delimitation from other corporate bodies

On closer examination of the advisory board in small and medium-sized enterprises, it is worth starting off by clarifying what is meant by such a body and how an advisory board distinguishes itself from other bodies, in particular the board of directors.

7.2.1 Concept of "advisory board"

There is no legal definition of the term "advisory board". However, an advisory board is generally defined as a body that can be formed by external experts and consultants and to which various tasks can be assigned either by the owner-manager or by the competent corporate body of a company.

It is a body set up on a voluntary basis, not a legally prescribed one. Ideally it can be made up even by one member only, although a collegiate body is more common.

The possibility to appoint an advisory board is contemplated by both NED Principles and the AIDAF–Bocconi Code, which do not, however, provide specific rules on its appointment and working mechanisms, but only introduce the concept and describe it as a useful means for improving corporate governance structure. The appointment of an advisory board is not ruled at all in the framework issued by Elite.

According to NED Principles 3 and 4 the establishment of an advisory board is aimed at introducing competent and outstanding professionals, who are able to "bring value to the stakeholders" and whose opinion is influential for the corporate needs.

The advisory board is not a corporate body like the board of directors, therefore it is not legally liable for the actions or omissions committed by its members, save for professional contractual liability of its single members or for liability due to gross negligence and wilful misconduct. In addition, advisory board members may be liable in those cases in which it can be proved that they were acting as "shadow directors" of the company.

The advisory board brings impulse to possible initiatives the company may adopt and is not provided with decision-making powers, as it only has advisory tasks on the specific subjects that the managers submit to it.

At the same time, an advisory board may act as consultant for either the shareholders' meeting or the board of directors. The presence of an advisory board could be temporary, since a board of directors should theoretically replace it at a certain point.

Since its statements and assessments are not binding upon the managers, the introduction of an advisory board may turn out to be particularly useful where the entrepreneur, being a sole manager, is afraid of losing its exclusive centralised powers through the appointment of a board of directors, a situation that is common in family owned companies. At the same time the advisory board has the advantage of providing real support to the entrepreneur with high-level consultancy, thus reducing the risks deriving from a blind management made by a sole director.

With particular reference to the starting-up period or a particular critical stage of a company, managers may need the support of professionals who are able to advise them in evaluating and adopting the most suitable choices, concerning the strategy as well as the approach and the development of internal measures of direction and control. Therefore, the advisory board is a means to collect competencies and share business views and actions, which can be replaced by a board of directors at a later stage, composed not only of shareholders or family members, but also of professionals, experts and independent directors.

7.2.2 Distinction from the board of directors

The legal form of a limited liability company frequently used in medium-sized or family owned enterprises does not initially provide by law for the formation of another body in addition to a shareholders' meeting (*assemblea*), the sole director (*amministratore unico*) or the board of directors (*consiglio di amministrazione*) and the board of statutory auditors (*collegio sindacale*).

Advisory boards are those boards that are set up without legal obligation, irrespective of the legal form or size of a company. Therefore, they can be set up only on a voluntary basis.

Unlike the main board, such a body lies outside the formal governance structure of the company. As a result, the decision-making powers of the owner-manager or controlling family on the main board remain undiluted. However, the advisory group helps improving the board's capabilities in terms of expertise and business contacts. Over time, members of the advisory group can be invited to join the main board as directors.

As the company grows in size and complexity, so should the board. Conversely, the advisory board should diminish in importance. An advisory group cannot exercise proper monitoring and oversight over the company.

Unlike a formal board, it cannot exercise significant influence over company strategy decisions.

7.2.3 Distinction from the committees inside the board of directors having advisory functions

The board of directors of small and medium-sized companies are entitled to appoint, depending on the specific needs and size of the company, one or more than one committee dealing with particularly significant topics. On the one hand, these committees differ from the advisory board since they are made up of directors, especially independent ones. On the other hand, the internal committees differ from advisory boards since they lack consultative as well as proponent functions.

The advisory board addresses its advice to different corporate bodies, depending on the one that appointed it, while the board committees only report to the board of directors.

According to clause 2.P.13 of the AIDAF–Bocconi Code the board of directors is entitled to appoint, depending on the specific needs and size of the company, committees dealing with particularly significant topics for corporate governance. Each of them could be provided with either proposal or advisory functions, in any case without binding effects.

As the advisory board organisations and functioning are not ruled by specific provisions (indeed the self-regulation codes for medium-sized companies do not contemplate provisions in this regard), the rules governing committees inside the board of directors set forth by the AIDAF–Code (as well as by the Corporate Governance Code) may be used as an example and a reference to be pursued by the companies.

The AIDAF–Bocconi Code sets forth several criteria relating to the appointment and the operation of the advisory committees established inside the board of directors, especially when the shareholders' structure is complex. Notably, the committees carry out the tasks listed in the resolution through which they were appointed, although such tasks can be revoked or modified by a subsequent corporate resolution. They are made up of at least two members, one of whom should be independent, unrelated to the family owning the company. The definition of independent directors is the same as the one used in the self-regulatory code for listed companies.

A chairman, who should be appointed among the independent members, coordinates the activities of the relevant committee. A budget for each committee should be resolved upon by the board of directors, to be used in case the committee needs external consultancy.

The committee is allowed to access the corporate information necessary for it to carry out its own functions and it should report on a regular basis to the board of directors on the activities carried out. Each meeting of the committee members should be recorded in minutes by the chairman.

Such committees inside the board of directors include but are not limited to the following ones: risks and controls committee, remuneration of the directors and officers committee and nomination committee. Each of them could be provided with either proposal or advisory functions, in any case without binding effects.

The committee for the appointment of the directors is required to advise on the balanced composition of the board of directors and it expresses opinions on professionals whose skills and competencies may be required inside the board or as managers. It suggests candidates in case of need to replace any resigning director or manager. It carries out enquiries in relation to succession of directors.

The committee for the remuneration of the directors is required to evaluate periodically the adequacy, coherence and effective application of the remuneration policy of the directors and officers with strategic functions.

It is empowered to express opinions or proposals to the board of directors on the remuneration of the directors provided with powers of attorney and on the business performance targets that are linked to the variable part of the remuneration, if any.

The remuneration committee monitors the actual implementation of the resolutions adopted by the board of directors and it verifies the effective reach of the predetermined goals, which, of course, should be as clear and precise as possible. Attendance at the remuneration committee's meetings is prohibited to those directors whose remuneration is the subject matter of the proposal under discussion at that meeting. Should the intervention of an expert be required to obtain information on the market practice relating to remuneration policies, the committee is required to verify in advance that the consultant in question is not in a conflict of interests position.

The committee for the controls and risks should be made up of directors provided with adequate accounting, financial and risk-management experience.

The committee for the succession plan is required to coordinate, programme and implement succession plans. In case of family owned companies, such committees should be made up of directors representing the various branches of the family and at least one independent director, the latter to ensure a better balance of interests.

7.3 Establishment, organisation and operations

According to Italian law, there is a principle of "close numbers" of corporate bodies types. The rights and duties of the (already existing) corporate bodies are therefore not changed by an advisory board, which provides advisory support in the direction of the business activity and contributes to the definition of the strategic goals.

7.3.1 Establishment

In principle, an advisory board can be set up in different ways: i) through the relevant implementation in the articles of association and the subsequent appointment by means of a resolution adopted by the shareholders' meeting or board of directors or by a decision of a sole director; ii) in case the articles of association do not contemplate a specific provision, the shareholders' meeting and the board of directors may appoint an advisory board; and iii) through the provision of a shareholders' agreement.

It is worth highlighting that the appointment of an advisory board involves costs in terms of remuneration due to its members. Therefore, the freedom to appoint an advisory board by the corporate depends on whether or not the company's budget envisages such costs.

Since advisory boards are never internal corporate bodies, they relate to the company and its corporate bodies on the basis of general civil law principles resulting from the Italian civil code.

7.3.1.1 Implementation through the articles of association

There are no explicit legal regulations for the establishment of an advisory board. The articles of association may allow for the creation of an advisory board having consultative functions, detailing its tasks and competencies.

In addition, the articles of association should set forth specific rules relating to its functioning as well as its composition and termination. However, in the absence of such rules, the resolution appointing the advisory board adopted by the shareholders' meeting or the management body could provide such provisions.

Finally, a self-regulation code governing the functioning of the advisory board may be envisaged by its members.

An advisory board can therefore be set up upon the company's incorporation or later by amending its articles of association.

7.3.1.2 Appointment by means of a resolution approved by the shareholders' meeting

The articles of association of a company may simply authorise or, if necessary, oblige the shareholders to set up an advisory board at a later date. In this way, in the event that the wish or need for an advisory board arises later, the shareholders can set up such a body without having to amend the articles of association.

The shareholders may appoint the advisory board directly, irrespective of a special provision contained in the bylaws, due to the mere consultative functions that the advisory may have.

Although uncommon, in principle nothing prevents the shareholders' meeting from appointing an advisory board, should certain specific business needs arise or also in case of the need for advice regarding succession plans.

Under no circumstances may the shareholders delegate their typical functions to an advisory board, since the delegation of functions is strictly regulated by the Italian civil code.

The powers of the shareholders remain those provided pursuant to the Italian Civil Code; as a matter of fact, none of the following powers may ever be delegated to an advisory board.

In SpA companies adopting either the traditional or the one-tier system, the ordinary shareholders' meeting must:
- approve the annual financial statements;
- appoint and remove directors;
- appoint the statutory auditors and the entity entrusted with the statutory audit of the accounts;
- establish the remuneration of directors and statutory auditors, if not established in the bylaws;
- resolve on the liability of directors and statutory auditors;
- resolve on other matters reserved to shareholders pursuant to the law or the bylaws and
- approve the procedural rules, if any, for the meeting.

In SpAs adopting the two-tier system, the ordinary shareholders' meeting must:
- appoint and remove the members of the supervisory board;
- establish their remuneration;
- resolve on their liability;

- resolve on the distribution of profits and
- appoint the entity entrusted with the statutory audit of the accounts.

In all SpAs (irrespective of the adopted management system), the extraordinary share-holders' meeting must resolve upon:
- amendments to the bylaws;
- appointment, replacement and powers of the company's liquidators;
- any other matter reserved to extraordinary shareholders' meetings pursuant to the law.

In Srls, the quotaholders resolve upon:
- the approval of the financial statements and the distribution of profits;
- the appointment of the directors, if provided by the Deed of Incorporation;
- the appointment of the auditors and the entity entrusted with the statutory audit of the accounts, if necessary;
- amendments to the bylaws;
- any decision to enter into a transaction that may involve amendments to the company's purpose or to the quotaholders' rights and
- other matters reserved to quotaholders pursuant to the bylaws as well as every other matter that the directors or the quotaholders representing at least one-third of the capital submit for their approval.

7.3.1.3 Appointment by means of a resolution adopted by the board of directors or by a decision of a sole director

The sole director or the board of directors may be entitled by the articles of associa-tion to appoint an advisory board having consultative functions.

The sole director or the board of directors may appoint the advisory board di-rectly, irrespective of a special provision contained in the bylaws, due to the mere consultative functions that the advisory body may have.

Under no circumstances, however, may the administrative body delegate its functions to an advisory board, since the delegation of functions is strictly ruled by the Italian civil code.

Specific management tasks may be delegated by the board of directors only to single board members or to a smaller group of board members. The board is also allowed to delegate specific functions and appoint persons outside of it to act as attorneys. In all these cases, the board of directors must establish the content and the limits of the tasks of managing directors and/or attorneys.

Even upon delegation of powers, the board of directors retains full managerial responsibility, meaning that it is free to give directives to the managing directors;

decide upon any transactions encompassed in the delegated tasks, whenever it is necessary in the interest of the company; and revoke the delegation of powers.

In any case, the following tasks may never be delegated:
- the issue of bonds, if delegated to the board;
- resolutions on the company's strategy;
- the drafting of financial statements;
- the increase of the share capital, if delegated to the board;
- the reduction of the share capital for losses, also in case of losses involving a decrease of the share capital below the legal minimum threshold and
- the drafting of merger or demerger projects.

The same rules apply to the members of the management board in companies adopting the two-tier system.

7.3.1.4 Advisory boards set forth by shareholders' agreement

All or some of the shareholders of a company can also set up an advisory board beyond the articles of association of the company in the form of a shareholders' agreement. An advisory board established under a shareholders' agreement is not considered to be a corporate body of the company. It cannot therefore make its own corporate decisions, as only a transfer of advisory/consultancy tasks is allowed.

Members of an advisory board under a shareholders' agreement only have a legal relationship with the company's shareholders. Their responsibility therefore depends exclusively on the content of the agreement on the basis of which they act.

If an advisory board is established in accordance with a shareholders' agreement, the rights and duties of the advisory board on the one hand and the advisory board members on the other – in particular information rights and advisory duties – result solely from the contractual relationship due to the lack of a position in the corporate bodies.

7.3.2 Members of the advisory board

The advisory board may be composed of external members only. The attendance of directors should be avoided since a director cannot hold direction and managing functions on the one hand and consultancy functions on the other. This would imply critical consequences also in terms of liability of the director concerned.

With regard to the size and composition of an advisory board, the shareholders are free to choose their own structure. The size of the advisory board should be based on the interests of the company, its expediency and efficiency. As for the number of members working on the advisory board, it is advisable to have from three to five members. The duration of the assignment is generally defined at the beginning of the relationship. In order not to be too constrained, it is advisable to propose a year with the possibility of renewal at the end of the same.

An adequate number of advisory board members should be "independent", meaning that they do not have, directly or indirectly or on behalf of third parties, nor have recently had any business relationships with the company, or any persons linked to the same, of such a significance as to influence their autonomous judgement.

Although some criteria are established, the Corporate Governance Code provides that the independence has to be assessed by the board of directors on a substantial – rather than formal – basis.

With regard to their responsibilities, members of the advisory boards are expected to always provide an independent, unbiased judgement on the proposed resolutions, since they are not directly involved in the executive management of the company.

7.3.2.1 Professional competence

In small and medium-sized enterprises and family owned companies, potential members may be requested to have strong territorial representation and might be chosen on the basis of criteria of authority and knowledge of a specific business sector.

The advisory board is especially effective at the beginning, in the start-up phase when reliance on credible partners is necessary.

7.3.2.2 Diversity requirement

The Code recommends listed companies to apply diversity criteria, including by gender, in the composition of the board of directors (and of the board of statutory auditors).

The relevant criterion, set forth by Law 120/2011 with the aim of fostering gender diversity, requires at least a "one-third quota" of the less represented gender both in the board of directors and in the board of statutory auditors.

The AIDAF–Bocconi Code proposes the presence in the board of directors of at least one non-family council, better still if independent (according to the regulation of listed companies) and that an adequate diversity in terms of professional background, age and gender is complied with.

The diversity criteria mentioned in this paragraph 3.2.2 should be adopted also with reference to advisory boards in SMEs and family owned companies for a more effective functioning.

7.3.2.3 Further requirements

Moving on to the practical side, those who want to experience the advisory board personally must first select trusted individuals who are willing to manage the assignment. This must be done considering the mutual esteem, the harmony between the two parties and the interest of the same in the company.

The internal regulation of the advisory board may set forth general criteria regarding the maximum number of management and control offices that the candidate may hold in other companies so as to be considered in line with the amount of time necessary for the proper execution of the office as member of the advisory board.

7.3.3 Appointment of advisory board members

The appointment of an advisory board member is the result of a decision-making process by the relevant corporate body. The parties may enter into a service contract setting forth the relevant terms and conditions; alternatively, such terms and conditions may be contained in the relevant resolution.

7.3.4 Compensation

It is advisable to provide for the payment of a remuneration based on the level of commitment requested (i.e., number of meetings), the seniority and experience of the single members. It is customary to pay members of an advisory board expense allowances.

The criteria for determining the remuneration should be contemplated specifically by the articles of association of the company or in the resolution adopted by the relevant corporate body (i.e., shareholders or the board of directors) or by a provision in the service contract or in the relevant shareholders' agreement.

If granted by corporate bodies and in cases other than the appointment of an advisory board pursuant to a shareholders' agreement, the remuneration should be included in the relevant periodic budget.

The remuneration itself should not be linked to the economic results achieved by the company, in order to avoid opportunistic advice.

For the same reason, the remuneration should not be part of incentive plans.

7.3.5 No transfer of representation to the advisory board

It is indispensable for the chairman and managing directors, together with special attorneys, to have the exclusive powers to represent the company as a body.

Hence, under no circumstances may the advisory board have the power to represent the company vis-à-vis third parties, because members of advisory boards remain consultants of the company and they are therefore not a part of an internal corporate body.

7.3.6 No transfer of competencies from the shareholders and/or managing directors to the advisory board

The tasks that lie exclusively with the board of directors and managing directors, as well as the shareholders, on the basis of a mandatory statutory regulation, may not be transferred to an advisory board.

7.3.7 Organisation and operations

The articles of association should contain specific rules regarding the organisation and operations of the advisory board. Alternatively, they may specify whether such rules are to be determined by the shareholders or the management body. Finally, each advisory board can prepare a self-regulation code setting forth, among other things, the frequency and place of the meetings and its functioning in general. In any case, such regulation should be separate from the articles of association and issued by means of a resolution by the relevant corporate body in order to avoid subsequent amendments.

The board appoints a chairman among its members. The chairman of the advisory board, who should have special leadership skills, convenes the meetings of the advisory board and chairs them. If the chairperson of the management board is a family member, the chairperson of the advisory board should be an external member (and vice versa) in order to form a counterpart.

The advisory board usually does not have its own office and it may even operate through virtual meetings on video chat communication tools and/or by email or in specifically designated areas of the company headquarters.

The meetings may be called, not necessarily on a regular basis, following the proposal also of a single participant.

Furthermore, its activities must be defined and administered internally, if possible with the support of a secretary appointed for this purpose.

Meetings must be convened sufficiently in advance to allow all members to prepare adequately.

7.3.7.1 Advisory board committees

Depending on the size of the advisory board and the tasks, it also makes sense to form internal committees in order to be able to process the tasks efficiently and effectively.

The activities of an advisory board committee are governed by the same principles as those of the advisory board itself.

7.3.7.2 Operations of the advisory board

The advisory board's activities may relate only to an internal impact and may not have an external one. An advisory board, which only provides non-binding advisory services, cannot make decisions. The advisory board may not have a specific duration and each participant has no constraints or commitments of any kind, and is free to voluntarily continue or resign.

7.3.7.3 Adoption of resolutions

Although the advisory board only exercises advisory and consultancy functions to corporate bodies, the members of the advisory board may pass resolutions having the effect to express the willingness of the board as a whole entity.

The work of the advisory board is coordinated by its chairman. The advisory board is called by the chairman in meetings for discussions and/or approvals of resolutions, generally according to the majority vote. The chairman may have a casting vote.

The minutes of the meeting, which have the aim of providing proof of and recording the resolutions passed and activities carried out, should be prepared by the secretary and signed by the latter and the chairman.

7.4 Members, breach of duty and liability

7.4.1 Eligibility requirements

Although not mandatory, the (minimum) legal conditions for eligibility set forth for directors should be applied also to the members of advisory boards.

The Italian Civil Code (ICC) sets forth a number of reasons of ineligibility related to the office of director. In particular, interdicted and banned persons, disqualified persons, bankrupt persons or those who have been sentenced to a penalty entailing interdiction, even temporary, from public offices or the inability to exercise managerial functions cannot be appointed as directors, and if appointed, they are revoked from their office.

Furthermore, special laws provide for numerous reasons for incompatibility (that operate differently from the above causes of ineligibility) with the office of director (e.g., civil servants, holders of governmental positions and members of Parliament cannot be appointed as directors). While a reason for ineligibility causes the appointment resolution to be null and void, should a reason for incompatibility arise, the appointed director must choose between one of the incompatible positions.

Additional reasons for incompatibility are provided by the ICC, depending on the management structure adopted and, in particular:
- For companies adopting the two-tier system, the members of the supervisory board cannot be:
  - interdicted and banned persons, disqualified persons, bankrupt persons or persons who have been sentenced to a penalty entailing interdiction, even temporary, from public offices or the inability to exercise managerial functions;
  - members of the management board;
  - persons who are employees of, or have any other financial or professional relationship with, the company or its subsidiaries or parent companies, in addition to those companies that are under the common control of the same entity, or any other professional relationship that may hinder the supervisory board member's independency.
- For companies adopting the one-tier system, at least one-third of the members of the board and all the members of the management monitoring committee must meet the following requirements:
  - not having been deprived of their rights, bankrupt or convicted with a judgment entailing interdiction, even temporary, from public offices or being unable to exercise managerial functions;
  - the spouse, relatives within the fourth degree of the directors of the company, directors and relevant spouse or relatives within the fourth degree of subsidiaries of the company and of its parent company, in addition to those companies that are under the common control of a same entity;
  - persons that are employees of, or have any other financial or professional relationship with, the company or its subsidiaries or parent companies, in addition to those companies that are under the common control of a same entity, or directors of the company and persons described in the paragraph above, that may hinder their independence, as well as, if provided by the by-laws, requirements provided for in codes of conduct drafted by trade associations or by companies managing regulated markets;
  - furthermore, at least one of the committee members must be selected among the certified public auditors registered into the relevant register.

The application of the eligibility requirements listed in this paragraph 4.1 may be extended to members of the advisory board in the relevant set of rules governing their establishment.

7.4.2 Service agreement

In addition to the appointment, it may also be necessary to enter into a service contract between the advisory board member and the company, which will be subject to civil law rules according to the ICC.

7.4.3 Rights and duties of advisory board members

If the goal is to allow the advisory board to be useful for the company, its tasks must be specified carefully and checked over time.

The personal rights and duties of the advisory board members generally correspond to those of consultants. Details, however, are derived from the individual tasks and structure of the respective advisory board.

In addition to the right to participate in advisory board meetings, the essential rights of an advisory board member are the right to be informed on the matters that are on the agenda, to have access to the necessary information and documentation in order to make assessment and evaluations, to vote, the right to receive minutes of meetings and a remuneration usually paid as well as reimbursement of expenses.

The tasks may be limited to a purely non-binding consultancy/advisory function, and they do not include monitoring and control duties.

In detail, the tasks vary as follows.

7.4.3.1 Consulting function

The typical and main function pertaining to the advisory board is merely "advising" the management and/or the shareholders, without binding effects. Based on their own specific and high-level skills and knowledge of the market in which the company runs its business, consulting tasks should include the following: giving suggestions and opinions on actions to be proposed to or proposed by the management body; proposing business strategies and ideas to foster business growth, long-term objectives and sustainability; finding new opportunities; simplifying relationships.

It can support the management body in the development and implementation of the corporate strategy and provide new ideas and thoughts.

The scope of the advice to be provided by the members of the advisory board depends upon the actual situation of the company and the mandate given.

7.4.3.2 Supporting function

The advisory board expresses its non-binding opinion on the development of strategies that the company must share promptly and transparently and suggests improvements, innovations and best practices considered effective for a better promotion and enhancement.

7.4.3.3 Monitoring and controlling function

Advisory board members, if specifically provided for in the relevant appointment, may be entrusted with monitoring the performance of the management, especially with regard to the progress made towards achieving company strategies and objectives. The board may then report to the board of directors or the shareholders' meeting the results achieved and then provide its advice.

The advisory board is not in charge of monitoring the management in terms of the legality, regularity and cost-effectiveness of its actions, since monitoring and control functions are strictly reserved to the board of statutory auditors and to the surveillance body (Organismo di Vigilanza or named also ODV).

The board of statutory auditors is made up of three statutory auditors and two alternate auditors and it is appointed by the shareholders' meeting that also resolves upon the relevant remuneration. The auditors have the following duties:
- acting autonomously and independently also from the shareholders who appointed them
- operating exclusively in the company's interest
- controlling the company's management carried out by the board of directors
- coordinating their activities with the auditing company and the internal control committee.

The board of statutory auditors is in charge of the surveillance and observance of law provisions and bylaws, of the principles of proper management and of the adequacy of the internal control system and management of the risks and on the organisational, administrative and accounting asset as well as of its functioning. It is also in charge of the implementation of the corporate management rules that the company declares to comply with; furthermore, it is called to provide a grounded proposal to the shareholders' meeting upon the appointment, revocation and relevant decisions on the remuneration and the office to the accounting firm.

Legislative Decree No. 231 of 8 June 2001 introduced regulations on the administrative liability of companies, providing that companies may be found liable and hence face penalties for crimes committed or attempted by directors or employees in the interest or to the advantage of the company. The company cannot be held liable if, inter alia, prior to the crime being committed, it adopted and effectively implemented organisational, management and control models designed to prevent said crimes and established a specific body responsible for monitoring the functioning of the models and compliance with the same. The ODV is appointed by the board of directors and its size depends on that of the company. A monocratic ODV is admitted. Such body is in charge of the surveillance and functioning of the model pursuant to Legislative Decree no. 231/2001 for preventing the commission of crimes (by way of example, crimes against the Public Administration, the breach of laws on safety at work, corporate crimes, market abuse, IT crimes and unlawful processing of personal data). It has its own internal regulation and operates on the basis of a specific surveillance programme. It meets at least on a quarterly basis and reports to the board of directors also through the internal control committee and to the board of statutory auditors.

7.4.3.4 Ethic functions

The strategic function of the advisory board is, with respect to the shareholders' meeting, and/or the board of directors and/or the director, to report management aspects of the company that, in its unanimous opinion, compromise one or more of the values listed in the specific regulation of ethic codes, if adopted. In addition, an advisory committee may be involved in non-financial performance issues and the relevant social and environmental impact.

7.4.3.5 Specific sectors

The advisory board may be established to provide consultancy and knowledge on any topic emerging from specific business markets.

7.4.3.6 Dispute resolution tasks

It is not common to delegate dispute resolution tasks to the advisory board when such litigation is between, by way of example, the shareholders and the managing directors or among the shareholders. In any case, should the advisory board be involved in this kind of activity, the relevant assignment must be specified in detail in the articles of association or in the relevant clause, and it will have the aim to facilitate an amicable settlement between the parties.

7.4.3.7 Generational handover

The advisory board may be set up for the purpose of providing mediation and handling support in the succession.

Support in the context of intergenerational transfers consists in the identification of the most effective solutions and instruments for the transmission of entrepreneurial assets. To begin with, the board collects data concerning the family owned company and it engages in the establishment of a dialogue with them and to identify the objectives and drivers for the subsequent feasibility study (progressiveness, continuity, segregation, financial impact). The advisory board may then support the shareholders in the subsequent implementation of the chosen solution.

7.4.4 Duty to act without conflicts of interests

The advisory board and its members are required to operate in the absence of conflicts of interests; in which case they should abstain from pursuing the relevant transaction or where applicable comply with the duty to abstain from voting. Where the conflict of interest is remarkable and could jeopardise efficient and loyal consultancy activities within the advisory board, the member bearing such conflict is expected to resign.

7.4.4.1 Duty of confidentiality

Members of an advisory board must undertake to keep confidential the information received by reason of their commitment to the advisory board, also for a certain amount of time after their termination. The company may adopt a procedure for the internal management and external communication of documents and information and each member of the advisory board shall be requested to operate in compliance with such procedure. In case of breach of the relevant provisions, the relevant member may be held liable and be revoked.

7.4.4.2 General duties

In addition, advisory board members are subject to the general duties of information, to act advisedly, with the appropriate skills, experience and knowledge of the company situation and to monitor one another.

7.4.5 Breach of duty and liability

Members of an advisory board who fail to comply with the standard of care incumbent upon them may be held liable for breaches of duty. The liability will be only towards the company and not vis-à-vis third parties. It is a contractual liability that can be assimilated to the consultants' one.

The advisory board members must operate according to and within the limits set forth in the instructions contained in the resolutions approved for their appointment or in the separate regulation or in the service agreement, if any. In this case, the members of the advisory board are obliged to comply with the relevant instructions; they may not carry out their own discretionary activities that are out of the scope of work assigned to them.

7.4.5.1 Breach of duty

The civil liability of directors cannot be restricted or limited *ex ante*. In fact, by operation of law, all directors are jointly liable if they have not made their best effort to prevent damages or to eliminate or mitigate the detrimental consequences thereof. It is possible for a director to avoid such civil liability in case evidence is given that: the director acted without negligence; documented his disagreement in the appropriate corporate document; or promptly informed the chairman of the board of statutory auditors. Under Italian law directors of a company may have:

(a) liability towards the company
Directors may incur liability towards the company. The directors' duties towards the company can be divided into (1) general duties (namely, the duty of care and the duty of loyalty), and (2) specific duties set out in statutory provisions of law or in the company's bylaws.

The assessment of whether directors acted with the necessary standard of care requires a case-by-case analysis.

Directors also owe the company a duty of loyalty that includes, inter alia, the duty to disclose any interest the director may have in a transaction to the board of directors and the board of statutory auditors.

As a general rule, directors may be held liable towards the company only when the breach of their duties has caused damage to the company itself.

The burden to prove the damage rests with the company claiming the directors' responsibility.

(b) liability towards creditors of the company
Directors are also liable towards company's creditors for any breach of their duty to preserve the company's assets in case the latter are not sufficient to satisfy the

creditors' claims. In principle, a company may not have enough assets to face its debts when due also without being technically insolvent.

(c) liability towards company's shareholders and third parties

Furthermore, any shareholder or third party may bring an action for damages arising from wilful misconduct or negligent behaviour of the directors, provided that it has suffered direct damages, different from those suffered by the company, and that are specifically and personally borne provided that the damage cannot be a mere consequence of the damage caused to the company.

The civil liability of the members of an advisory board is different from the civil liability of directors and shareholders. However, in the case of legal suits brought against any of them, each of them, as the case may be, could sue, in turn, the advisory board members in case the activity of such body is the reason for or contributed to determine the reason for the action suffered from third parties. In this case, the corporate bodies may request the advisory board to be held harmless and indemnified.

Furthermore, the members of the advisory board may be liable for a breach of the service contract. Any non-performance gives the aggrieved party a right to damages either exclusively or in conjunction with any other remedies. The recovery of damages may include the loss suffered by the aggrieved party, as well as the loss of gains.

7.4.5.2 Standard of diligence

Advisory board members are required to act with the diligence imposed by the nature of their appointment and their specific competence. In general, they have to take all the necessary actions in order to prevent any damages to the company.

7.4.5.3 Non-competition obligation

The company shall be entitled to claim damages from a member of the advisory board in case of breach of a non-competition obligation. It is advisable to insert a specific clause in the service agreement, if any, or to envisage the signing of a statement whereby the non-competition obligation is undertaken, specifying the kind of activity, the geographical area of interest and the duration, which may not exceed 5 years.

7.4.5.4 Limitation of liability

Due to the contractual freedom in ruling advisory boards, there are no fundamental objections to include liability limitations in favour of the advisory board members in the articles of association, or in the relevant appointment resolutions or the individual service agreements, save in case of gross negligence or wilful misconduct.

7.5 Termination

There are no legal regulations on the termination of advisory board members; therefore, the general principles of company law apply.

The members of the advisory board may leave their office for different reasons. Termination of the assignment can be regulated by a statutory clause, by the minutes adopted by the competent corporate body approving their appointment, by the internal regulation that the board has decided to establish or that has been established by other corporate bodies or by the service contract. However, there are no rules contained in the ICC or in other regulations that govern the termination of the assignment.

The reasons for the termination of the advisory board membership in a medium or small or family controlled company are detailed in the following paragraph 5.1.

7.5.1 Termination with regard to a certain member

The membership may be automatically terminated at the expiry date of the board or upon fulfilment of the tasks assigned to it and the achievement of the purpose for which the advisory board was set up.

Termination may occur by dismissal or resignation from office.

7.5.1.1 Automatic termination

The assignment can cease because it was granted for a fixed term or in case of overcoming absence of the eligibility requirements.

Another cause of termination of the assignment is the death of the member or the abolition of the advisory board.

If the member in question has taken on the task by virtue of a service agreement, the same may provide for an expiry date.

7.5.1.2 Revocation by the competent appointing body

Revocation can be caused by the non-fulfilment of duties and by failure to perform the tasks assigned. Generally, the revocation finds its foundation in the loss of the relationship of trust.

It should not be based on a mere disagreement with the revoked member.

However, pursuant to a notarial orientation, it is possible to provide in the articles of association that no compensation is due for damages caused to directors who have been revoked without just cause. This rule could be contemplated by clauses in the articles of association governing the advisory board.

7.5.1.3 Resignation

Each member of the advisory board may resign at any time. The presence of a just cause is not necessary, and it is not necessary to accept the resignation. Among other things, resignation could depend on the existence of significant conflicts of interests that jeopardise the action of the relevant members inside the advisory board.

7.5.1.4 Termination of service contract

The termination of the service contract may take place by a member of the advisory board or by mutual agreement.

A consensual termination of an advisory board mandate is possible at any time and does not require a good reason.

Ivan Kaisarov and Victor Mukhin

Chapter 8
Russia

8.1 Introduction

In Russia,[1] the law only provides for a mandatory supervisory body – a so-called supervisory board or board of directors – for public joint stock companies (JSCs) and for non-public JSCs with more than 50 shareholders. In all other cases, a supervisory body (board of directors) is voluntary.

In most cases, medium-sized enterprises, and in particular family owned businesses, are not established in the form of JSCs. As it was mentioned, for them, the only question that usually arises is the formation of a voluntary supervisory body (board of directors). The term "advisory board" could be used as a generic term for the various forms of advisory bodies, including supervisory boards (boards of directors) with appropriate advisory functions.

The concept of advisory boards (not in the form of supervisory boards) is quite new and is not regulated by current legislation or judicial practice, nor has it been addressed by legal doctrine. We have found several articles on advisory boards and their applicability in Russia from a business perspective;[2] however, we did not find any detailed legal analysis in this regard.

Russian law does not prohibit the creation of such bodies as long as there is no violation of the corporate structure imposed by mandatory legal provisions, including in the intersection with other bodies' mandated competence. In view of this, various alternatives are used today when establishing advisory boards in Russia.

On 1 January 2019 there were 3,458,812 commercial companies in Russia and 3,345,098 of them were limited liability companies (LLCs).[3] LLCs (Obshestvo s ogranichennoy otvetstvennostyu (OOO)) are particularly prevalent among medium-sized and family enterprises in Russia. The following considerations therefore focus on this particular form of incorporation.

---

1 We would like to thank the following contributing authors: Daria Atamanova and Daniil Nikolskiy.
2 For example, https://cyberleninka.ru/article/v/sovet-direktorov-kak-organ-upravleniya-srednimi-i-malymi-kompaniyami (accessed 31 October 2019), http://nand.ru/professional-information/and_library/17148/ (accessed 31 October 2019).
3 https://www.nalog.ru/rn77/related_activities/statistics_and_analytics/forms/7243238/ (accessed 31 October 2019).

https://doi.org/10.1515/9783110666182-008

8.2 Concept and definition, delimitation from other corporate bodies

On closer examination of the advisory board in medium-sized and family owned companies, it must first be clarified what is meant by such a body and how an advisory board distinguishes itself from a supervisory board or board of directors.

8.2.1 Concept

Initially, advisory (consulting) boards were established under federal and regional government bodies in Russia, for example, the Scientific Advisory Board of the Supreme Court of the Russian Federation[4] and the advisory board on the implementation of state national policy in St Petersburg under the government of St Petersburg. Such boards were therefore in Russia usually associated with public authorities.

Subsequently, with the development of economic activities, advisory boards began to appear in state-owned companies, and then in private companies, including medium-sized and family enterprises. Unfortunately, medium-sized and family enterprises do not publish information on whether they have an advisory board; however, we have found advisory boards in large private companies, for example, the advisory board of the public joint-stock company VTB Bank.[5]

As stated above, the concept of advisory boards is not very familiar in Russian law, except advisory boards in the form of supervisory boards or boards of directors with advisory functions. There is therefore no legal definition of the term. However, and despite the lack of such regulation, the Russian business community had adopted the general concept of "advisory board" from Western countries and nowadays sometimes establishes such bodies in its corporate structures.

In general, an advisory board can be defined as a voluntarily established body that lacks the functions of the governing bodies in a company or other legal entity (like the general meeting of shareholders, the board of directors or an executive body), the ultimate purpose of which is to advise the company's owners or management and to make recommendations on strategic issues in business activities.

---

4 https://www.vsrf.ru/about/structure/?section=scientific_advisory (accessed 31 October 2019).
5 https://www.vtb.ru/akcionery-i-investory/informaciya-dlya-akcionerov/konsultacionnyj-sovet-akcionerov/ (accessed 31 October 2019).

8.2.2 Distinction from supervisory boards (board of directors)

Advisory boards are often confused with supervisory boards or a board of directors. Supervisory boards and a board of directors are in this regard quite similar and we will only use the term "board of directors" in the following. The main distinction between a board of directors and an advisory board is whether the board has a governing function.

A board of directors is a governing body for JSCs or LLCs, whose competence, activities and liability are regulated by Russian Federal Law No. 208-ФЗ of 26 December 1995 "On Joint-Stock Companies" (hereinafter the Law "On JSCs") and Russian Federal Law No.99-ФЗ of 08 February 1998 "On Limited Liability Companies" (hereinafter the Law "On LLCs"). Members of boards of directors may adopt resolutions that are binding on the executive body, and must bear responsibility for these decisions. In some cases, as was mentioned, the creation of a supervisory board is mandatory (Article 64 (1) and Article 97 (3) of the Law "On JSCs").

Generally, boards of directors perform the following functions (one of them or their combination):

- a supervising function: The board of directors controls the activity of the executive body and provides approval for certain transactions or actions to ensure that the interests of the company's owners are safeguarded
- a management function: The board of directors defines strategic plans for the development of the company and its activities, and supports the executive body in its management functions
- an advisory function: The board of directors provides advice and recommendations to the executive body, top managers, or shareholders

Usually the board of directors performs mostly supervisory functions in Russia. That is why in most cases, a board of directors is indeed established in large firms, to control the activity of the executive body and to ensure that the interests of the company's owners are safeguarded.

In contrast, advisory boards lack such a governing function. Decisions made by advisory boards are considered as recommendations and do not have any binding power upon the executive body. The creation of an advisory board is always voluntary.

Additionally, we would like to address the issue whether a board of directors could function only in an advisory capacity. We believe that a board of directors without any binding authority, including management function or supervisory function, could be considered as a separate body and not as a board of directors. We do not have relevant court practice in this regard; however we assume that an advisory board in the form of a board of directors should have some supervising or management functions and binding powers; otherwise it should be considered as a separate body.

Therefore, there is a certain dispute in the doctrine regarding the role of advisory boards in Russia. Some authors consider an advisory board as an intermediate step to the formation of a board of directors, since the range of tasks addressed by these bodies is similar.[6] Others believe that an advisory board is a body that is in no way connected with the board of directors and has completely different goals.

Thus, advisory boards will be analysed according to the two following approaches in this document:

- the advisory board as a board of directors, including any committees of the board of directors, with advisory function or its elements among other functions
- the advisory board as a separate body in the company's governance structure on the basis of the articles of association or of other local regulations

8.3 Establishment, organisation and operations

8.3.1 Establishment

As stated above, there are two options available to establish an advisory board in Russia: in the form of a board of directors, or as a separate organ in the company. An advisory board can be set up at the same time as the company is founded or at any later point by amending its articles of association or adopting additional internal regulations. In any case, questions related to the establishment of the body itself, to its internal organisation, and to its subsequent activities, must also be regulated.

In most cases, however, advisory boards are only established at a later point after the company's incorporation if a specific need arises for its establishment due to a particular development or business problem to be resolved.

8.3.1.1 Establishment of an advisory board in the form of board of directors

Certainly, the concepts of advisory board and board of directors are fundamentally different. However, due to the flexible regulation of supervisory boards in Russia, especially for the LLCs, some companies establish an advisory board in the form of a board of directors with an advisory function among other (supervisory and management) functions. One of the main reasons for doing this is the similar nature of key issues that are handled by members of advisory boards and boards of directors in medium-sized companies, with the real managerial power being in practice concentrated in the hands of the shareholders.[7]

---

6 http://www.bossmag.ru/rubrics/boss-v-pomoshh/menedzhment/advisory-board-ili-nedostayushhee-zveno.html (accessed 12 October 2019).
7 https://iims.hse.ru/data/2015/02/04/1105766226/материалы_для%20семинара_НСКУ.pdf (accessed 16 October 2019).

The Law "On LLCs" contains a minimum of legal norms regulating how boards of directors function. Under Article 32 (2), the company's articles of association may provide for the formation of a board of directors in the company. Also procedures regulating the formation and functioning of the board of directors, as well as the termination of the mandate and the powers of its members and chairman, should all be determined by its articles of association. In addition, shareholders may approve internal regulations to provide a more detailed regulation of the board of directors, including the establishment of different committees answering to the board of directors.

An advisory board in the form of a board of directors may already be decided in the company's original articles of association before it commences its operations at the incorporation stage. Another option is that shareholders of the company may resolve to establish a board of directors at a later stage of development of the company. In this case, it is necessary to amend the articles of association and to register these amendments in the Russian state trade register of companies (EGRUL).

Once a board of directors is established in the articles of associations, its members are appointed by resolution of the general meeting of shareholders, according to the procedure decided in the articles of association. The number of directors in the board of directors should be regulated by the articles of association. If the executive body of the company is collegial, members of the executive should not constitute more than one-quarter of the board of directors; see Article 32 (2) of the law. If the company has a sole executive body (general director), this person cannot simultaneously be chairman of the board of directors.

Different specialised committees may also be set up, either as part of the board of directors, or separate to it but under its authority. Under earlier versions of the Law "On JSCs", the creation of committees within the board of directors was not regulated by law, but was considered by the Corporate Governance Code[8] as best practice for joint-stock companies, and such constructions could also be used for LLCs. Usually, such committees are regulated in additional internal regulations approved by the shareholders, and not in the articles of association.

If the committees are an integrated part of the board of directors, they normally only include members of the board of directors who are specialists within a particular area. Committees that are established separately from the board of directors could in contrast include other individuals who are not members of the board of directors and may be tasked with carrying out auxiliary functions that contribute to increasing the efficiency of the board of directors,[9] for example, reviewing materials, giving conclusions and presenting draft decisions. Usually the documents prepared by such committees are of an advisory nature and are

---

8 Note of the Bank of Russia "On the Corporate Governance Code" dated 10 April 2014 No. 06-52/2463.
9 https://www.mrsk-1.ru/common/upload/docs/polowenie_kkiv_0108.pdf (accessed 27 October 2019).

prepared for the board of directors. Such external committees are in their nature very similar to the establishment of an advisory board as a separate body (please see Section 8.3.1.2).

8.3.1.2 Establishment of a separate body

Article 53 (1) of the Russian Civil Code stipulates that the legal entity shall acquire rights and duties through the actions of its corporate bodies, in accordance with the law, other legal acts and with the company's incorporating documents. The formation and competence of the various bodies is regulated by law and by the company's incorporating documents; cf. Article 53 (1) of the Russian Civil Code. According to Article 12 of the Law "On LLCs", the articles of association may also contain any other provisions that are not incompatible with mandatory provision of this law or other federal laws.

Thus, the establishment of separate bodies in a legal entity, independently and additionally to the bodies that are prescribed by law, is not prohibited. All details regarding the composition, tasks and competence of such separate bodies should be anchored in the articles of association. It is important to avoid any gaps in regulation by adopting very detailed provisions, since such voluntary bodies are not regulated by legislation. To avoid making the articles of association too detail-heavy, a hybrid solution that can be recommended would be to only include there the basic provisions establishing the body, but to move most of the details of procedures and specifics to a separate internal regulation.

Despite the fact that any gaps in the regulation of the advisory board should be avoided, which requires a detailed regulation of its activities, the operations of such an advisory board should be approached in a flexible manner. Meetings may be held as many times as necessary. A strict agenda is not necessary; the course of the discussion itself forms a list of current issues to be resolved by this body. A conversation at a meeting can go in different directions, but will meet the important challenges to find answers.

In this respect, it is advisable to provide most of the details of the procedures of the advisory board in the separate internal regulation to facilitate making subsequent changes rather than frequently making amendments to the articles of association. The chairman of the advisory board, who should have special competence as a leader, summons and chairs meetings of the advisory board. It is recommended that meetings should be summoned long enough in advance to allow all members to prepare sufficiently.

Potentially advisory boards can be established by the company's shareholders in internal regulations without any references to such body being made in the articles of association. Strictly speaking, such an approach does not meet the requirements of Russian corporate law, because, as aforementioned, the establishment and competence of corporate bodies should be as regulated by law and by the company's incorporating documents (articles of association). However, if a separate body is only to provide recommendations to other bodies or to the shareholders, and does not violate the interests and competences of other bodies, we do not see the impediment in setting up separate bodies in this way as a purely internal matter.

Name of the advisory board as a separate body

Article 53 (1) of the Russian Civil Code gives broad competence to shareholders to regulate all issues concerning the establishment and functions of the legal entity's corporate bodies in the articles of association. Since there is no specific regulation for separate non-governing bodies, shareholders have absolute powers in determining which name a separate body should have.

There is no doubt that the terminology used in the body's name cannot be decisive for its function and competence, however, it may be illustrative and reflect to some extent the role played by that body in the corporate structure.

In Russian business practice, such advisory bodies are described in different ways. The most commonly used names are board of recommendations (*recomendatelniy sovet*), consultative-advisory body (*konsultativno-soveshatelniy organ*) and expert board (*expertniy sovet*). In some cases, companies also add a reference to a particular governing body in order to indicate a nexus between them, for example, a "shareholders' advisory board" or the "general director's consultative board". A range of different names are thus available for separate advisory boards.

8.3.2 Organisation and operations

8.3.2.1 Organisation and operations of advisory boards in the form of a board of directors

Pursuant to Article 32 (2) of the Law "On LLCs", the authority of the board of directors shall be determined by the company's articles of association and in accordance with the law. The law provides an indicative and non-exhaustive list of competences that may be assigned to the board of directors:
- formulating fundamental principles for the company's activities
- establishing, appointing and dismissing executive bodies, as well as any decision to outsource the executive functions to a third-party commercial organisation (management company) or to an individual entrepreneur (a "manager"), the appointment of such a manager and the terms of the corresponding managing agreement entered into

- deciding on the amount of remuneration and compensation to the sole executive body or to members of the collegial executive body, as the case may be, or
  to the manager
- deciding on the company's participation in business associations or other co-
  operation forums for commercial organisations
- endorsing major transactions where provided for by the Law "On LLCs"
- other issues provided for by the Law "On LLCs", as well as issues provided for
  by the articles of association and that are not given to the authority of the general meeting of shareholders or to the executive body

Russian legislation provides wide opportunities for the shareholders to define the
powers and role of the board of directors. Nevertheless, the authority of the board
of directors should not overlap with the imperatively established competence of the
general meeting of shareholders and the executive body.

Thus, shareholders can decide that the advisory function of the board of directors is its main function, or merely one of its functions among others (supervising,
managing, etc.).

The operations and procedures for meetings of the board of directors in LLCs
are not regulated in detail in the law. Therefore, the shareholders must adopt the
necessary provisions in the articles of association, in particular the board's competence, the procedure for the election of its chairman, how many meetings should be
held per year, which form the meetings should have (in person, via conference
calls, etc.), the procedure of the call of the meeting of the board of directors, the
number of members, the procedure for the adoption of decisions, etc.

8.3.2.2 Organisation and operations of advisory board in form of a separate body

Like with a board of directors, the shareholders are free to define the authority and
procedures for the functioning of the advisory board, in the articles of association
or in other local regulations. As a separate body, the advisory board may adopt resolutions to the address of shareholders or the executive body, which do not have
any binding power for the addressees.

In the form of a separate body, the advisory board only exercises advisory or
consultative functions, and therefore the members of the advisory board are not
obliged to adopt written resolutions on the relevant agenda items; however, it is
recommended to record somehow the issues that were discussed and possible resolutions for them, so shareholders can consider them when they adopt strategic
decisions. Nevertheless, a different approach could be used, including written resolutions and minutes.

8.4 Members, breach of duty and liability

8.4.1 Members

The shareholders are free to choose the structure, composition and number of members of any advisory board. The size of the advisory board depends on the interests of the company, its type of business and goals justifying the establishment of the advisory board. Usually this is a group of professionals assembled by the owner with the aim of exchanging experience and developing solutions that require a thorough discussion. In most cases, the group is formed by owners (shareholders), according to one single criterion, namely what competences are needed in the business at that moment.[10]

The advisory board is composed of its members. Only physical persons (and not legal entities) may be members of the advisory boards no matter whether as part of a board of directors or as a separate body. Also, the tasks and powers delegated to the advisory board shall be exercised by its members personally. If the advisory board is in the form of a board of directors, there is a direct prohibition to delegate members' votes to a different person. We assume that the same approach should be used for advisory boards as separate bodies in the corporate structure; otherwise it would make this body useless if members do not personally participate in discussions.

A member of the advisory board may be appointed from among the company's shareholders, from among the company's employees or indeed it is possible to appoint individuals who neither hold shares in the company nor are employed by it. However, to best perform the board's advisory functions, it is recommended to appoint independent experts who may provide "third-party opinions" on the issue discussed.

Once the appropriate candidates have been determined, they must be appointed by the shareholders decision. Additionally, the shareholders may decide to conclude with elected candidates employment agreements or so called "civil law" contracts specifying the rights and duties of the members of the advisory board. If the members of the advisory board violate their duties, they may be held liable.

8.4.2 General duties

8.4.2.1 Advising duty

Usually, in medium-sized companies shareholders hold most of the powers and make all strategic and main decisions, while other bodies just follow them without having

---

10 http://nand.ru/professional-information/and_library/17148/ (accessed 12 October 2019).

broad independence.[11] Therefore, such owners are initiators to establish the advisory board to receive "third-party opinions". The duties of the advisory board members result from the competence and tasks assigned by the shareholders. The tasks of the advisory board can be very different according to the purposes pursued by its appointment. However, in Russia the competence usually is limited to a purely non-binding consultancy/advisory function, except if it is in the form of a board of directors, which can perform broader functions, including management and supervision.

Thus, the main duty of the advisory board in Russia is to provide advice and consultation to shareholders. Due to this, the scope of the advice to be provided by members of the advisory board depends upon the particular circumstances and business situation of the company; the more difficult or crisis-driven, the more intensive the advisory services should be rendered.

The expert opinion of the advisory board is required, both for specific questions of the owners of the company, but also unsolicited, if the advisory board identifies a corresponding need. This is a permanent, continuous task that is future-oriented and serves to resolve current issues in the most efficient way. This requires a constant flow of information from the side of shareholders and operational management.

8.4.2.2 Duty of loyalty and good faith

The advisory board and its members are committed to the interests of the company. Russian Civil Code in Article 53 (3) directly provides that members of the body of the company must act reasonably and in good faith. The interests of the company's shareholders should only be taken into account to the extent that they are compatible with the overall interests of the company to be considered by the advisory board. At the same time, considering that an advisory board may be established as a separate authority and such bodies are not very common in Russia, it is recommended to directly include such duty for the members in the articles of association, contracts with the members or other internal corporate regulation.

In addition, the interests of the company must be safeguarded and there is an obligation not to take into account any of their own or other interests in the exercise of the advisory board rights and duties and thus conflict of interest provisions and procedures should be additionally established, including a duty to inform the owner of the company or other body about it and, possibly, not to participate in certain meetings.

---

11 https://secretmag.ru/opinions/igor-rozanov-zachem-privlekat-v-biznes-storonnih-lyudej-chem-konsultativnyj-sovet-luchshe-soveta-direktorov.htm (accessed 25 October 2019).

8.4.2.3 Duty of confidentiality

Members of an advisory board must maintain confidentiality regarding certain information related to the company's activities that have become known to them through their activities on the advisory board. The obligation to maintain confidentiality should apply to all confidential information related to the business of the company, its intellectual property and other information, which are not intended to become known according to an objectively assessed need for secrecy on the part of the company. For this reason, it is highly recommended to conclude non-disclosure agreements with the members of the advisory board or to include equivalent provisions in their contracts. In some cases, for example for trade secrets or know-how, additional internal regulations are required in this regard.

Considering that the duty of confidentiality is mostly contractual in nature, it is necessary to provide for liability if there are violations. The type of liability will depend on the type of information that was disclosed and the type of contract that was concluded with the individual member of the advisory board. For example, disclosure of a commercial secret may lead to criminal liability under the Russian Criminal Code. At the same time, disclosure of ordinary confidential information may lead to civil liability in the form of damages or penalties only.

If employment contracts are concluded with the members of the advisory board, their liability will be limited to direct damage only, and, usually, in such cases, it is hard to bring an employee to material liability for disclosure of confidential information. Thus, employment contracts are not very efficient for cases related to confidential information, except if it is commercial secret information or know-how, which have special regulation and carry a particular liability in Russia.

8.4.3 Advisory board in the form of board of directors and liability of the members

8.4.3.1 Legal relationships with members of the advisory board in the form of board of directors

Employment contract

According to the position existing in the legal literature, which is sometimes used in practice, it is possible to structure the legal relationship between the members of the board of directors and the company using employment contracts. However, there are many disadvantages with such an approach, as Russian employment law has mostly peremptory norms that aim to protect the rights and legitimate interests of employees and are not flexible when it comes to the terms of employment contracts. Boards of directors frequently gather on an ad hoc basis, while, as a general rule, employment contracts have to be concluded for an indefinite period. This circumstance may cause unnecessary expenses related to the payment of salaries for periods when members of the board did not conduct any activities.

Moreover, it is not possible to terminate a contract with the employee without cause. The list of causes is listed exhaustively in the labour code, and is not flexible. Therefore, a situation may happen when a term of appointment of a member of the board will end, but it would be still impossible to terminate the employment contract at the company's discretion if there are no breaches of contract from the side of the board member.

Thus, the practice of concluding individual employment contracts with the members should be assessed as quite inconvenient and inefficient.

Service contract

The possibility of regulating the company's relations with members of the board of directors by concluding service contracts is more appropriate, as service contracts are more suitable for the nature of a legal relationship existing between the member of the board and the company. Under a service contract, the company would not be obliged to provide the same guarantees that must be provided under an employment contract. Moreover, service contracts allow to stipulate a more flexible remuneration system; i.e., it would be possible to pay remuneration only for those periods when a member actually takes part in the board's meetings. Additionally, service contracts allow unilateral termination by any party, thus, a situation of it being impossible to terminate the contract will not happen. Therefore, we consider the service contract being the best option for structuring a company's relationships with members of the board.

In practice, it commonly happens when a person is appointed to a board of directors by the general meeting of members (shareholders [owners]) of the company that no contract is concluded with this person at all. We consider these situations as highly precarious, since in a case of litigation the full status of this person will remain unclear and this will entail questions regarding the legal relationship between the company and the member of the board.

Remuneration

Members of the board can exercise their authorities on both a paid and unpaid basis if a service contract was concluded. Employment contracts always require remuneration.

Options

Large companies in Russia (especially in the oil industry) frequently choose not to use a traditional remuneration system for their board of directors, but instead they implement option programmes. Option programmes allow the members of the board to obtain shares in the company upon achievement of certain financial results. Nevertheless, throughout the duration of the option programme, the members of the board remain the owners of options that guarantee the right to acquire shares in the future. Options programmes may provide several methods for transferring rights to the acquired shares. Such programmes are generally good motivators and allow for achieving decent financial results and could be used in medium-sized and family companies also for advisory board members.

8.4.3.2 Liability of members of the board of directors

The liability of the members of the board of directors is regulated by the Russian Civil Code (Article 53.1) and the Law "On LLCs" (Article 44). According to these provisions each member of the company's various bodies must act reasonably and in good faith. If the actions (or omissions) of the members of the board of directors cause damage to the company, it is possible to claim damages from them. Any claim may be brought against either present or former members of the board of directors. Also, under Article 53.1 (5) of the Russian Civil Code, the liability of members of the board of directors could be limited under a separate agreement.

A breach of duties can lead to the (immediate) termination of the corporative relationship to the company. It also may lead to the termination of service contracts for good cause without notice period if such was provided by the service contract. If an employment contract was concluded, it may be difficult to terminate it, because under Russian employment law there is exhausted list of grounds for termination and none of these grounds are appropriate for such a situation.

However, it should be noted that regarding advisory functions it would be quite difficult to bring members of the board of director to liability. One of the main reasons for dismissal of claims against members of the board of directors is the lack of regulation of the specific obligations of the members of the board. Unlike the sole executive body, a member of the board does not act on behalf of the company and as a general rule does not have representative powers towards third parties. Thus, a causal connection between the actions and damage caused is not always obvious, especially regarding the board's advisory function.

Damages cannot be recovered from members of the board of directors who voted against the decision that caused damages to the company (or those who abstained from voting).

8.4.4 Advisory board in the form of separate body and liability of the members

8.4.4.1 Legal relationships with members of the advisory board in the form of separate body

Advisory boards are not directly regulated in Russian legislation, however, the instruments to structure the legal relationships with members of the board that were described above in relation to the board of directors, as well as the remarks regarding remuneration that were given, are also applicable to advisory boards as separate bodies.

8.4.4.2 Liability of the members of the advisory board in the form of separate body

As for the responsibility of members of such a body, since any document that is prepared by the advisory board typically has an advisory nature, internal regulations usually do not contain provisions on liability. Nevertheless, based on the general provisions of Russian civil law, it is possible to hold members of the advisory board liable if they commit actions that are obviously aimed at causing harm to the company. However, we are not aware of such cases in practice. At the same time, members of the advisory board bear responsibility related to the duty of confidentiality as a contractual duty if a contract to that effect was concluded (please see Section 8.4.2.3).

8.5 Termination

Regarding the termination of advisory boards, it is necessary to distinguish between the termination of an advisory board as a body and termination of the legal connections between its members and company they serve.

8.5.1 Termination of advisory boards as a body

8.5.1.1 Board of directors

The termination of an advisory board in the form of a board of directors is a procedure involving two decisions.

First, upon deciding on termination, the general meeting of shareholders should strip advisory directors from their governing powers. This is done by passing a respective resolution by majority of voices of shareholders who attended the meeting. Such termination of powers will take effect on a date specified in resolution.

Changing the company structure to remove the board of directors is an extra step that should be taken to prevent any competence from becoming "vacant". Decisions on changing the board's structure (amendments to the board's statute or termination of the advisory committee) is passed by a simple majority of votes.

After these decisions are made, the board of directors no longer exists as a part of the company and its functions are transferred to other bodies according to legislation and the company's articles of association. The articles of association must be amended to reflect the new corporate structure and then registered in the Russian state trade register of companies (EGRUL).

8.5.1.2 Separate governing body

As Russian corporate legislation provides relative freedom to the shareholders to establish non-defined bodies inside the company, it also does not limit them from choosing ways to terminate such bodies. Therefore, the termination of an advisory board as a separate governing body is a process wholly regulated by shareholders' will as defined in the articles of association or in internal regulations.

The most common and legislation-friendly procedure for termination is by a resolution of the general meeting of shareholders' decision that is carried out according to the same procedure as mentioned in Section 8.5.1.1. Alongside the decision on termination, shareholders can redistribute the ex-advisory board's powers to other bodies and rescind superfluous internal documents.

Other procedures for the termination of the board's activities can be established by the articles of association, and the competence for the advisory board to establish and terminate such contracts could be held by different bodies.

After fulfilling all steps of termination provided by the company's articles of association the separate governing body of advisory board is duly terminated. If there were any amendments to the article of association these must be registered in the Russian company registry (EGRUL).

8.5.2 Termination of legal connections with advisors

Russian law provides for a lot of ways for a company to establish legal connections with its advisors, and each type is terminated according to procedure specified in different sections of legislation.

8.5.2.1 Corporate connection

An advisor as a part of a governing body has a special corporate connection with the company established by the resolution of its authorised body. The relationship between the company and the members of its board of directors or advisory board, which are established by the articles of association, are terminated by reverting the appointment decision, or by passing a resolution on dismissal. Such decisions are only regulated in the internal regulations of Russian corporate law, and are not subject to any limitations or restrictions.

8.5.2.2 Employment

If members of the advisory board have concluded employment contracts, their termination is regulated by employment law. The Russian Labor Code has a full chapter (no. 13) that provides for the termination of employment contracts. Most grounds for termination can be classified into the following categories:
– by common will of both parties
– by the unilateral will of the employer or the employee
– certain circumstances due to which the employee no longer can be employed

While the first one's procedure is rather simple (termination is carried out by an agreement on the contract's termination), unilateral termination is strictly regulated by the Labor Code. It names more than a dozen situations when the employer can terminate the contract (Article 81 of the Russian Employment Code), but all of these are rather specific: liquidation of the company, contractual breach by the employee, fraud, etc. Thus, dismissal could be a significant issue for the executive body of the company (general directors must sign employment contracts in Russia and dismiss employees).

Therefore, Russian companies prefer to terminate employment contracts by common agreement and negotiate with the advisor his future dismissal. This procedure causes less negative impact for both parties and does not take longer than a few days, which is useful in a change of control.

8.5.2.3 Service

As mentioned, companies usually would like to avoid entering into employment contracts with advisors who are considered more like freelancers than actual workers. To legally justify compensation for their knowledge and service, many companies conclude service contracts under the Russian Civil Code.

Such contracts, thanks to the general freedom of contract, provide for high level of flexibility as to the termination of the agreements. As with establishing the advisory board under the articles of association, the procedure to terminate the service contracts is to be fully agreed between the parties. It is possible, for example, to tie the termination to a different body in the company adopting a decision to dismiss the member, or by expiration of a member's mandate.

Anthony Turner
Chapter 9
United Kingdom

This chapter looks at the role and structure of advisory councils in the United Kingdom. The focus of the chapter is principally private corporate entities, and it does not focus on companies that are listed on public markets.

The chapter refers to advisory councils in the context of private companies, but the principles are equally applicable to all other entities, for example, limited liability partnerships, public companies and profit and not-for-profit companies. The principles in this chapter apply as equally to small domestic companies as they do to large international groups.

9.1 Introduction to advisory councils

An advisory council is a body of two or more persons appointed by a company to fulfil a particular role or function. As the name suggests, it is generally advisory in nature and it does not have the authority to make decisions in relation to the company, and nor will it be expected to do so. The advisory council's role will need to be defined – frequently a bespoke process – but it will generally be to advise or produce recommendations to the board, which will make the relevant decision.

The term "advisory council" is not a term of art and it may be referred to as an "advisory board", an "advisory committee", an "advisory body" or a "family council".

Advisory councils are not widely used in the United Kingdom and, although there are a number of examples of their use, they are not commonplace.

Advisory councils are not creations of statute, and there is no existing legal framework or body of law that helps define what an advisory council is and how it should act. As such, they will often be bespoke creations put in place by a company in order to fulfil a specific function or role, or achieve a specific result.

The benefit of the lack of a legal framework is that they can be used for a wide variety of purposes and are not necessarily restricted in terms of structure or function. This flexibility is therefore an advantage but, given the lack of a default framework, the creation and management of an advisory council will often need detailed thought.

There is also no prescribed role of an advisory council and it can therefore be incredibly flexible, in order to support companies at all levels. The advisory council may serve to support the board, the employees or to act as a body that represents the view of shareholders or a company's wider stakeholders. It can be temporary or permanent and may look at a single issue or a range of issues.

https://doi.org/10.1515/9783110666182-009

An advisory council is not a substitute for other management and executive roles in a company. For example, a company must have a board of directors that should be comprised of a balanced selection of appropriate individuals so that alone it can operate as a fully functioning board. In the United Kingdom, company directors have a number of statutory and non-statutory duties, and these are duties for the board of directors and not any advisory council. The advisory council should therefore be in addition to, and not a replacement for, boards of directors. The same principles apply where an advisory council has a role representing the views of shareholders; it will not replace the shareholders or assume any of their rights, even though it may act as a conduit for the views of the shareholder base.

Advisory councils do not generally have any authority in relation to the company. As such, they cannot instruct the board or any employees to take, or not to take, any action, and the role is purely advisory. All decisions of a company should be taken by the board or employees (as appropriate) even though the recommendations of the advisory council may be persuasive. This is an important limitation to the role and remit of advisory councils: they should provide wise, and independent, counsel but not take decisions. This is particularly important given that the members of an advisory council are generally not subject to any formal duties or liability in terms of their decision making and actions. It would, therefore, in many cases, be inappropriate for the advisory council to take any decisions without there being clarity of their duties and accountability for any decisions they take.

It is important, for other reasons, that the advisory council does not exercise in practice any meaningful decision-making powers. In the United Kingdom a 'shadow' director is a person that has not been formally appointed as a director but on whose instructions the board of directors of a company is accustomed to act. This is a reasonably high standard, but care needs to be taken both in the setting up of the advisory council and in its continued management that the board of directors does not in any way abdicate its decision-making responsibilities in favour of that advisory council.

If a person is treated as a shadow director, they will be subject to all of the duties and obligations of directors. This will be particularly unattractive to individuals on the advisory council as they will not see themselves as having this role (nor will they often want to). This risk may be more acute in the context of smaller, early stage companies who may be fast moving and are still in the process of putting in place governance arrangements at a company level; here it may not be too difficult for an engaged advisory council by default to become involved in the direction and management of the company.

In creating an advisory council, there does need, as with a board of directors, to be a balance in the composition of that advisory council for it to be effective. Therefore, the composition, function and terms of service of those sitting on the advisory council is important and a great deal of thought should be given to this at the early stages of the process.

9.2 Why appoint an advisory council?

There are an infinite number of reasons why a company might appoint an advisory council and therefore there is no one size fits all in relation to this. However, there are several fairly common reasons for doing so, which are set out below.

Perhaps the most usual use for an advisory council is to provide independent strategic advice to the board of directors of the company. The advisory council is created to bolster the resources available to the existing board of directors and to act as a sounding board or as a discussion forum for the board of directors.

Advisory councils should therefore at least be a body of experience and knowledge, either in relation to the specific sector in which the appointing company is involved, or as a counterbalance where they have relevant knowledge that the company does not have but would benefit from. In many cases, those involved in advisory committees will have significant prior experience that is directly relevant to the appointing company.

An advisory council should not be a substitute for a balanced board of directors, but it may fill existing or temporary gaps in experience or knowledge while board appointments are made.

An advisory council may be appointed to deal with a specific issue affecting the company, such as international expansion, where the existing directors and employees do not have local knowledge of the relevant new countries or the complexities involved. Alternatively, it may be appointed for particular projects where the company and the board is not able to focus specifically on those projects, or they are at an early, feasibility stage and an advisory council could take a lead role in forming an initial view of the particular project.

An advisory council could be used as an informal dispute resolution mechanism where it would provide an independent view on particular issues where the board for whatever reason is struggling to reach an agreement. The advisory council would not make a decision or provide the answer but may provide a view on the issue in dispute that would be persuasive, or it may act as a form of mediator, helping the board reach a consensus position. The advisory council would know the company and its business – and would therefore be able to respond quickly – and could fulfil this role in a confidential way without additional cost or the need to put in place agreements with third parties.

The advisory council may have a purely business development role and its function would be to go out and sell the relevant company and to create strategic opportunities, or act as ambassadors. An allied reason may simply be to demonstrate credibility by having on its advisory council well-known or high-profile names. Where it is not appropriate for those advisory council members to be directors, the role of an advisory council may well suit this purpose. For example, those with the relevant credibility and experience to sit on an advisory council may not want the full time and onerous role of being a director of a company, and an advisory council allows them to be involved and to provide the company the benefit of their wisdom and experience but without necessarily a great time commitment.

In addition to providing a body of experienced people representing the company, an advisory council will often help show gravitas, good governance and an aspiration to grow into a company that is of a sufficient size and complexity to warrant a separate advisory council.

An advisory council could have a role as a mentor to the company, or key staff within it. It does not therefore need to be solely available to support the board of directors. There are examples of advisory councils being used as a sounding board for senior management, who can try out ideas and present to an advisory council, which can then help refine and shape the offering that is ultimately proposed to the board of directors.

In early stage and growth companies, an advisory council is often a useful support to the entrepreneur who is running the company. The entrepreneur may not want to be constrained by the formal appointment of other directors to the board (and may not be able or want to pay them) but will nonetheless want, or need, a body of people to turn to for advice and to discuss strategic objectives in confidence. The advantage of an advisory council, rather than an individual mentor, is that there is the benefit of collective discussion as well as a wider pool of experience to draw from.

Often an advisory board will represent the shareholders, or wider stakeholders, of a company. This is particularly relevant in the context of family businesses and sport bodies, each of which is considered below. An advisory council may also be used to provide a forum for key customers or potential customers of a company to comment on services, products or brand perception; here it is more a point of focus to receive and distil comments from these stakeholders than a body that gives advice.

It may also be a conduit for employee engagement, to allow employees to air their views (in a way that they would not do in front of their employer) and for the advisory council to form part of the process for wider employee engagement and grievances.

Finally, the advisory council can form a check and balance on the board but in a soft way. As it is unlikely to have any formal power to challenge the board, they will not be able to supplant any decisions made by the board. However, where an advisory council (made up of individuals with experience and knowledge) feels that the board is not acting in a proper way, it is often sensible to allow them to challenge the board and raise these concerns. From the perspective of the board, this should be a helpful check and ensures the directors review and test what they are doing since by definition the advisory council's view is likely to carry weight. Of course, a board has the final responsibility to make any decisions and they may nonetheless choose not to follow the recommendations of the advisory council.

9.3 Creation of an advisory council

There are several ways of constituting an advisory council.

9.3.1 Informal arrangements

There is no legal requirement to put in place any legal structure or documents to define the role and relationship of the advisory council, and it may be entirely informal. This is how, in many examples, an advisory council is set up and run. It is therefore possible to create an advisory council simply through discussions with the members; there is no need to formalise the role of the advisory council in writing.

Furthermore, there are no registration requirements for an advisory council; it does not need to be registered with Companies House and, as it is not a trading body, with the tax authorities (although the individual members may need to account for tax if they are remunerated). There is also no limitation on a company publicising the creation or existence of its advisory council.

The advantage of formalising the relationship is so that the advisory council has a clear remit and purpose. It is always helpful for there to be clear rules and an understanding of what is expected of the members of the advisory council. There is not a great deal of point in having an advisory council (unless it is purely as a figurehead) if the members of that council are not engaged in the role and adding value to the company. The company will also want to define (and in many cases limit) the role of the advisory council so that it is focused, and it does not spend time and effort in other areas that the company does not want it to.

Structure is also important for the members of the advisory council, so that they know what is expected of them and how and where they can contribute to the company. Equally, the members of the council will want to know what information and support they will be given by the company.

Even in informal arrangements, certain provisions should be legally binding between the company and the advisory council, namely:

- Confidentiality is often key, especially where confidential or sensitive information is given by the company to the advisory council, and this does need to be legally enforceable against the individual member of the advisory council on a breach. In many ways, putting in place binding agreements will give the company the confidence that it can freely share information with the advisory council, and this will be a benefit to both.
- Where the advisory council members are remunerated, there needs to be clarity on their status and appropriate provisions put in place to reflect the timing and the nature of the payment and any liability for tax. In many cases, the advisory council member will be a contractor to the company and will be responsible for

their own tax arrangements, and this should be reflected in the agreement together with appropriate protections for the company.
–   The advisory council will have limits. It is not a legal entity and cannot contract
or incur liabilities on its own behalf. Crucially it should not be able to incur liabilities on behalf of the company, and this needs to be clear to the advisory
council members. It would also be sensible when promoting the existence of the
advisory council to make clear that its members cannot make decisions or otherwise bind or incur liabilities on behalf of the company.

9.3.2 Committee of the board of directors of a company

An advisory council will often be appointed by the board of directors as a committee
of the board. This is a reasonably simple step to take and, provided that it is permitted by the company's constitution (Articles of Association (Articles) in the United
Kingdom), the board can resolve at any time to appoint an advisory council on terms
that it determines. These terms are normally set out in a formal board minute and
terms of reference that will define the role and scope of the committee. Although a
committee of the board, there is no objection in calling the committee an advisory
council, or any other similar name.

As a matter of company law in the United Kingdom, a committee of the board is
not required to include members of the board. As such, it is possible for a committee of the board to comprise persons who are not directors (and generally the directors will not sit on an advisory council), and this therefore allows the appointment
of an advisory council as a committee of the board.

There are a number of key points in the context of a committee that should be
borne in mind. The board does not (and should not) delegate any decision making
to the advisory council and the board needs to exercise sufficient oversight of the
committee. The board cannot delegate their duties as directors to that committee
and they will therefore need to ensure that there is a clear and robust purpose and
reporting lines in relation to that committee.

9.3.2.1 Contract

In practical terms, this is the usual way to appoint an advisory council. The contract
is often a series of individual agreements with the members of the advisory council
as well as terms of reference for the role of the committee.

A company could appoint a number of individuals on specific terms, such as a
consultancy agreement, to provide the "services" of an advisory council. The terms
of reference would probably (but do not need to be) contractually binding and
would set out the obligations and responsibilities of the relevant members of the

advisory council as well as the process for the appointment and functioning of that advisory council (see further in Section 9.4). The advantage of this structure is that the terms of reference can be changed by the company over time without the express need for the agreement of the advisory council.

9.3.2.2 Articles of association

It is possible to build the concept of the advisory council into the Articles of a company (i.e., the company's constitution). This is rarely done in a commercial context – but is more usual for sports and non-profit organisations (see Section 9.6) – as it will enshrine in the company's constitution the roles and responsibilities of the advisory council. Those Articles can only be put in place and changed by a special resolution of the shareholders (75 per cent of voting shareholders) and therefore if the advisory council is constituted in the Articles, control over the advisory council may, to a large extent, be taken away from the directors of the company.

There are advantages of this approach, especially where the company needs or wants to demonstrate positive commitment and engagement with a wider range of stakeholders. Enshrining the essential elements of the advisory council in the constitution is a powerful way of demonstrating this.

9.4 Terms of an advisory council

Given that there is no statutory or legislative model for advisory councils, there will need to be full terms of reference setting out the role and responsibilities of that advisory council. We have set out below several areas that we suggest should be covered. These are suggestions and, given the lack of formality required for an advisory council, it may be appropriate not to be too prescriptive in each case. However, the key is that it is absolutely clear about the role and purpose of the advisory council so as to make the most of it as a body. The terms of reference for an advisory council should reflect the creation, operation and termination of the council.

– Role of the council – this is the mission statement of the advisory council and should set out with clarity and in sufficient detail what is expected of the advisory council.
– Composition – the number of persons and any particular role that they might have on the advisory council should be set out. This may be prescriptive, and narrowly define the role of each member of the council, or it may be more flexible and simply appoint a number of individuals to the council with no formal roles or titles. An advisory council should not be too large to be unwieldy and it is usual therefore to include a maximum number of members of the advisory

council. The advisory council should be diverse and include a membership that has a balance of skills and personalities.

- Chair – any effective body needs an effective chair, and a great deal of thought will need to be given as to the identity of that chair. The chair will have certain specific obligations under the terms of reference, for example, running meetings and being the point of engagement with the board.
- Membership – the terms of reference would ideally set out the manner in which the advisory council members will be appointed or removed. We would expect the company to have an overarching power to appoint and remove members of the advisory council, but it may be appropriate for the advisory council itself to be able to appoint, or remove, additional persons to the advisory council.
- Terms of office – generally it is better to address the expected length of service of the members of the advisory council, ideally so there is a balance of long-term knowledge and experience combined with fresh thinking and a reasonably regular overhaul of the membership.
- There should be a great deal of flexibility here and if, for example, an individual feels that they are not able to commit the time and attention needed to contribute validly to the advisory council, then they too should feel that they are able to step aside.
- Confidentiality – to perform their role properly, the advisory council will probably need access to a degree of confidential information about the company. While United Kingdom law does impose obligations of confidentiality where confidential information is disclosed, it is sensible to ensure that legally binding terms of confidentiality are put in place between the company and each member of the advisory council. This could be set out in the terms of reference or, probably better, in the relevant appointment letter with the individual or a separate code of conduct that is signed by the relevant member.
- Access to information – a corollary of confidentiality is that the individuals will need to be given access to information for them to perform their role properly and effectively. The extent to which they are given (or are able to access) information will depend very much on the nature and role of the advisory council but in many cases it will not be appropriate for them to have full access to all aspects of the information of the company. It would also be normal for any information to be channelled through the board, which would need to consider in each case whether this was the correct information to be given to the relevant individuals of the advisory council.
- Conflicts – almost by definition members of an advisory council will have other commercial interests. In many cases, this breadth of interest will be an asset to the advisory council and may well be one of the reasons that the individual is appointed. However, it is good practice that the terms of reference include provisions dealing with actual or potential conflicts of interest of the relevant member of the council.

- At the very least, these should require that any such interests be disclosed, both to the company but also to the other members of the advisory council and a formal record of this should be kept. It is in the interests of all parties for there to be full transparency on conflicts so that appropriate action can be taken. It may be that because of a conflict the conflicted member will not be involved in certain roles of the advisory council or, in extremis, it may no longer be appropriate for them to continue to be a member. This disclosure process should at least be carried out before confirming an appointment to the council, and regularly updated as appropriate.
- Termination of membership – clearly a number of circumstances will lead to immediate termination of membership. Bankruptcy or any reputational issues will be key and should permit both the advisory council and the board to remove individuals as members of the advisory council forthwith in these circumstances. It may be useful to encourage participation to state that individuals will cease to be a member if they do not attend a certain number of meetings in any given period.
- Meetings – given it is a council of individuals, it is going to be useful for them to meet periodically. This should be at least twice a year (depending on the purpose of the advisory council) but may be more, or less, frequent as is felt appropriate. The manner in which meetings can be called, where they can be held and how they should be held would ideally be set out.
- Remuneration – members are not always remunerated, and it is a question for the company in each case. It may need to pay to ensure that it has the right persons on the advisory council or, because of the nature of the company or the relationship with the advisory council members, there may be no payment. Payment may be in cash, shares in the company or any other acceptable remuneration. The actual remuneration to be paid will need to be considered in each particular case and be documented.
- Employment – it is not expected that any member of an advisory council will be an employee as a result solely of membership of the council, and this would be unusual. If this is the case, then additional thought will need to be given to that role, and separate employment contracts put in place. Where the individuals of an advisory council are remunerated, it will often be appropriate to put in place a separate letter of appointment setting out the basic terms of their appointment and dealing with payment and related liabilities.

9.5 Family businesses

An advisory council can fulfil several useful functions for a family business, particularly one that has many family members not all of whom are shareholders. In these companies, the engagement between the (wider) family members and the company are important and the standard company law structures in the United Kingdom do not easily cater for the dynamics of a large family business.

There is often the balance (and tension) between, on the one hand, ensuring that the company is run in a professional and focused way for the financial benefit of the company (and therefore its shareholders), and reflecting the views and wishes of a family that may not have a direct involvement in the running of the company but that have a financial interest and an emotional attachment to the business.

This position is often particularly acute in the context of a family business where it is important that there is clarity of roles between the family and company (in order that the company is sufficiently well run for the benefit of the wider family) but recognising that in family companies there needs to be a greater level of engagement between the family (as shareholders or otherwise) and the company. This engagement will cover all relevant areas from the commercial decisions taken by the company, strategic change, the amount and frequency of distributions to shareholders and succession.

As such, an advisory council (perhaps better called a family council) is often an incredibly useful independent body to act as a conduit between the family on the one hand and the company (generally through the chair) on the other. This role for family companies is important both at the inception of any family governance arrangements, for example, the putting in place of a shareholders' agreement or a family charter for the family, as well as afterwards to ensure the efficient engagement between the family and the company.

The role of the family council is therefore double headed. On the one hand, it should engage with the shareholders and wider family to ensure that there is a process for engagement and interaction with the family council in relation to the family business. This may be time consuming and require meetings with the individual members as well as holding meetings for the wider family. This is distinct from shareholder meetings, which are proposed and run by the company for those persons who are shareholders only.

On the other hand, the family council should engage with the company. In order to do so there will need to be an active engagement with the board of the company, and it should have access to some of the key business plans and strategy of the company. The family council is advisory to the company in the sense that it represents the wider family and distils the view of the wider family of the way in which the company should be run.

The family council therefore acts as a conduit between the company and the family. This role cannot be underestimated, and a well-run family council will be a hugely important body in ensuring harmony. From the company's perspective, this takes a great deal of time off their hands and may put some sensible distance between the wider family (not all of whom are shareholders) and the business of running a company.

9.6 Sports bodies

The use of more formal advisory councils is not unusual in the context of sport governing bodies in the United Kingdom.

Perhaps the principal reason for this is that those governing bodies need to engage fully and properly with a wider stakeholder base of those who may not have a formal role in the governing body but who have an interest in the relevant sport, and an advisory council is one way of doing this.

This could, of course, be achieved in any of the ways set out above but often it is felt that to enshrine the role and powers of an advisory council in the Articles of the company is seen as an important and positive step of stakeholder engagement. Accordingly, these bodies choose to enshrine elements of the role and function of the council in their Articles. These bodies may also go further and give the advisory council specific obligations under the Articles. For example, they may need to consent to specific actions taken by the governing body, and they may be able to put resolutions to meetings or have access to remuneration of the members of the board.

It remains clear, however, that these councils, although enshrined in the Articles, are not the same as a board of directors nor are they members of the company and they have their own specific defined purpose within the Articles.

The current Code for Sports Governance in the United Kingdom – which applies to sports organisations that seek certain government funding –recommends a council and defines it as:

> A body forming part of the constitutional or organisational structure of a sport's national governing body . . . representing some or all of its stakeholders in some capacity, and having powers or rights with respect to its governance but which is not the board of the NGB [National Governing Body] (or a committee of the board) or the shareholders in general meeting.[1]

The role of the advisory council is to ensure engagement with stakeholders as part of ensuring a healthy democracy within the organisation, for the benefit of the organisation itself but also, principally, for the wider benefit of the sport.

Under the Code for Sports Governance, it is for the relevant sport organisations to determine the role of its council but the suggested roles that might be given to them are advisory and consultative. For example, they could include rights to an audience with the chair of the board or the board as a whole, the power to call a meeting of the members and to put resolutions to it and the power to be provided with information and to be consulted in relation to strategic matters.

---

1 https://www.uksport.gov.uk/resources/governance-code

Sabrina Bruno
Chapter 10
United States of America

10.1 Introduction

In USA there is no mandatory advisory and controlling body for corporations of any dimension. The corporate governance structure is the one-tier board where the general meeting of shareholders appoints the board of directors. No other body, apart from the board of directors, is contemplated under US legislation for corporations. Within the board, listed corporations may appoint internal committees with audit functions but this practice is not regulated under hard law and, in any case, the audit committee is not a separate body from the board of directors. This practice, however, is limited to listed corporations.

10.2 Concept and practice of voluntary advisory board

There is no legal definition under US law of the term "advisory board". Traditionally, colleges and universities or non-profit organisations (belonging to many sectors, from arts to foundations) voluntarily have appointed advisory boards to offer guidance, time, support, social and financial capital. These boards are mainly comprised of prominent volunteers from the community and industry who receive no compensation and who, actually, are expected to make donations to the institution. Commonly, there is no limit in the terms they may serve, and their appointment can be renewed. They usually meet a few times per year, but, in case they don't attend a certain number of meetings, may be relieved.

More recently, however, also profit organisations are starting to voluntarily appoint advisory boards: It happens with start-up or venture capital-backed companies (where advisory boards represent the interests of these investors) or other companies, both closely held family controlled or medium-sized entities and public companies. The aim is to receive support to grow and become established business. The sense is to avoid a myopic attitude in running an enterprise. This practice is becoming more and more relevant and advisory board programmes are organised to help business leaders in finding the right member to appoint in the advisory board. Sometimes business leaders join each other's advisory board to exchange the favour.

https://doi.org/10.1515/9783110666182-010

Another possibility, lately proposed, is to appoint a stakeholder advisory board within corporations to increase stakeholder consideration and improve social responsibility of firms; reference is made to representatives from all the major corporate stakeholder groups (from employees, vendors, customers, creditors, etc.).

10.2.1 Distinction from board of directors or board of trustees

The responsibilities of advisory boards are different from those of boards of directors or boards of trustees as they do not have authority – fiduciary, policymaking or otherwise – over the entity. In case of non-profit organisations members serve as ambassadors of the institution and because of their career and contacts, in business, public service, medicine, etc., can contribute to the institution's prestige and credibility. They mainly perform organisational activities to link to key stakeholders to strengthen ties and make them cooperate with the institutions also for fundraising purposes. In case of corporations the role of the advisory board is to give management and strategic advice.

Because there is no piece of legislation, there is a great deal of latitude on when and how to set up an advisory board. When it comes to start-up or other corporations, advisory boards can be structured both to help with the direct operation of the company and to release information on various business, legal and financial trends that may affect the business. Members may have various expertise – legal, accounting, marketing, financial or human resources – or they may be successful entrepreneurs from other industries who understand the basics of business and will view different business with a fresh eye. Of course, advisory boards do not have an active management role and they do not assume any liability for the company or for the advice they offer. Also, in cases of start-up or other corporations, advisory board members are rarely compensated. The idea is that, actually, advisory board members will benefit from such a role in a variety of tangible or intangible ways – such as being exposed to new ideas and perspectives and expanding their own networks.

10.3 Duties and liabilities of members of advisory boards

Members of advisory boards are not elected but chosen by invitation even though there is usually an agreement regulating the relationship between the advisory board and the entity. As said, they have no authority to make business decisions and do not owe fiduciary duties to the shareholders or other constituencies of the entity by virtue of their advisory role. This is the main difference from companies' directors who, by contrast, owe fiduciary duties and are subject to liability arising from any breach of those duties.

There is little case-law or other legal authority addressing the rights, duties and potential liabilities of board advisors.

It is believed that reference shall be made to basic principles of corporate law and corporate authority to structure the arrangements with advisory board members. Given the absence of any piece of legislation there is great latitude also with reference to the contents of such agreements. Usually they are written agreements and fix the precise duties and responsibilities depending on the entity's particular needs and objectives; but they may also have no formality and be made verbally. In both cases duties and responsibilities may vary from one entity to another. Commonly, such agreements clearly limit the advisory board members' exposure to liability. Generally, duties consist of providing the company with knowledge, expertise and connections that expand those of the entity's management and directors. In many cases, investors in companies financed by venture capital or private equity firms have a contractual right to appoint board observers to attend meetings and receive information available to the directors. A board observer represents the interests of the investor that appointed the observer, and therefore, from the company's perspective, the board observer is a mandatory requirement driven by the investors' rights and needs. For this reason, while observers may provide valuable advice and perspective to the board and company management similar to those by advisors, they may face some hostility from directors or management because they primarily protect the investor group they represent. Like board advisors, board observers attend and participate in meetings of a company's board of directors and are typically entitled to receive all information provided to board members. Also, like board advisors, board observers have no voting rights.

The imposition of fiduciary duties on members of board advisory boards by case-law would not be consistent with corporate or trust law that underpin fiduciary duties. Fiduciary duties arise whenever somebody manages an asset for the benefit of another party and, therefore, he shall comply with duties of care and loyalty in managing the asset for the beneficiary. In a corporation, directors owe fiduciary duties to the shareholders. By contrast, members of advisory boards are not elected by shareholders or other constituencies, do not manage somebody else's assets, have no authority to make business decisions for the company and therefore cannot be deemed, under corporate or trust law, owing fiduciary duties just because of the advisor role.

However, as for any other individual, members of an advisory board shall behave in good faith; otherwise potential liability may arise whenever the advisory board collectively, or one or more of its members, release advice that happens to be prejudicial for the entity or other parties and is proven to have been given negligently or fraudulently.

To clearly distinguish the role of the advisory board members from directors, it is fundamental that in the agreement between members of the advisory board and entities the former are clearly identified as "advisors" and distinguished from directors. In addition, the advisory board shall not, even in practice, perform duties traditionally reserved for a director (such as participating in the board or on a committee by voting or deciding business or managerial issues). Finally, members of the advisory board shall not exert (or appear to exert) control over one or more members of the board of directors. Otherwise, in the latter two cases, members of the advisory board might be qualified as "shadow" directors and be held liable as any director.

10.4 Advisory board agreements: Key provisions

The relationship between entities and members of the advisory board is usually regulated under written agreements or policies – even though as said they may be verbally made. Usually these agreements or policies regulate members' roles, limit their liability exposure and protect the company's interests, including confidentiality and intellectual property rights. Some companies also adopt bylaw provisions and separate advisory board charters. In any case, the company's or other entity's board should formally approve the creation of the advisor relationship or advisory board with resolutions or a written consent, including adoption of the advisory board agreement.

Key provisions are those on duties, terms of service, compensation, information and participation rights, confidentiality and privilege, intellectual property and disclosure of conflicts of interests.

With reference to duties, the agreement usually specifies that the role is to provide consulting services to the board of directors or to management and makes clear that the advisor has no power to act for, represent or bind the company and cannot take action that implies it has this type of authority. Generally, the agreement also specifies: (1) the number of meetings, conference calls or other events the advisor must attend; (2) any preparation the advisor should complete in advance of these meetings or events, including reviewing materials such as business plans or budgets; and (3) any other duties the company and advisor have agreed upon (e.g., identifying business opportunities or assisting the board with management communications).

With reference to term of service, members of advisory boards generally serve at the will of the board or the entity's management. Sometimes a term is provided to encourage advanced planning and ensure the mutual commitment expected. Even if the agreement specifies a term, it is possible for either party to terminate the agreement at any time, with or without reason.

As far as compensation is concerned, as said, members of the advisory boards may be compensated or not. In non-profit organisations usually they are not compensated while in companies they might. In any case the agreement usually specifies which party is responsible for expenses and how expenses must be reported. If the advisor is compensated, amounts and timing of payments are also specified. Sometimes compensation may involve an equity component.

Given that members of the advisory board have no right to attend directors' or management's meetings at law, usually the agreement specifies if notice of meetings, materials, reports or other information shall be given by the entity to the advisor. The right to access company information such as books and accounts is, in most cases, expressly reserved for the company or the entity.

If board advisors are given, under the agreement, access to board or management meetings it is generally specified that all sensitive corporate materials, all confidential and proprietary information released to the advisor shall remain property of the entity, and any use or disclosure of such materials is prohibited. In order to avoid that the confidentiality restrictions are drafted so broadly as to interfere with the advisors' own business activities, the entity carefully considers any conflicts of interest that might develop in light of its business and any advisor's other activities and commitments.

An Illinois decision has confirmed that the attorney–client privilege – i.e., the client's right to refuse to disclose and to prevent any other person from disclosing confidential communications between the client and the attorney – generally speaking, does not extend to advisors: see *BSP Software, LLC v. Motio, Inc.* (N.D. Ill., 12 June 2013). This includes discussions during board of directors' meetings with counsel regarding privileged matters. As a practical matter, this means that advisors should be asked to step out of any meeting when privileged matters are being discussed, and privileged documents should not be shared with advisors.

BSP Software, LLC v. Motio, Inc. (N.D. Ill., June 12, 2013)
BSP Software, LLC ("BSP") did not have a board of directors but assembled a group of four persons to act as an advisory board. The four persons were selected on the basis of long standing relationships and familiarity with an officer of the company (e.g. his boss and mentor during his previous employment, an attorney etc.). There was no written agreement between the company and the four persons because, in light of the relationships, "a handshake agreement was stronger than anything that could have been reduced to writing". The mission of the advisory board was to "impart business and financial advice" in an informal manner; they were not employed nor paid for their services; they possessed no binding authority over BSP or its owners. In a previous order the Court held that four email chains from the company to its advisory board were privileged in the origin. In those emails BSP disclosed certain privileged information from BSP's counsel to the advisory board in order to get its business and financial advice on whether to file suit against Motio – biggest BSP's competitor – for abuse of intellectual property. In the motion before the court, the company sought a ruling that it did not waive the privilege by disclosing the protected material in the four email chains to its advisory board and that members of the advisory board understood their communications with BSP to be confidential and treated them in that manner. On the contrary, Motio contended that BSP waived the privilege in the attorney-client communications by sharing them with the members of the advisory board. BSP tried to claim that there was no waive because sharing the information with the advisory board was like sharing them with a duly constituted board of directors as the advisory board should be treated as the functional equivalent of the board of directors. But the Court dismissed the motion stating that the attorney-client

privilege, being in derogation of the search of truth, must be strictly confined. According to the Court, BSP did not properly show the functional equivalent test, for example the existence of a close working relationship with the advisory board on matters critical to the company's position in litigation, the possession by the advisory board of information by no one possessed in the company. The Court clearly distinguished the advisory board – with no decision making authority or primary responsibility for a key corporate job – from the board of directors highlighting that BSP could create a formal board of directors vested with authority instead of relying on non-binding advice from the advisory board. Finally, the argument brought by BSP that the communications were received and treated by the advisory board as confidential was not accepted by the Court that does not consider confidentiality alone sufficient to establish the privilege or to avoid waiving it by disclosure to a third party.

In addition, the company or the entity also protects in the agreement any intellectual property its advisors may create while performing their roles. Developments or other works created by advisors generally would not be deemed work-for-hire owned by the company; as a result, any intellectual property rights would generally be retained by the advisor. Therefore, the agreement should contain an express assignment to the company or the entity of any developments or works created by the advisor within the scope of his engagement, or that otherwise arise from the use of the company's confidential or proprietary information.

Commonly, the company or other entity consider potential conflicts of interest of its advisors or prospective advisors: They may not want to engage an advisor who is also serving on the board of, or consulting with, a competitor or company in a related industry. Those circumstances create conditions for potential cross-over discussions of proprietary information or trade secrets, which may lead to disputes over intellectual property (IP) rights. For this reason, agreements often clarify whether the advisor's role with the company is exclusive, and the advisor should represent and warrant that his duties under the advisory board agreement do not conflict with any arrangement with another company or venture.

Another clause that may be inserted within an agreement between the company or entity and its advisory board refers to the possibility for the latter of being sued by shareholders or other plaintiffs, together with the entity's directors, due to participation in board meetings and access to materials. This might be particularly true for start-up companies when an advisor often has a net worth greater than the corporation itself (and therefore may be viewed as a "deep pocket" by potential litigants). Even though, at law, the role and liability of the advisory board is different – as explained – from those of the board of directors, this possibility remains. That is why companies or entities typically provide in the agreement the indemnification for members of the advisory board for any advance expenses in connection with any suits or proceedings brought against them by reason of their role within the company or entity.

The relationship between corporations and entities and advisory boards is governed by the law of the jurisdiction in which the corporation or the entity is incorporated or in which its principal place of business is located. The agreement also provides that disputes be resolved in a specified jurisdiction and venue. Since disputes are likely to be business disputes among sophisticated parties, the parties should waive the right to a jury trial. Alternatively, the parties may provide that disputes arising under the agreement be submitted to binding arbitration – in which case the agreement should specify the provisions that would govern the arbitration proceedings.

10.5 Conclusion

Board advisors are being used more and more in practice also by corporations of any dimension because of the great value they can provide to a company's board and management. It is advisable to regulate the arrangement by contract to precisely fix rights and obligations for both corporations and advisory boards. Even though, in practice, sometimes the agreement is made verbally. In the absence of statutory or common law provisions, written agreements can ensure the coverage of key issues that are important to the parties, including limitation from any exposure of liability by members of the advisory board.

About the editor

Daniel Graewe is an attorney-at-law and full professor of law based in Hamburg, Germany. He specialises in the fields of compliance, commercial and corporate law, corporate governance, mergers & acquisitions and directors' liability. He is also member of two advisory boards of medium-sized enterprises in Germany.

Daniel studied law and political science in Germany, Switzerland, the U.S. and Japan. For about ten years, he worked as a corporate law attorney with White & Case and CMS in Hamburg, London and Munich before starting his own boutique law firm in 2016. In the same year, he was appointed as Professor of Business Law and Director of the institute of applied business law with Nordakademie University of Applied Sciences in Hamburg. He is also a faculty member of the Institute of Mergers, Acquisitions and Alliances in Vienna and in 2019 he was a visiting scholar at the University of California, Berkeley.

https://doi.org/10.1515/9783110666182-011

List of contributors

Sabrina Bruno is Full Professor of Private Comparative Law at University of Calabria (Italy) and Adjunct Professor of Law and Economics at Luiss G. Carli, Rome (Italy). She is an M.Litt. from Oxford University (Linacre College) (U.K.), and Ph.D. from University of Florence (Italy). She was Visiting Scholar at Stanford Law School (U.S.A.) in 2019, and Fulbright Visiting Scholar at Harvard Law School (U.S.A.) in 2010. She is the author of two monographies (on "Civil liability for financial information" and on "Role of general meeting in corporate governance") and of several articles and chapters published in international and Italian editions on corporate governance, sustainability, climate change, and Italian, English and American company law. She has been a non-executive director in various Italian listed companies and banks and is currently Non-executive Director at Carige Bank (Italy).

Julius Ecker is an associate at Haslinger/Nagele with a focus on company law. Before joining Haslinger/Nagele in 2019, he was a university assistant at the Institute for Civil Law and the Institute for Environmental Law at the Johannes Kepler University Linz. In addition to his frequent publications in civil, company and environmental law, he continues to teach as a lecturer at the Johannes Kepler University Linz.

Jan Holthuis is Managing-Partner of Buren's China Practice and lives predominantly in China. He is a Dutch qualified lawyer and a solicitor in England and Wales. He is a registered arbitrator at China International Economic Trade Arbitration Commission (CIETAC) and the Shanghai International Arbitration Commission (SHIAC) since 2016. Since 2017, he has been the Chair of the Agriculture Law Section of the International Bar Association.

Jan founded HIL International Lawyers & Advisers in 1995. HIL became the first Dutch law firm licensed in China by the Chinese Ministry of Justice in 2004. In 2016 Jan merged the HIL practice with BUREN.

Jan has handled sensitive China inbound and outbound investments and is considered an expert in the field of China law and policy. He has more than 25 years of experience in China.

Jan is also a guest lecturer on Chinese law at Erasmus University and Wageningen University.

Li Jiao is Partner within Buren's China Practice. Li Jiao became a qualified Chinese lawyer in 2007. She is well versed in cross-border M&A, joint venture projects and corporate restructurings. With her expertise in Chinese corporate law and general knowledge of international corporate law, in-depth understanding of Chinese local market, and sound business sense, Li can effectively represent multinational clients in negotiating with Chinese counterparties and provide commercially pragmatic advice to achieve clients' objectives.

Li is also a guest lecturer on Chinese law at Erasmus University and Wageningen University.

Ivan Kaisarov is a senior associate at Eversheds Sutherland. Ivan has extensive experience providing legal support to international and Russian clients. He mostly gives advice on corporate, commercial and M&A issues. Ivan also has several years of experience advising clients on intellectual property issues, privacy and data protection. Ivan obtained his master's degree in Law from Saint Petersburg State University and later completed a postgraduate program in Law at the same university. Ivan is a frequent speaker in seminars and forums on a wide range of legal issues.

https://doi.org/10.1515/9783110666182-012

Antje Luke, Berg&Moll Rechtsanwälte Avocats, specialises in corporate law, cross-border mergers and acquisitions, corporate restructuring, and joint ventures. She also advises her corporate clients, banks, investment funds and French, German and international investors on all matters relating to commercial law, contract drafting and negotiation as well as compliance matters. In addition to her truly international experience, Antje Luke is known for her extensive knowledge of the German and French cultures and legal systems, and her dual education in German and French law. Antje regularly publishes on matters of corporate law and compliance and also teaches at universities. Since 2015, she has been President of the "DAV Frankreich" (Association of German Lawyers in France).

Dietmar Lux is Partner at Haslinger/Nagele since 1998. His main areas of practice are contract and company law with a focus on banking law and arbitration. After his move from academia to advocacy, Dietmar Lux maintained a close relationship with the Johannes Kepler University Linz, lecturing in civil and company law. Together with Norbert Nagele, he commented the chapters "Amendment of the Statute" and "Corporate Actions" in the renowned Manz commentary on the Stock Corporation Act (Aktiengesetz), edited by Prof. Artmann and Prof. Karollus.

Victor Mukhin is an associate in the Corporate and M&A practice group of Eversheds Sutherland. He provides legal support to foreign and domestic clients on various aspects of Russian law. Victor primarily advises companies across multiple industries on a wide range of corporate and commercial matters. He also has experience with providing consultation to clients on various regulatory matters concerning their business activities in Russia. Victor obtained his bachelor's and master's degree in Law from Saint Petersburg State University. A native Russian speaker, Victor is also fluent in English.

Paulo Penna is a senior partner of the Brazilian law firm Novotny, Ney, Saldanha, Penna, Ponte, Vianna & Corrêa Advogados. With over two decades of experience, his practice focuses on general corporate matters, corporate governance, M&A, joint ventures and private equity deals, representing both international and domestic clients. Paulo is also a lecturer on business law at the Law School of Pontifícia Universidade Católica do Rio de Janeiro and has written a number of legal publications. He holds a master's degree in Commercial Law from Pontifícia Universidade Católica de São Paulo (2010) and a postgraduate degree in Finance from Ibmec Business School (2002). Paulo is also Vice-President of the Capital Markets Committee and a member of the Business Law Committee of the Rio de Janeiro Bar Association. He is fluent in Portuguese, English and Spanish.

Francesca Ricci is Partner at Ughi e Nunziante, an Italian independent law firm established more than 50 years ago, in Rome and Milan. Francesca achieved a consolidated experience in commercial and corporate law, assisting Italian and foreign companies in extraordinary transactions, including M&A transactions and listings on both the regulated market and multilateral trading systems, in corporate governance matters of listed and unlisted companies and in the management of the company secretary office. She has acted as defense attorney in proceedings before the Italian Securities Authority for market abuse. She assists companies in drafting and negotiating international commercial agreements. Among the clients assisted on an ongoing basis are companies operating in energy, aviation and pharmaceutical sectors.

Luisa Shinzato is an associate of Brazilian law firm Novotny, Ney, Saldanha, Penna, Ponte, Vianna & Corrêa Advogados. Her practice focuses on general corporate matters, corporate governance, M&A, real estate and data protection, representing both international and domestic clients. She has a specialisation degree in Business Law from Fundação Getúlio Vargas in Rio de Janeiro (2017) and is a member of the Golden Key Honour Society since 2013. She is fluent in Portuguese, English and Spanish.

Anthony Turner is an experienced corporate partner with a broad transactional and advisory practice. Anthony undertakes the full range of corporate transactions for corporate and individual clients, advising on M&A, complex domestic and international structuring and equity investments. Anthony has particular experience in the area of governance for corporate entities and large family businesses. Anthony is recommended by Legal 500 as a corporate lawyer. He is an editor of the Butterworths Corporate Law Service, a member of the Company Law Committee of the Law Society, and sits on the committee of the UK branch of the International Business Structuring Association.

www.ingramcontent.com/pod-product-compliance
Lightning Source LLC
Chambersburg PA
CBHW081101220326
41598CB00038B/7189